THE WORLD OF DAVID WAGONER

THE WORLD OF DAVID WAGONER

Ron McFarland

University of Idaho Press
Moscow, Idaho
1997

Copyright © The University of Idaho Press
Published by the University of Idaho Press
Moscow, Idaho 83844–1107
Printed in the United States of America
All rights reserved

01 00 99 98 97 5 4 3 2 1

Library of Congress Cataloging-in-Publication Data

McFarland, Ronald E.
    The world of David Wagoner / Ron McFarland.
        p.   cm.
    Includes bibliographical references and index.
    ISBN 0-89301-200-9 (alk. paper)
    1. Wagoner, David—Criticism and interpretation. 2. Northwestern
States—In literature. 3. Middle West—In literature.   I. Title.
PS3545.A345Z79   1997
818'.5409—dc20   96-44322
                                                                       CIP

Permission to quote works written
by David Wagoner courtesy David Wagoner.

CONTENTS

ACKNOWLEDGMENTS

ABOVE ALL, I OWE DAVID WAGONER a debt of gratitude for his co-operation during the years I have put this book together. After that, I am grateful to the University of Idaho for providing a sabbatical leave during which I completed much of the work on this book. And I thank Wagoner's former students, Tess Gallagher, Sandra McPherson, and Mary Ann Waters, whose comments helped me through the last chapter. Special thanks to the University of Idaho Research Office, and particularly to Corinne McKean, who bailed me out by teaching me how to use the scanner when my computer crashed and left me high and dry. And last but not least, to my wife, Elsie, who fortunately has all of the patience with life that I lack, and to my daughters, Kim and Jen, and my son, the downhill skier and linebacker, Jon.

Ron McFarland

INTRODUCTION

TO WRITE A BOOK ON THE FICTION and poetry of David Wagoner is not to sail uncharted seas, but it is to navigate with only a few partially reliable maps, none of which account for the entire destination. One might argue that the accumulated ten novels, fourteen books, and one chapbook of poems, along with assorted stories, essays, and interviews constitute ample cartographic materials. All are primary evidence. Sum up what you have before you, and you have an analysis or at least a survey of "the world of David Wagoner." But even with the publication in the fall of 1987 of his *New and Selected Poems* and the forthcoming publication of his collected poems in 1997, Wagoner's odyssey continues. Now, at age seventy, he has taught at the University of Washington for more than forty years, and he remains vigorous, is happily remarried, and is the father of two adopted daughters.

If it is true that David Wagoner has remained consistent in his thinking, in his values and ideals, it is equally true that his perspectives have shifted and that his broad range of voices and modes appears to take some new direction with every book. A student of Wagoner's work, then, could probably predict certain directions a collection of his poems might take at the turn of the century, but no student of his work would be so foolish as to make such a prediction in anything other than general terms.

In the absence of substantial scholarly response to Wagoner's poetry and fiction, I have called upon the less certain body of secondary evidence provided in book reviews. As atlases go, these are tantamount to those free road maps that cover vast sections of the country—the Northwest, the Midwest. Yet the range of the book review is almost always very narrow. A single volume is examined, often without reflection on previous work. Frequently the reviewer chooses to focus on a single poem, as if a close look at Seattle's King County would suffice for all of Washington. But the reviews— most of them glowing, a few glowering—do provide useful subsidiary maps.

Why Wagoner's poems, in particular, have not attracted greater critical or scholarly interest remains something of a mystery. His critics have suggested that he is too "accessible," or that he does not take sufficient "risks," or that his voice is too mild or quiet. There is also what some critics have recognized as a sort of Midwestern flatness in the tone of some poems. One of his more scholarly admirers, Sanford Pinsker, whose study groups the poems of Northwesterners William Stafford and Richard Hugo with Wagoner, observes that Wagoner's ear is "conditioned by the Midwest," that his "characteristic pitch is a flat, almost wry combination of the matter-of-fact and the mildly self-deprecating," and that these traits are manifested "in a quiet astonishment, at once a reverence for the intrinsic magic that is life and a continual surprise as one encounters it again and again" (*Northwest Poets* 113–14). The penetrating commentaries by Laurence Lieberman in *Unassigned Frequencies* (1977) and Hyatt Waggoner in *American Visionary Poetry* (1982) have ably suggested the nature and depth of Wagoner's contribution, which Hyatt Waggoner describes as "poems treating experience in nature more concretely and more realistically than Whitman, less subjectively than Roethke, poems that explore the natural world and our relation to it without apparent preconceptions or psychic idiosyncrasies" (196).

What has not been charted hitherto is the journey itself, the development of Wagoner's poetic craft. Nor has the range of his odyssey been adequately accounted for, even by those scholars who have produced the most valuable atlases. Wagoner is rarely given credit for his keen observations of human nature, even though some of his most powerful poems concern people and events altogether divorced from the coastlines, riverbanks, rain forests, mountains, and deserts with which most readers associate his poems. His novels have been largely overlooked or disregarded, but while they are not as central to his achievement as a writer as are the poems, a thorough consideration of his writing should also take them into account. Consequently, I have attempted a sort of integration of his fiction with his poetry by alternating chapters on the novels and the poems. Because I wish to represent a developing portrait of the man and his work, I have proceeded linearly, following the dates of publication. Moreover, I have included pertinent biographical information, not intending to produce a critical biography but to set contexts that might prove interesting or valuable to the reader. My major sources for biographical data have been the autobiographical essay that Wagoner composed for the *Contemporary Authors Autobiography Series* (1986) and the writer himself, whom I have pestered off and on for several years.

My study begins with the publication in 1953 of Wagoner's first collection of poems, *Dry Sun, Dry Wind*, so it remains for me to supply information about what might be called the formative years. Wagoner begins his autobiographical account in *Contemporary Authors* with the statement, "Geography had a lot to do with it" (397). Born in Massilon, Ohio, in 1926, Wagoner left the small-town Midwest with his brother and sister (nine and seven years his senior) in 1933 when the family moved to the industrial corridor between Gary, Indiana, and Chicago, where his father was to work in the steel mills at Whiting, Indiana. He describes the move from the hills and dales of Eastern Ohio to the flat, industrial wasteland as alienating, and that response informs the poems of his first book. His omission of any poems from *Dry Sun, Dry Wind* in his *Collected Poems 1956–1976* may reflect not so much his rejection of them as products of an apprenticeship, as his recognition that in moving to the Northwest at age twenty-eight he no longer felt alienated from an environment which he could only depict as sterile or moribund.

Wagoner's poetic debts, as recorded in an interview I conducted with him several years ago, are to his generally acknowledged mentor, Theodore Roethke, and to Yeats, Auden, Dylan Thomas, Stanley Kunitz, Wallace Stevens, and James Wright ("Interview" 16). But his first efforts at poetry, written at age ten or eleven, he describes as modeled after Longfellow and Whittier. By high school he had "added a few love poems and some overwrought Poe-drenched nightmarish narratives" (*Contemporary Authors* 400). His reading list from youth includes the works of Edgar Rice Burroughs, the Bomba the Jungle Boy series, the Sherlock Holmes adventures, the Oz books, P. G. Wodehouse, H. G. Wells' travel books, and "whole shelves of detective novels" (400).

Wagoner acted in high school plays and won prizes for oratory. Listening to the radio, he became aware of the "disembodied human voices" (400) which he was later to employ in his poems. He was also fascinated with magic, and he remains a member of the Society of American Magicians. As he describes it, Wagoner spent "the vast majority" of his time in high school "becoming a mediocre forward in basketball" and a "slightly better center in football" (402), following in the footsteps of his father, who had played in the trenches at Washington and Jefferson College where he graduated *magna cum laude* in classical languages. He describes his father as "very strong, very short-tempered, very opinionated, and most of the time silent" (400). But his most vivid portraits of his father are recorded in several poems in which he is the central figure. He describes his mother, who was born in Canada, as "almost pathologically self-effacing" (401).

He was accepted into the Naval ROTC program at Pennsylvania State University in 1944 and "jammed through four years of college work in three calendar years" (402), including basic engineering and naval training courses. These classroom experiences are reflected in several of his poems. He also found time for writing workshops taught by Roethke (poetry), Edward J. Nichols (fiction), and Warren Smith (drama). One of his one-act plays was performed by the Penn State Drama Department in 1946, but "it was Roethke's workshop that really changed the direction, quality, and meaning of my life" (403). Wagoner has flirted with the stage throughout his career, so the dramatic reading of his poems by the Seattle Repertory Theater (March 20 and 21, 1987) was an especially fitting tribute.

By the time he graduated from Penn State, Wagoner was committed to a life as a college English teacher and poet. Accordingly, he entered the graduate writing program at the University of Michigan, transferring after a year to the English Department at Indiana University, where he studied creative writing under Peter Taylor, who assisted him in the publication of his first short story, "Holiday," in the *Kenyon Review*. At about the same time, "Marsh Leaf," the first poem he had written for Roethke's workshop, was accepted by *Poetry*. So began his oscillation between prose and poetry. In the 1981 interview for the special Wagoner issue of the *Slackwater Review*, he lists as influences on his fiction—besides Peter Taylor—Kafka, Welty, Graham Greene, Wodehouse, and Conrad. He received his M.A. in February of 1949 and began teaching as an acting instructor of creative writing at Indiana that spring.

In the fall, he moved to DePauw University where he taught for one year, wrote his first novel (never published), met Dylan Thomas, and married for the first time. The marriage lasted less than two years, during which time he was an instructor in the Penn State Extension System in the Philadelphia area. In 1952, Wagoner began teaching on the main Penn State campus after some summer work as a reporter with the *Hammond*

(Indiana) Times, and in 1953, his first collection of poems was published by the Indiana University Press in its new poetry series. He began teaching at the University of Washington in Seattle, at Roethke's invitation, in the fall of 1954, and there he has remained.

If a single motif may be said to dominate David Wagoner's fiction and poetry, it is that of the journey. But his characters, personae, and speakers are rarely "on the road." They are, rather, adrift in the world, whether in Chicago, on the frontier of the American West in the nineteenth century, on Dungeness Spit, on Sammamish Slough, or in some unnamed city, forest, desert, or stream. Although adrift, Wagoner's travelers are seldom aimless or desperate. They may be confused or uncertain as to just what it is they seek, but with the exception of some protagonists in the urban novels, they are not simply on the lam or seeking refuge. The literal or symbolic goals vary and sometimes change as the work progresses. In search of gold, Ike Bender, of *The Road to Many a Wonder*, finds it and love as well. The persona of the "Travelling Light" sequence, who at first appears alone and seeking simply to survive in what he sees as a hostile wilderness, finds both love and enlightenment in the "world of our first selves where believing is once more seeing" (261).

Wagoner's use of the second person in many of the poetry sequences causes the reader to identify with the questing persona. The speaker in such poems, the disembodied voice of a sometimes sardonic teacher, seems often to be neither a character in the poem nor the poet himself. If we tell ourselves that the speaker "must" be the poet, we discover that the persona probably is the poet as well, and we are led to the likelihood that we are witnessing an inward voyage, perhaps a quest for self-identity and unity of being.

Wagoner's journey concerns not only discovery, which entails the finding and leaving of temporary refuges, but also change, both of scenery and of self. Transformations and metamorphoses lie at the heart even of those novels and poems which appear to involve no journey at all (poems involving magic, for example, or those concerning Wagoner's parents). Change must be endured and even embraced as a facet of the human condition, and of course the change of death is the ultimate case in point.

In both the poems and the novels, including even the bizarre thriller, *The Hanging Garden* of 1980, the most fortunate travelers are those accompanied by their beloved. There is no antidote for change any more than there is for death, unless death itself is the antidote, but love softens the trial and makes the rigors of the journey more endurable. For all his specific knowledge of flora and fauna—and Wagoner is an avid naturalist—his best poems are not so often nature walks as they are the travels of lovers in a world which must be treated with respect, even though it cannot be fully understood or charted.

THE APPRENTICE WORK:

Dry Sun, Dry Wind and A Place to Stand

THE YEAR 1953 SAW THE PUBLICATION of Theodore Roethke's fourth collection of poems, *The Waking*, for which he was to win the Pulitzer Prize, and of David Wagoner's first collection, *Dry Sun, Dry Wind*, which shows clearly the impact of Roethke, to whom it is dedicated, as well as the influence of what might be regarded as the "formalist project." In 1948, W. H. Auden, who had reversed T. S. Eliot's course and become an American citizen two years earlier, won the Pulitzer Prize for his long poem, *The Age of Anxiety*. A proponent of high craft and formalism in poetry, Auden was to exert considerable influence on the course of American poetry and poetics at midcentury as editor of the Yale Series of Younger Poets (1947–59). Auden was a significant influence, for example, on the work of William Meredith, whose evolution as a poet from strict formalism toward freer, more conversational lines is similar in some ways to that of Wagoner.

But it was most immediately Roethke's workshop at Penn State in 1946 that changed the direction, quality, and meaning of his life, Wagoner reports in the *Contemporary Authors Autobiography Series* (403). In his essay for *American Poetry Review*, Richard Hugo, himself a student of Roethke in 1947 when he went to the University of Washington, observes that "through his fierce love of kinds of verbal music," Roethke "could be overly influential," and he notes Wagoner's "long painful time" breaking away from that influence ("Some Stray Thoughts" 50). Nevertheless, X. J. Kennedy has suggested it was probably "useful for Wagoner, so given to order and common sense, to have a wild man for an early trainer" (136).

1. DRY SUN, DRY WIND

Examples of Roethke's impact abound in *Dry Sun, Dry Wind*, for instance in the poem entitled "Toward the Interior" (29) or in such quirky lines as

"Farewell, farewell, / Love sleeps beside the chamberpot" ("Home for Old Ladies" 24). But perhaps "Marsh Leaf," one of Wagoner's first published poems, appearing in *Poetry* in 1948, will sufficiently illustrate the nature of Roethke's mark. It was the first poem he wrote for Roethke's workshop.

> *A coward may run from grief*
> *Or hide desire from his eyes;*
> *But the shape of a russet leaf*
> *Reechoes the dry wind's cries;*
> *One leaf, lying underfoot,*
> *Speaks, though dead and fallen and deaf.*
>
> (Dry Sun, Dry Wind 22)

Rhythmically, the poem is reminiscent of the interplay of iambs and anapests in Roethke's "River Incident," also published in 1948:

> *A shell arched under my toes,*
> *Stirred up a whirl of silt*
> *That riffled around my knees.*
> *Whatever I owed to time*
> *Slowed in my human form. . . .*
>
> (Collected Poems 49)

The alternating rhyme scheme of Wagoner's first four lines is not sustained throughout the poem, but like Roethke, he does enjoy playing with sound. The long *i* that echoes throughout the stanza, particularly in the second line, is one case in point. Wagoner also demonstrates in these early lines a very subtle ear. Note, for example, the assonance that connects grief, desire, leaf, reechoes, leaf, and speaks and also the pairing of "dead" and "deaf" in the last line, in which he creates the eye rhyme of "deaf" with "leaf." Elsewhere in "Marsh Leaf" one hears other echoes of Roethke; for example, in the third line, "Cold watermouths move and sing." The echoes are ones of tone or a manner of phrasing, however, rather than thefts from this or that poem.

The relationship, too, between the persona in the poem and his environment is similar to that found in Roethke's poems, except that Wagoner's "I" is almost infinitely subdued by comparison. The poems of his first collection show little influence of Roethke's colloquial wildness. Wagoner never comes close, for example, to the playfulness of this quatrain from "Praise to the End!" (the title poem of Roethke's 1951 collection):

It's a great day for the mice.
Prickle-me, tickle-me, close stems.
Bumpkin, he can dance alone.
Ooh, ooh, I'm a duke of eels.
(CP 81)

Wagoner's persona or speaker appears only twice in "Marsh Leaf": "I look for a hopeful thing, / But the mud and reeds have been troubled long" and "I look for a mooring place, / But leaves are light."

Roethke's persona is generally more aware of himself and more at ease in the world than Wagoner's: "Alone, I kissed the skin of a stone; / Marrow-soft, danced in the sand." ("A Field of Light," *CP* 63); "I woke in the first of morning. / Staring at a tree, I felt the pulse of a stone" ("The Visitant," *CP* 101). In "Marsh Leaf," however, Wagoner's speaker is searching for his place in the natural world but not finding it. At this early stage of his development, Wagoner shows no close or intimate contact with nature, but instead finds himself, as in "Finale," in a world where "broken glass / Blooms where the iris was" (*DSDW* 19). In the last stanza of "Marsh Leaf" he abandons the first person for a more general comment: a coward may try to avoid grief or conceal his desires, but a single leaf, even though it is fallen and dead, still "speaks." This does not reflect despair or alienation, though, for the "I" continues to look for a "hopeful thing" and a "mooring place," and the speaker remains capable of making pronouncements on cowards and can yet hear the cry of a single leaf.

Perhaps another way of expressing it is to say that even in this early effort Wagoner anticipates but clearly does not realize what Hyatt Wagoner has called the "visionary poem": a poem that "begins in direct perception, not in reflection or thought" and that assumes "no dichotomy between the perceiver and the perceived" (12). At this stage of his growth as a poet and as a person, David Wagoner tends to express unfulfilled desire and the awareness of lack, of what is not available to him in a natural world that readers in the fifties might have seen as a lyrical reflection of Eliot's waste land. Having said this much about the influence of Roethke and other poets on Wagoner, I will put that ghost to rest with Hyatt Wagoner's observation that while he finds David Wagoner a true "heir" to Roethke, that does not make him a "follower or disciple" (181).

During the year before the publication of *Dry Sun, Dry Wind*, David Wagoner underwent a divorce and accepted an instructorship at Penn

State, where he had received his B.A. in 1947. The book was published at Indiana University, where he had received his M.A. in creative writing in 1949, and it received a handful of reviews appropriate to a first collection. John Ciardi, writing for the *New York Times*, offered a balanced and carefully selected assortment of observations beginning, "David Wagoner's first book shows him working toward a sound poetic manner." He praised the "terse rhythm" and "deliberate diction," but he noted a "deliberately 'made' quality of the diction" that seemed to "tip the poem into stylistic eccentricity" (10). Some fifteen years after its publication, Richard Howard in *Alone with America* characterized the volume as "twenty-two rigorously inhuman lyrics" and "eight dramatic monologues delivered from beyond the grave" (622).

Certainly the first several poems of *Dry Sun, Dry Wind* live up to the spareness and desiccation implied by the title. Consider, for example, the opening lines of the first three poems in the book:

> *Overturned by the hills*
> *And the plow of stones,*
> *Drier than left husks. . . .*
>
> ("Sun, Wind" 13)

> *Like retarded water*
> *Sweeping to a shore of houses,*
> *The dunes alter.*
>
> ("Afternoon of Sand" 14)

> *Day wavers at the flagstone wall.*
> *The bird-bath on a pedestal*
> *Dries underneath the scalding moon. . . .*
>
> ("Lawn Design" 15)

Of course there are signs of life in the three poems, even signs of human presence, but more common is the humanized or personified landscape. The "I" who appears briefly in the next two poems seems almost to be an intruder, not appearing in "Vigil" (17) until the sixteenth line of the twenty-line poem.

It is difficult to detect a "voice" at all in these poems, and virtually impossible to detect a distinctive, consistent voice, but then these are the efforts of a young poet still in his apprenticeship, a fact that Wagoner acknowledged tacitly by excluding all poems of this volume from his 1976 *Collected Poems*. Nevertheless, the poems of *Dry Sun, Dry Wind* do reflect some of Wagoner's talent aside from his keen ear. This includes a sharp eye for natural detail, an almost classical sense of form, and some range or variety in both form and content, which anticipates the considerable range and variety to come.

The first poem of the collection, the title poem, "Sun, Wind" (13), exemplifies Wagoner's commitment to form, a commitment that he has maintained over the years, though with considerably greater flexibility than in these poems. In fact, one might argue that form is something of a crutch for Wagoner in the earlier poems, providing a way of seeing the poem through to an end which seems sometimes more of an escape than a conclusion. The opening stanza of "Sun, Wind" sets the form and tone of the poem:

> *Overturned by the hills*
> *   And the plow of stone,*
> *Drier than left husks*
> *   Where fields were mown,*
> *Wind takes no whitened seed—*
> *   Older than trees,*
> *It moves down pallidly*
> *   To die like these.* (13)

Note the short, accentual lines (alternating three and two beats per line); simple, balladlike rhyme scheme (abcb, defe); predominance of blunt monosyllables (27 to only 5 polysyllabic words); elemental imagery (hills, stone, husks, wind, seed, trees); the charged words indicative of sterility and death (drier, older, pallidly, to die). Wagoner seems committed to distancing himself as poet and persona from the dry, lifeless landscape.

The second stanza is a formal reflection of the first, introducing "sun" at the same place occupied by "wind" in the initial stanza:

> *Overworn by its fire*
> *   And the twists of sky,*
> *Drier than frilled lichen*
> *   Where the oaks lie,*
> *Sun carries death to leaves—*
> *   Older than air,*

It burns through flower and fern
    With its straight flare. (13)

The parallels in construction, down to the punctuation marks, between this stanza and the first are so obvious as to require little comment. Words like "dried" and "older" not only recur, but also recur at the same locations in the stanza. Monosyllables continue to predominate in this extension of the stark sterility of the landscape. Only the music of this stanza distinguishes it from the first. Note, for example, the long *i* (fire, sky, drier, lichen, lie) in the first four lines and the growling *r* sounds beneath the more obviously alliterative *f* in the last two lines (burns, flower, fern, flare, through, straight). Again, however, the scene appears to be devoid of humanity, and Wagoner represents that fact through his presentation of flat, unadorned images.

In the concluding stanza, perhaps predictably, given the tight construction of the first two, Wagoner draws the dry sun and dry wind together and stresses the past tense, which had been introduced briefly in the fourth line of the poem ("Where fields were mown"):

Dry sun, dry wind,
    And both aloft
Where once birds were
    Or under the least tuft
Of moss where earth was cool—
    O drier than time,
They know no counterparts
    But love and rhyme. (13)

The elemental imagery which is resumed in this stanza (birds and the tuft of moss) dissolves in the last three lines with the apostrophe, a fairly common device in Roethke's poems and traceable perhaps to the Romantics. The device may be intended to sound vatic in some way, but this apostrophe heralds no "wild west wind," the "breath of Autumn's being." The birds in Wagoner's poem did not fly or soar, but simply "were." The apostrophe leads to a series of abstractions: time, love, and rhyme. In what sense, his reader may ask, do "sun" and "wind" resemble "love" and "rhyme"? The fact is that while this poem stops, it does not really end. It is a conclusion in which nothing is concluded, a handsomely lyrical ligature. The terms "love" and "rhyme" remain flat abstractions, more likely desire for than promise of regeneration, healing, or even consolation.

"Sun, Wind," therefore, illustrates both the strengths and the weaknesses of Wagoner's early poems. Frequently the lyrics of *Dry Sun, Dry Wind* end with abstractions or with a sort of flatness that leads nowhere. Eyes, in the next poem, "Afternoon of Sand," are "tossed like sandburs" by the wind and "Buried at random with the tree, with love, / With last year's certain light" (14). The "lull" in a poem by that title "melts all the houses, / And the vague yard / Is full of strangers, things" (16).

Throughout *Dry Sun, Dry Wind* (and in at least a dozen poems from the next volume, *A Place to Stand* [1958]) the apostrophe intrudes, almost always drawing attention to itself rather than to the powerful perceptions of the speaker's epiphanic revelation. The concluding sestet of the sonnet, "Foreshadowing," begins, "O the rain comes slowly from its anchorage" (21); in "Toward the Interior," Wagoner concludes the first stanza, "O all distance turning cold / With age, stilting the white lake" (29). Occasionally Wagoner does use the apostrophe with greater effect, for example, in the last two lines of "Home for Old Ladies": "O holy, holy, / The walls are sprouting to the Lord" (24). Here we also find Wagoner punning playfully as he does throughout his work, testing the ambiguities of language as a sort of protodeconstructionist poet. Wagoner's signifiers often insist on plurisignification. Although the impact of Wagoner's wordplay probably varies with the reader, his "play" is generally in earnest from these early poems to his most recent. In "Home for Old Ladies," where "eyeless mice" strut like "bawdy-belles in heat," the puns are apt enough and the apostrophe is part of the fun.

In the first line of the last stanza of "Warning," the apostrophe announces a personal flash of recognition via memory, which justifies its use: "O once I dropped a sunfish on a pier. / Its gills were flecked with roses" (27). The poem is reminiscent, in miniature, of Elizabeth Bishop's "The Fish." Out of pity, the speaker (a child) turns a hose on the fish in Wagoner's poem, but it dies: "Now, as the straight wind lunges at my side, / I gasp, recalling the warning and the fear: / Too much to breathe, think, see." With the publication of *The Nesting Ground* in 1963, the apostrophe all but disappears as a trait of Wagoner's lyric style.

Another way of characterizing the poems of *Dry Sun, Dry Wind* is to reflect upon some lines that illustrate the predominant themes of passing time, the cold emptiness of autumn and winter, old age, and the failure of energy and love (that is, of vitality). In fact, a sort of entropy seems to have befallen the world of these lyrics. "Lawn Design," where "[d]ay wavers" and "October pulls the awnings down," concludes, "And the bright images are gone" (15). "Like white ice," we are told in "Lull," "The light itself can father / Nothing around the houses." The speaker complains, "Still air / Has stolen time from me" (19). "Song from the Second Floor" ends, "The husk / Of memory is aired with dreams, / And dust goes dancing in the room" (20). When the lyrics focus on people rather than the barren landscape, the characters are women at a home for the aged, a blind man, a nurse ("[a]ll lightness and a cold caution" [32]), and an old man at the beach.

In "Bedrock," at a quarry, no bones or fossils are discovered, and the "dangling roots" do not suggest fertility, as in Roethke's greenhouse poems, but a pit in which "nothing has grown" and near which rests "An empty box of dynamite" (26). Wagoner could hardly have chosen a more appropriate symbol for the powerless world of *Dry Sun, Dry Wind*. The effect of the waste landscape is cumulative. In "Sudden Frost" a crow "cracks at the earth," but "it will not loosen." The killdeer and the wasp are "Arched to pierce . . . all who threaten / To live." This tightly constructed sonnet, composed entirely in slant rhymes and consonance, ends: "In an air already greyed to the thinnest light, / The thinnest noise, the first snow falls too late" (28). Such is the vision of David Wagoner's first lyrics, a severe, impotent chill depicted with remorseless eye and ear.

In the dramatic monologues of the second part of *Dry Sun, Dry Wind*, Wagoner demonstrates his ability to fashion character and to sustain narrative, while at the same time maintaining his sharp sense of sight and sound, as shown in the lyrics. The first of the eight monologues, "Cora of Pigeon Run" (37–40), is the most ambitious and perhaps the most successful as well. Richard Howard's observation that the monologues are all "delivered from the grave" should not be construed, whatever his intention, as meaning that they are somehow morbid or lifeless (622). The poems are written in the present tense, not in the reflective past tense of Edgar Lee Masters's Spoon River poems. Moreover, most of the poems are not monologues delivered at the "ultimate moment" or afterward, though most of them do involve the contemplation of death, and the word shows up in all of them in one way or another. Edmond of New Hope, a canal man, describes his "victory" as "[s]light as a dog-whelk's death" (43). The tightrope walker, The Great Bellado, says, "Death is straight below, / There, to be tiptoed surely, like a spark, / And balanced in the head" (45). Erich the printer says, "Names are a death, / And numbers are the clockmarks toward it" (47). Even Silas the tree surgeon, contemplating his last sick tree, describes the sumac as "[w]ashed like a dead possum in the creek" (49). The monologues offer the first significant examples of Wagoner's more human (and humane) voice and also, most significantly, of his great sense of humor.

Each of the speakers in the poems is allotted a lifespan, Cora's being 1820 to 1859, and then the monologue itself, or its subdivisions, is dated. Cora is about sixteen in the first section of her monologue (1836), and she is pregnant. In the opening verse Wagoner develops a metaphor of spinning, which may pertain not only to Cora's patient domestic task, but also to the idea of fatality:

> *A spindle winds the wind into the south,*
> *And the long day follows, warping*
> *The light awry and down the furthest*
> *Of the world, drawn thin as mist*
> *Through the lowering air.* (37)

As in his lyrics, Wagoner's ear is sharp, especially for assonance: spindle/wind, light/awry, thin/mist, through/looming. The wordplay on "looming" in the last line of the stanza is typical of Wagoner's verbal legerdemain. An avid magician, Wagoner has never tired of the special magic inherent in words. Sanford Pinsker, in his essay, "David Wagoner: The Poem is Quicker than the Eye," observes, "Like the magician, the poem's voice controls the situation and its reality. Language is, in this sense, the 'inexhaustible hat' out of which all manner of 'rabbits' pop" (113). That is, Pinsker points out at the end of his essay, Wagoner's magic is "lyrical."

Cora cannot understand the restlessness of her husband, who "whispers of creeks as long / As summer, wearing into a new country" without her (37). Each of the three sections concludes with a question, which she answers with varying specificity. "Why should he dream / Of land beyond the window?" Cora asks here (37). She answers herself in an apostrophe that closes the first movement of the poem:

> *O here*
> *Under the swelling of my dress,*
> *The child grows slowly into an open space,*
> *Curving, and there the world*
> *Lies wheeling out the great round years*
>
> *That draw the wind, the light, then dark,*
> *Into the hidden spindle of my womb.* (38)

Just as the baby will expand into the open, changing world, so does her husband yearn for the freedom of the wind on the prairie. Wagoner returns Cora to her opening metaphor in these last lines. Key words like "world," "wind," "light," and "spindle" recur, but with new significance. The spindle that winds the wind in the opening stanza, an apparently fanciful metaphor, becomes the mythic, eternally feminine, "hidden spindle" of the womb at the end.

The second section of the poem is dated 1844, which would make Cora about twenty-four. Her eight-year-old daughter plays as her husband works on a new roof, his hammer flashing in the sun, the symbol which replaces the wind in this section (as the hammer may supplant the spindle). But the sun in the dramatic monologues is as merciless as that in the lyrics. It lights the hen's blood that "glitters" in the opening line as a kind of portent. Cora has forgotten "The claws flicking like twigs, the neck / Wrenched backward to my apron," but for some reason she cannot wash her hands (38). Because the sun is the predominant symbol in this section, Cora is quite conscious of passing time. At dawn her husband "waved love" toward her as she stood in the doorway holding the hen, but it is a "stern love" that has "nailed him to a place among roofs / And wagons and a lisping daughter" (38). Ridden with guilt for having deprived her husband of his freedom, Cora sees herself now as "like time," and she converts her twisting of the hen's neck into thwarting her husband's desire to move; that is, to "strangling / All distances in about his neck, / While the West breathed" (38). The question Cora proposes to herself in this section is, "When was I alive?" (38). Her answer is, "At noon, as the hen bled and the young / Girl pleated the shafts of dust / Athwart the light with her tipply dancing" (38). The past tense anticipates the coming pain, as her husband falls from the roof to his death. The blood she cannot rinse from her hands is probably his. In the last lines of the section we see why Cora has "forgotten" the flicking claws of the struggling hen, as Wagoner returns to the earlier phrasing: "He is somewhere: / I have forgotten noon and his hands" (39). In death, presumably, Cora's restless husband discovers his mysterious "place."

The third section of Cora's monologue is dated ten years later; she is thirty-four (the attentive reader realizes she has just five more years to live) and her daughter is about eighteen. As in the first lyric in the book, sun and wind are brought together, but love and rhyme correspond more clearly to the symbols of this dry landscape than in "Sun, Wind" because of the dramatic context. Cora watches her daughter and a boy kissing "among the fray / Of straw" (39). The weather cock, a male symbol replacing the hen of the previous episode, "treads" the dry wind over them, and her daughter's dress "Flames against the straw and takes / The low sun from behind the poplar / Windbreak." Cora's question here is simply, "O why?" In answer, she traces the arrival of the boy who came down the dry creekbed and stood "Against the reddening furbelows / Of the sky" (40). Her daughter ran to him, "flashed her hair / Like mine under the arbor" and "spun / My dress about her smoothest knees" (40). In short, Cora's daughter seems destined to follow her mother's path in life. The poem ends with a recapitulation of images from the first lines of the third section:

> The sun goes, fleck by fleck, up
> From the doorframe, and the muffled room
> Silences the creak of the weather cock,
> And they are kissing, kissing, where the straw
> Spills burning from our wagon. (90)

Like Cora, all the speakers in the monologues are very conscious of time, which, as Max of Wolf Lake observes in the last poem, "has no love for circles or the things / That spin" (53). (Perhaps by coincidence that passage also applies very well to Cora.) After presiding over races of everything from motorcycles to greyhounds, Max anticipates another year when "It will be turtles or bullfrogs, then fleas, then germs, / And then the floating ghosts" (54).

2. A PLACE TO STAND

Although Wagoner was to build on this dramatic style of narration in later poems, usually introducing a voice of his own rather than using these assigned voices, his next collection, *A Place to Stand* (1958), offers neither an array of distinct characters nor a clearly definable first-person speaker, that is, with one or two exceptions, a speaker with a distinctive voice. Shortly after the publication of *Dry Sun, Dry Wind*, Wagoner's first novel, *The Man in the Middle*, was accepted by Harcourt, Brace, and he spent the winter of 1953 at the Yaddo writers' colony in Saratoga Springs, New York, writing another novel. Early in 1954, Theodore Roethke called him from Seattle with a job offer at the University of Washington, and propelled by his excitement, Wagoner finished the novel (*Money Money Money*) that spring. It was accepted by Harcourt before the first novel appeared later that year.

His move west, Wagoner writes in his autobiographical essay, "expanded my previously confined world in a way that frightened me with what seemed like too many possibilities" (*Contemporary Authors* 405). When he drove out of the Cascades into Seattle, however, his "extreme uneasiness turned to awe": "I had never seen or imagined such greenness, such a promise of healing growth. Everything I saw appeared to be living ancestral forms of the dead earth where I'd tried to grow up." Wagoner calls the Pacific Northwest "a part of the country where . . . the promises of the earth hadn't been broken yet" (406). On several occasions he has recounted his first trip into the Olympic Peninsula where he took a hike off an abandoned logging road and was lost in a rain forest for about an hour. By the time he relocated his car, Wagoner reports, "I didn't know what I was, but I was certain I'd been more or less lost all my life without knowing it. It was the beginning of my determination not to be lost in any of the woods, literal or figurative, I might explore after that." He followed his "strong impulse" to learn about the fauna and flora of his new habitat, and he writes, "I began to learn how to write about my own life more directly and less from overly literary metaphors about it" (406). On the other hand, the literary metaphor of a person lost in the world and struggling to find his or her way home, was to become the dominant symbolic pattern of Wagoner's poems and of his fiction as well.

Those who pick up *A Place to Stand* or his third novel, *Rock*, published the same year, however, will be disappointed if they expect to discover significant evidence of the impact of the Northwest on Wagoner's writing. That impact has been extensive and deep, but it was not immediate. Wagoner has described the process as "gradual" and "still going on" (*Contemporary Authors* 406). A Guggenheim Fellowship that took him to London in 1956 may have somewhat delayed his assimilation of the rich new world of images and experiences, and perhaps, too, his reentry into the orbit of his mentor delayed his discovery of a voice to reflect his own new vision. Wagoner is quite aware of the approximate moment of that discovery and consequent turning point in his writing, which coincides with his second marriage in the summer of 1961, but the first products of that event appear in his third collection of poems, *The Nesting Ground* (1963).

The lingering influence of Roethke in *A Place to Stand* can be striking at times, as in the final lines of "The Balance": "Going by darkness, coming false by light, / I sway at my center, balanced, drawing breath" (30). The speaker in these poems is clearly evident as a passionate "I" cast on the Roethkean edge. The interplay of dark and light is common throughout Roethke's poems, and "sway" is a recurrent verb, as in his favorite among his own poems, "Words for the Wind" (*CP* 118–21). The last stanza of Wagoner's "The Crisis" resonates with Roethkean rhetoric:

> *O the forked oaktree planted at my birth*
> *Is split upon the turning point of love.*
> *I wait to be consumed where my life began,*
> *My hands behind me, eyes on either blaze:*
> *The heart's immediate fire against the bone,*
> *The mind's impossible flare through paradise.* (56)

The imagery is reminiscent of Roethke's as is the contemplation of the regressive journey into the self. The poem consists of three sestets in blank verse, and only three of the lines are enjambed. The stanza above is typical. Despite the impassioned utterance here, the form is classical, as the balance at the medial caesura in the fourth line and the close parallelism of the fifth and sixth lines demonstrate. The long *i* predominates in the last four lines, and music is also provided by such assonantal pairs as began/hands and flare/paradise.

But *A Place to Stand* (1958) is several strides beyond *Dry Sun, Dry Wind* in many ways. The thirty-six lyrics range in length from the twelve long lines of "Admonition" to the sixty-two lines of "The Hero With One Face" (a playful reference to Joseph Campbell's *Hero with a Thousand Faces*), which is arranged in quatrains composed of tetrameter couplets, heavy with slant rhyme and consonance. An increased liveliness in these poems results not only from a change of theme, but also from a shift in point of view. Of the first twenty-two lyrics in *Dry Sun, Dry Wind* seventeen are written in the third person, none are in the first-person plural, and of the five poems in the first-person singular, two use the personal pronoun only once. In effect, the poems are dehumanized, or at the very least depersonalized. In *A Place to Stand*, however, the first person, singular and plural, is dominant, appearing in twenty-six of the thirty-six poems. The inevitable effect is an increased intimacy, a warmth provided by a human presence which is missing from most of the lyrics in Wagoner's first book. Few of the poems in *Dry Sun, Dry Wind* focus on people, while most of the poems in *A Place to*

Stand involve characters represented dramatically or the speaker himself. Wagoner appears to have recognized the advance of this collection over his first, for he included ten poems from it in his *Collected Poems* of 1976.

The critical response to this book was also more positive. Richard Howard argues that by the end of *Dry Sun, Dry Wind* Wagoner has "not yet created himself" (623), but in *A Place to Stand* he has "found a way to introduce himself into his language, has found, that is, a way to identify *his own life*" (627). Although Robert Cording detects in this volume too many echoes of Roethke, particularly in the song poems, he suggests that in the second poem, "To My Friend Whose Parachute Did Not Open," we find "Wagoner's best work to date" (350). These are relatively recent critical judgments, but the reviewers' responses to this collection in 1958 are also of interest because they anticipate some of the critical bywords, both positive and negative, over the past forty years. The most extravagant in his praise was W. T. Scott, writing for the *Saturday Review*: "In its kind it is the most brilliant work since Richard Wilbur first came on the scene. Wagoner is a splendid lyric poet who gives us not mood alone but intellect and, above all, responsible imagination" (13). In effect, it is the stuff of which book-jacket blurbs are made. More important to Wagoner may have been the positive reception of such fellow poets as Thom Gunn, who admired the poems for their clarity (302); William Meredith, who commended the "fine ear and good sense of form" (10); and James Wright, whom he had met at the University of Washington and who praised the "wide range of emotional and intellectual experience," the "superb technical resourcefulness," and the "almost flawless ear" (49).

The reviewers also commented on shortcomings among the poems of a sort that have continued to draw comment reminiscent of that occasionally aimed at John Updike's fiction. In general, these may be characterized by such terms as "too cerebral," "academic," and "too consciously finished." Meredith, for example, perceived a "contrivedness" in the diction (10). Scott observed an "overmechanization of structure" that could "chill" the lyrics (13). Gunn complained of "a sort of grotesque dynamism," which he suspected Wagoner of indulging "when he is short on substance" (31). Collectively, these reservations suggest that Wagoner's greatest strength as a poet, his technical mastery of the craft, is also his greatest weakness; it is the suspicion that Wagoner sacrifices substance or conceptual depth for verbal cleverness and reliance on sheer (or mere) technique. Such reservations may constitute the major hurdle to be cleared for Wagoner to be accepted as a major poet, a John Donne, rather than simply a fine poet, a Robert Herrick. At what point, one might ask, does polish become glitter? When does "solid structure" or "admirable sense of form" become "lifeless mechanization" or "predictability"? The artistic tastes of an age, culture, or class are rarely so firmly legislated as they were in late seventeenth-century France, and literary tastes were never farther from being standardized than they have been in the late twentieth-century United States. But those who cannot abide the writing of a master of language would do well to avoid Wagoner's poems. He has remained unblushingly a poet with a deep commitment to craft and a persistent delight in language.

The landscape of *Dry Sun, Dry Wind* is so alien that the speaker can only observe it, for the most part; he cannot really be part of it, nor can he define himself through it, since he cannot generally find himself in it. In *A Place to Stand*, however, the speaker is located in the poems, and he is clearly seeking out his identity, as implied in the title poem, in which the question of early explorers and cartographers is turned toward the reader: "Where are we now?" (11). The poem ends in a series of unanswered questions, which may be especially appropriate for the first poem of that book. More than half of the poems involve specific questions, and though some of those are relatively inconsequential, a good many point toward some serious self-interrogation. "Song at the End of Winter," for example, offers several questions and answers, the last of which is, "When shall I follow? 'Now'" (15). In "The Eye of the Storm" the speaker asks, "What place is this?" (20). "What vague imbalance in our hearts / Leaned us together then?" he asks in "The Feast" (26). "Admonition" concludes with a flurry of questions: "What called me? Why? When will the flame and foam make sense? / How shall I quicken? Who are these animals? Where *am* I?" (29). "What was the truth that first appeared?" he asks in "Credo Admiration" (31). "Part Song" poses three fundamental questions in the search for self-identity: "What am I now?" "What was I once?" "O what will I be?" (51). Each of the three stanzas of "The Recognition" ends with questioning, and the last lines provide a resolution:

> *This body and this thought*
> *Are strangers saying, "What has filled us now?"*
> *O love, I recognize myself by you.* (61)

Several poems in *A Place to Stand* indicate that love is the answer to the speaker's dilemma; for example, "The Eye of the Storm" concludes, "We leaped above the water and cried, Love" (21). The penultimate poem in the book, "The Recognition," begins, "I recognize myself, but not by sight" and continues, "I am no longer skin . . . I am no longer vision" before concluding with the triumphant apostrophe, "O love, I recognize myself by you" (61).

Fittingly, the last poem in the book, "The First Word," which Wagoner includes in his *Collected Poems* of 1976, also concerns love and ends with questions, but these contribute to the theme of "recognition" (of the self and of its place in the world). The premise of this poem involves speculation on the first word (not the plural) uttered by man (the speaker is male). "Deep in his cave" primal man heard the sounds of nature (e.g., falling water, bees), but so far "his tongue was but a thing" (62). The speaker speculates, "Was it death-noise first?" and, seeing the sun, "Did he call it *day*?" He concludes in the negative, but asserts that primal man did raise his eyes and saw at the entrance of his cave "[a]nother . . . like a god," and then "A voice stirred in the wilderness of his head. / Was it *yes* or *no*? Was it *you* or *me* he said?" Presumably, these questions are rhetorical.

The first lines of the first three poems from *Dry Sun, Dry Wind*, quoted earlier in this chapter, demonstrate not only the austerity of that landscape, but also the similarity, at least in tone, of many of the lyrics in that collection. Some sense of the variety among the poems of *A Place to Stand* may be gained from a similar procedure with opening lines, this time of the first four poems:

> *On ancient maps they stood,*
> *Explorers, cartographers—*
> *Between the dew-lapped god. . . .*
> ("A Place to Stand" 11)

> *Thrown backwards first, head over heels in the wind*
> *Like solid streamers from wing to tail,*
> *You counted whatever pulses came to mind. . . .*
> ("To My Friend Whose Parachute Did Not Open" 13)

> *What are you wearing?* "Snow."
> *Send two feet after two*
> *On the Glazed Meadow. . . .*
> ("Song at the End of Winter" 14)

> *After the murder, like parades of Fools,*
> *The bungling supernumeraries come,*
> *Sniffing footprints, looking under rugs. . . .*
>   ("Murder Mystery" 16)

The academic conjectures of "A Place to Stand" give way to the profound
personal speculations and metaphysical leaps of "To My Friend." Then
"Song at the End of Winter," a nature lyric rooted in turf and bracken,
yields to the playful romantic comedy of "Murder Mystery." Of course
such virtuosity can backfire on a poet. In writing about everything, some
critics might argue, one risks saying nothing. But part of the risk Wagoner
takes is just that virtuosity. Like the Renaissance *uomo universale*, who
could be clergyman, naturalist, politician, and poet all at once, Wagoner
assumes multiple identities while remaining true to the self at the core.

Although he did not include it in his *Collected Poems*, "Credo Admiration," located at the midpoint of the book, attracts attention because it is
something of an *Ars Poetica*, though Wagoner's exclusion of it may indicate that he has had second thoughts. The poem begins boldly:

> *The Metaphor shall be God. The host*
> *Of Sound beyond the hand and mind,*
> *His son. And while light's fountains spume,*
>   *O grace of the blind,*
> *Words shall triangulate the ghost,*
> *Vision shall crucify the past.* (31)

Wagoner locates sound in a realm apparently beyond the conscious control of craft, but it is difficult not to see the hand and mind of the craftsman
here, as elsewhere in his poems. His masterful control of the complex
stanza (rhyming abcbaa) throughout this ten-stanza poem may have some
origins in the unconscious, but it is the craftsman's hand that carves out
such skillful consonances as dust/must/lost, burn/born, blood/god/should,
and gems/dreams. These he mingles with pure rhymes and slant rhymes to
create a subtle music.

One may be reminded of the hard craft that lurks beneath the wildness
of Dylan Thomas's poems and be reminded, too, of Thomas's definition of
poetry as "only the sudden, and generally physical, coming of energy to
the constructional, craftsman ability" (Kreshner 193). It is probably more
than coincidental that one of Thomas's best-known poems, "If I Were

Tickled by the Rub of Love," concludes, "Man by my metaphor" (*CP* 15).
Wagoner met Thomas when the Welsh bard was on tour in Indiana in
1952, and he and fellow graduate students spent "two wonderful days of
beer drinking, poetry reading, and memorable storytelling" with Thomas
at a private home in the country (403). They met again in 1953 in New
York, where Wagoner "became one of his White Horse Tavern and
Chelsea Hotel acolytes during those last weeks" (*Contemporary Authors*
403). (The initial publication of "Credo Admiration" in 1954 suggests that
it may have been triggered by Wagoner's meetings with Dylan Thomas.)

The rhythm of "Credo Admiration" is also indicative of Wagoner's sure
sense of craft. The first line of the poem has nine syllables, and the first
line of the second stanza, "Tree, grass, the bloom in dust," has only six, but
the metrical norm is established in the second line, and although Wagoner's line is essentially accentual in this poem and throughout his canon,
it does not wander far from an accentual-syllabic standard. The second
line of the poem is quite regular iambic tetrameter, as is the last line of the
second stanza: "Through caves whose ax and bow were lost." I would say
that while Wagoner's metrics do not stray far from the accentual-syllabic in
this poem, they do wander far enough; sufficiently to ensure that the
reader will not get locked into a jog-trot pace and to sustain the dynamics
of the poem. For example, of the nine shortened fourth lines, all of which
are two-stress lines, only one is cast in conventional (pure) iambic dimeter.
The reader can never rest assured in a rhythmic pattern, but there is a
strong pulse in nearly every line.

The "father" and "son" in the trinity of Wagoner's poetic godhead are
metaphor and sound, but the "holy ghost," measured out in words, as if
surveyed, remains mysterious, associated with "light," "grace," and "vision." Following his conclusion in the last line of the opening stanza, that
"[v]ision shall crucify the past," Wagoner explores a renewed world in
which trees, grass, and flowers "[r]ise into flame" (second stanza), crows
and hornets ascend, "[w]orms enter pebbles," and "the hare, / Like wind,"
is filled "[w]ith barbs of sunlight" (third stanza). In the first line of the
fourth stanza the speaker asks, "What was the truth that first appeared?"
The simple, elemental truths are rehearsed in the remainder of the fourth
and in the fifth stanza: "Sandstone, pounded, will make sand . . . / Leaves
vanish, and the slanting snow / Will stagger the lake . . . love / In a curve lies
born" (31–32). Wagoner's many allusions to insects and animals may also
be influenced by Thomas's imagery.

The next two stanzas are comprised of a Yeatsian evocation of the *spiritus mundi*, and the symbolism is clearly that of the mystic, perhaps the Rosicrucian, announcing triumphantly the unity of man and nature:

> *From* Spiritus Mundi *these descend:*
> *Rock in the womb, Fire on the tongue,*
> *Beast in the breast, Snake in the groin,*
>   *Rose in the dung,*
> *And Bird in the tall clouds like the mind,*
> *Sun at beginning, Sun at end,*
>
> *The stretched man becoming Cross,*
> *The Water quick, and Water dead,*
> *Earth clutching Air like brick to quoin,*
>   *O Star in the head,*
> *And Bone resurrected by clean moss,*
> *The Tree of all, Sweetness in dross.* (32)

The latter stanza is somewhat reminiscent of "My Jack of Christ born thorny on the tree," also from Thomas's "If I Were Tickled" (*CP* 15).

"Credo Adoration" concludes firmly in the last two stanzas that the business of the poet, speaking for all the "[c]reatures of light," is to "give praise." In the midst of a material world in which "atoms spin themselves to doom," man's part, similar to that of the angels in Rilke's *Duino Elegies*, is to "Strike fields of aureoles in flesh . . . / Fountain and flash / In sight of ghost, loud son, and god." The poet is also to "[c]all splendor from the wheel of days," in effect, to redeem the time. The closing couplet is powerfully affirmative: "Accept, as Mother, soil and blaze, / Blaze, sea and wind; and give back praise" (32).

In an interview with the editors of *Crazy Horse* in 1972 Wagoner describes three voices he has discovered in poetry, including his own work: "the Searching and Questioning Voices, the Warning and Accusing Voices, and the Healing and Celebrating Voices" (40). In poems like "Part Song" and "The Recognition" Wagoner uses the voices of searching and questioning, which seem to dominate *A Place to Stand*, and in "Words Above a Narrow Entrance" we encounter an early example of the voices of warning and accusing, which have become his most distinctive. Wagoner surmises, however, that all poets would "prefer to concentrate on healing and celebrating if only they could" (41). "Credo Admiration" is a good example of a poem of celebration, and what is almost certainly the finest poem of this volume, "To My Friend Whose Parachute Did Not Open"—the lead poem in his *Collected Poems*—exemplifies the healing aspects of that voice.

"To My Friend" (13) also bears testimony to Wagoner's strong sense of formal structure. It is set up in five five-line stanzas with variable rhyme patterns, composed, as is usual with his lyrics, of slant and eye rhymes and consonance. Each stanza includes a fairly obvious pair of end rhymes, varying from the pure rhyme of sound/ground in the last stanza to the consonance of then/thin in the penultimate and the eye rhyme of cloth/both in the third. The poem begins almost playfully as the friend tumbles from the plane:

> *Thrown backwards first, head over heels in the wind*
> *Like solid streamers from wing to tail,*
> *You counted whatever pulses came to mind—*
> *The black, the bright—and at the third, you pulled,*
> *Pulled savagely at the ring clenched in your hand.* (13)

At the last line of the stanza, the hint of desperation occurs in the word "savagely," but instead of pursuing that lead into a study of the parachutist's fear, the speaker turns to physics in the second stanza, then returns to his friend's dilemma in the third:

> *Down the smooth slope of trajectory,*
> *Obeying physics like a bauble of hail,*
> *Thirty-two feet per second per second hurled*
> *Toward treetops, cows, and crouching gravity*
> *From the unreasonable center of the world,*
>
> *You saw the cords tail out from behind your back,*
> *Rise up and stand, tied to a piece of cloth*
> *Whose edges wobbled, but would not spread wide*
> *To borrow a cup of air and hold you both.*
> *O that tall shimmer whispered you were dead.* (13)

Despite the laws of physics, the world, with respect to the parachutist, is "unreasonable," and he becomes a "bauble of hail"; but although he is hurtling through the air, he can still see his predicament. Wagoner shows the absurdity of his friend's condition by reducing the parachute to a "piece of cloth" with wobbling edges, and then by introducing the domestic metaphor of borrowing a cup of sugar (here, "of air"). This homey metaphor clashes with the mathematically asserted figures for the acceleration of gravity in the dependent clause of the previous stanza. But the last line of the stanza, stated in an apostrophe, confronts us with the inescapable reality of the situation—the death of the speaker's friend. The use of the second person, which was to become quite frequent in Wagoner's poems, has almost inevitably the effect of involving the reader in the context. Traditionally, the use of the second person is exceptionable in rhetoric because the attentive reader may rebel against being told what he or she thinks or does and because it can become accusatory. In fact, in a number of poems, Wagoner uses the second person for precisely the latter effect, to accuse or even to intimidate the reader. But in this poem the effect of the second person is to equate the reader with the doomed parachutist. His dilemma becomes our dilemma.

Now the question becomes, how does the parachutist and how do we respond to imminent death? As quickly as he recognizes death, the parachutist's mind surpasses reason (thought), as the last two stanzas indicate:

> *You outraced thought. What good was thinking then?*
> *Poor time—no time for lunging into luck*
> *Which had, like your whirling, weightless flesh, grown thin.*
> *I know angelic wisdom leaped from your mouth,*
> *But not in words, for words can be afraid:*
>
> *You sang a paean at the speed of sound,*
> *Compressed miraculous air within your head*
> *And made it fountain upward like a cowl.*
> *And if you didn't, then you struck the ground.*
> *And if you struck the ground, both of us died.* (13)

Just as luck is not sufficient at such a time, so does ordinary language fail. Only the miracle of poetry can create the metaphoric "cowl" to replace the failed reality of the parachute. At the point of the miraculous, however, when logic seems most vulnerable or dispensable, Wagoner turns with a paradoxical, Donne-like pivot for his conclusion. If his friend did not pull off the miracle, then he hit the ground. And if his friend hit the ground, both he and his friend died. And implicitly, if both died we have no poem. Yet we readers presume that the friend did hit the ground and die, but that the speaker is alive to write the poem we have just read. Is the speaker wrong, lying, or illogical?

Intellectually, we have been playing an odd game throughout this poem, and at the end we are confronted with the consequences of it. We have gone along with the speaker from the first when he said that his friend ("you") "counted whatever pulses came to mind." We conceded the point because it seemed appropriate from what little we knew about parachuting (you count three and pull the ripcord, or the D-ring, or whatever it is). We were encouraged in our trust of the speaker when he offered us science in the second stanza, so we had no trouble seeing ourselves as the doomed friend watching the parachute fail in the third stanza. And so it went with us throughout the poem, until we realized that we were caught in this paradox, which requires us to accept the miracle via logic because we have been accepting it all along. The record of the friend's desperate "paean at the speed of sound" is, of course, this poem we have just read and believed. True to the elegiac tradition, the poet has assured us that his Lycidas or Adonais is not dead, and of course it is poetry (sound transcending words) that saves him.

Some critics say there is in "To My Friend" a "necessity" that had not appeared before among Wagoner's poems. In this poem he makes believers of us. He compels us to accept the paradox. Of course not all or even most of the poems of even the best poets compel belief, though it could be argued that all poems implicitly request it. As Randall Jarrell has observed, that sort of poem takes a "lifetime of standing in thunderstorms," and a good poet is the one who is lucky enough "to be struck by lightning five or six times" (148). Wagoner has been struck more frequently as he has matured as a poet.

The lyrics and monologues of *Dry Sun, Dry Wind* (1953) constitute a coherent collection in the sense that most of the poems in each of the two sections are consistent in mode, theme, and tone. They reflect the sterility of the industrial suburbs of Gary, Indiana, where Wagoner's father worked in the steel mills. "It was a hard place for anything to put down roots or put out leaves for long," Wagoner notes. "The soil was sandy and poor, the winters harsh; in several vacant lots where I used to play, the weeds were taller than the trees" ("An Interview" 39). But although Wagoner was not destined to become the poet of industrial wastelands, *A Place to Stand*, despite the title, does not indicate just what sort of poet Wagoner would be, even in the best poems of that collection. Instead, the title poem itself suggests the directions being sought, and the coherence that does not exist among the more varied poems of this book evolves from the search for self-identity and a tone or mode of questioning. It was in the next two collections, *Nesting Ground* (1963) and *Staying Alive* (1966), that David Wagoner was first to express the voices, stances, and ideas that would come to distinguish his best work. In the meantime, however, he was busily establishing some identity for himself as a writer of fiction.

"WHERE WEALTH ACCUMULATES":
Wagoner's Urban-Midwest Novels

DAVID WAGONER'S FIRST PUBLISHED fiction, a short story entitled "Holiday" published in the summer of 1949, anticipates in several ways the settings, characters, and motifs of his five novels set in the urban Midwest. As in nearly all of Wagoner's novels, the theme pertains to money, the dependence on or pursuit of which destroys either the dreams, the ideals, or the lives of the usually innocent protagonists. Twenty-four-year-old Ted works in the supply room of United Steel Foundries, apparently buoyed with a textbook image of chrome desks, *Business Week*'s advice to young executives, and mottoes from Horatio Alger. When these notions dissolve in the wake of his boss's sudden decision to quit for no apparent reason after nearly thirty years, Ted also walks out, leaving the dreary office as one coworker slings a whiskey bottle through the window and another tearfully enters purchase figures in the wrong account book. All the workers are disenchanted with their dull, aimless, joyless routine. The setting, which prefigures those of the urban novels, contributes to the dismal atmosphere:

> Beyond the knocking radiators and windows, he could sense the piles of scrap iron and the tracks that switched out in all directions. When he looked, the snow was dirtier than he had remembered, and the clouds were draining down the sky to the rusty powerhouse. (441)

Ted's vision of grime and of deteriorating power was to become standard in Wagoner's urban-Midwest fiction, perhaps because growing up in the steel mill suburbs of Gary, Indiana, and having a father who worked in the foundries, it was the novelist's most vivid impression of reality. In an interview, Wagoner describes the people as "secondary and rootless" among the "mills, refineries, smelting plants, foundries, soap and chemical factories, dumps, slag-filled swamps, innumerable railroads" where he lived ("An Interview" 38–39).

The tone of the passage from Wagoner's story is echoed five years later on the opening pages of his first published novel, *The Man in the Middle* (1954), when Charlie Bell reflects on his job as a railroad-crossing tender.

> This was no kind of life. He hated the trains, hated the way they rumbled, shot steam, clanged. He stared beyond the ditches and heaps of ties at the way the pale, reflected sunlight still creased the trees along the beach and lit the bricks of the filtration plant. (9)

Similarly, Willy Grier, the thirty-six-year-old protagonist of *Money Money Money* (1955) looks past the "red smudges of Indiana Harbor" to observe "the squat silhouette of the pumping station, made tall only by the smokestack that came out of its middle" (3). And twenty-eight-year-old Max Fallon, of *Rock* (1958), sickens as he enters the Chicago suburbs on a bus that stops near one of the Standard Oil entrances "where an open catwalk arched over the highway, over the stationary grit-laden tops of cars and trucks" (1). Sooner or later in all of the urban novels, Wagoner's protagonists are confronted by the industrial ugliness and filth of their environs.

"Confronted by" is the appropriate phrasing here, for it is not accurate to say that the characters actively confront or somehow deal with the dirt and noise around them, despite their awareness and occasional outspoken resentment of it. Attempting to escape his pursuers, a couple thugs from the mob, Charlie Bell remembers "passing patched-together wrecks of houses . . . weedy lots, a boarded-up drugstore" (104), but he does not really respond to the shabbiness. Rather, he takes it for granted as part of the atmosphere which the reader recognizes as a by-product of human greed. The dirt and ugliness of the industrial midwestern cities derive from the pursuit of money. On the last page of the novel, Charlie stares "through the stream of cattle-smell" and sees "the soap factory poking up out of the dark like a yellow cloud" (248). Throughout the chase Charlie has grown dirtier and sweatier until, at the end, he is dehumanized, like the cattle in the railroad cars, and his head feels as though it is stuffed with dirty straw (247). He becomes, in effect, a scarecrow, Yeats's "tattered coat upon a stick."

The setting is not so significant a factor in *Money Money Money*, but setting haunts Max Fallon throughout the pages of *Rock*. Returning to a working-class Chicago suburb after an eastern college education, an office job, and a failed marriage, Max finds a brother who had idolized him but has become disenchanted and rebellious. Like Charlie Bell in *The Man in the Middle* and Willy Grier in *Money Money Money*, Max is estranged from those around him, most notably from his family. Ironically, since he is also alien to the rock music world of teenagers, Max ends up working as a lifeguard on Lake Michigan. But his surroundings are not those that we might ordinarily associate with those of lifeguards at a public pool or beach:

> To the left, in the long, interrupted crescent of Lake Michigan, he saw the ruins of four piers—black, snaglike stumps in a line, going out a hundred yards into the water—and beyond them, hazy with distance, the bulk of the generating plant at the Chicago city limits, then the forms of steel mills, then nothing. And to the right, the gray, brown, and buff industrial buildings and sheds were closer, the smoke stacks and towers more individual; but they too became a fog, a nothing, in the northeastward curve. On the lake itself, aside from the stationary, derrick-like pumping station a half-mile out, the only shape was a long, seemingly motionless ore boat on the horizon, fouling itself as its smoke was blown forward over its bow. (54)

I have quoted at some length here because this passage represents many to be found in Wagoner's first novels and because such passages contribute to a sameness of tone which the reader is likely to perceive in each. Smoke, haze, or dirt are prevalent elements in such passages, and colors like black, gray, and brown predominate. An almost inevitable feature of Wagoner's urban landscape is the smokestack or the power plant. The power source of the urban monster is plain to see in its ugliness: "the bulk of the generating plant," "the forms of steel mills," "the smoke stacks and towers," "the stationary, derrick-like pumping station." In this particular portrait, Wagoner undercuts any real potency such images might conjure by insisting that each is somehow swallowed up. The generating plant and steel mills are "hazy with distance" and they dissolve into "nothing," and the closer industrial sheds and smokestacks also become "a fog, a nothing." The pumping station, despite its association with energy, is "stationary," and the ore boat on the horizon, which carries the raw material for this urban leviathan, is "seemingly motionless" and "fouling itself" with smoke. One may be reminded here of Gerard Manley Hopkins's "God's Grandeur," in which "all is seared with trade; bleared, smeared with toil."

In his useful but somewhat oversimplified paradigm for "Wagoner's basic story" in the four urban novels, William J. Schaefer states that an "innocent man . . . is involved unwillingly or accidentally with corruption" (71). He is then "pursued relentlessly by evil forces, becomes himself corrupt . . . and is therefore damaged or destroyed" (72). This formula holds fairly well for the first two novels, but not very well for *Rock*, in which the protagonist is not altogether innocent, is not pursued by what can truly be called "evil forces," and is in fact better off at the end of the novel than he was at the outset. The model does not really apply at all to *The Escape Artist* (1965), since the protagonist clearly prevails over the corrupting forces, nor does it fit the fifth Midwest novel, *Baby, Come on Inside* (1969), which had not been published when Schaefer wrote his essay. Schaefer's insights are valuable, however, and his essay is the only serious and extensive consideration of Wagoner's urban fiction to date. He accounts well in general terms for what Wagoner has done, and as I will demonstrate hereafter, Schaefer's paradigm can be adapted to apply to Wagoner's comic Westerns.

In all of Wagoner's novels, however, and in some of his poems as well, it is clear that what Schaefer says about the theme of *Money Money Money* holds true: "The crux of the theme [is] *cupiditas radix malorum est* . . . in a double-edged way he shows that both the love and the ignorance of money are roots of evil" (76). In her review of *Money Money Money*, Sylvia Stallings concludes that the novel is "a morality play for our times" on the subject of corruption via the cash nexus (3). This view applies, moreover, to nearly all of Wagoner's fiction, including the Westerns. The connections between money, power, and corruption are biblical, of course, from Deuteronomy 8:10–15 to 1 Timothy 6:9–10. "Absolutely speaking," as Thoreau declares in his essay, "On the Duty of Civil Disobedience," "the more money, the less virtue" (246). Wagoner's perspective is similar, I think, to that of Norman O. Brown as he expresses it in *Life Against Death* (1959): "The alienated consciousness is correlative with a money economy. Its root is the compulsion to work. This compulsion to work subordinates man to things, producing at the same time confusion in the valuation of things (*Verwertung*) and devaluation of the human body (*Entwertung*). It reduces the drives of the human being to greed and competition (aggression and possessiveness, as in the anal character). The desire for money takes the place of all genuinely human needs. Thus the apparent accumulation of wealth is really the impoverishment of human nature" (237–38). It is from this conceptual perspective that I will comment on the characters and themes of Wagoner's five urban novels set in the Midwest: *The Man in the Middle* (1954), *Money Money Money* (1955), *Rock* (1958), *The Escape Artist* (1965), and *Baby, Come on Inside* (1968).

1. THE MAN IN THE MIDDLE

Charlie Bell of *The Man in the Middle*, whom Schaefer characterizes as "a dull and innocent man in his early forties" (72–73), becomes involved in corrupt power politics when he tries to assist a reporter who is on the run from a pair of hit men. An early reviewer notes that Charlie is a "refreshing anti-hero for a thriller" (Sandol 8) but goes on to observe that Wagoner appears undecided as to whether he is writing a novel or a thriller. Schaefer argues that Wagoner adapts the "rhetoric and paraphenalia of the detective thriller" in these novels (72), but how successful his adaptations have been is a matter for individual judgment. *The Man in the Middle* and Wagoner's most recent novel, *The Hanging Garden* (1980), are indeed thrillers, if such a line of demarcation can be drawn, but the remainder of his fiction, while it may show signs of the thriller (nearly constant action, as provided by the pursuit motif; flat characterization, particularly of those other than the protagonist; thematic simplicity), is clearly of a more serious nature.

As another reviewer asserted, Charlie Bell lacks the usual traits of the pursuit hero: intelligence, physical prowess, quick wittedness (Boucher 15). Moreover, perhaps as a result of his antiheroic characteristics, Charlie is much more realistic than the protagonists of most thrillers and films. If we lose patience with him as he wanders through the back streets of Chicago dirty, hungry, and dazed, perhaps it is because he does not offer what the hero of the thriller generally does: release from ourselves. Presumably, most of us would like to think that we could respond to danger like Agent 007, James Bond, but more likely we would find ourselves trapped, confused, and terrified, like Charlie Bell.

In a familiar plot, the senator's hit men murder the reporter and leave her body in Charlie's apartment after knocking him out, in order to frame him. Charlie must avoid detection by the police and the public as he roams Chicago, attempting first to collect his wits, then, in order to understand the mystery, contacting the newspaper for which the woman had worked. Charlie never gets the upper hand, however, and he never makes much sense out of his dilemma. Wagoner assures that the reader comprehends the maze in which Charlie is trapped by alternating short chapters (7 to 10 pages) pertaining to the pursuers with longer chapters (24 to 38 pages) narrated from Charlie's point of view. The short chapters sustain the impression of corruption, of the power of money, and of the cold inhumanity of Charlie's tormentors. Frequently the hit men, whom Schaefer characterizes as "fumbling all-too-human thugs" (74), appeal for more money, and the senator is described as a millionaire. At the heart of the case is money, in the form of a bribe offered by the senator's agents to a news editor. The reporter has left with Charlie a recording and photostatic copies of checks which would incriminate the senator.

What distinguishes *The Man in the Middle*, then, is a sort of contrariness on Wagoner's part. He will not produce the conventional thriller, in which the victim is in fact a superman, nor will he bail out the "man in the middle" by a stroke of luck or through the assistance of others. It does not mar the novel that Charlie does not get a clear sense of what is happening to him: that is the whole point of the novel. Charlie is the vulnerable champion of right. An old leg injury plagues him throughout, leaving him physically unable to compete, and his limited experience and paralyzing fear compromise his ability to deal even with a pair of inept thugs. That, as Schaefer points out, leads to an element of comedy in this otherwise tragic story. What sustains Charlie Bell, a loner like most of Wagoner's protagonists and in fact rather like Wagoner himself, appears to be little more than a simple sense of right combined with sheer determination and will.

Without friends or relatives to turn to, Charlie happens upon a group of communists at a book store. While they understand his predicament and the significance of his evidence, they are more interested in exploiting the situation than they are in helping the man. People with complex motives confuse him.

> People like these and the ones whose names were on the checks baffled him. They were like train engines: he didn't know what they meant, what they were doing, where they were going, or who made them that way. He always wished for people to be simple like a glass of beer, having only one, possibly two purposes. (149)

When he does fall in with a "simple" elderly woman who offers him a ride and then accompanies him on the latter part of his odyssey (a bizarre detour into the black South Side of Chicago), Charlie discovers that she is too simple. She is sixty-one and is somewhat addled, taking Charlie for a soldier and believing that he intends to marry her. In short, she is interested in the man but seems incapable of understanding his predicament.

Because he is a crossing tender, time, in the form of train schedules, has been central to Charlie's life, but in his initial encounter with the hit men he is roughed up and his watch is broken (21). Thereafter, Charlie is lost in time. He cannot get used to daylight savings time, we are told: "His instinct was geared to something near sun time, but the way clocks flipped backwards and forwards had ruined it, and he began to feel really uneasy for the first time at the hopelessness of being without a watch" (79). Wagoner reminds the reader of time throughout the novel by providing datelines for the chapters, from the beginning on a Thursday night to the end the following Saturday afternoon. Time is a recurring symbol in the novel: Charlie has lost it (he often reflects that he doesn't know what time it is), yet it seems always to be at his back.

> He fumbled automatically for the watch in his vest pocket. No pocket, no vest, no watch. He'd forgotten that. And as he glanced around inside of the restaurant, he could find no clock. Never could get things located right in time anymore, never could feel that things were clicking and turning at the right speed. (221–22)

Charlie might be described as the natural man. He is instinctively geared to the sun, and in losing track of time he also loses track of place. In effect, it is a loss of speed that destroys him. Time becomes a matter of the simple mathematical equation where time equals the distance to be covered divided by the rate at which one is moving. When Charlie can no longer move after having his legs crushed and suffering internal injuries in an automobile accident, he attempts to escape by pulling himself onto a passing train, but it moves "like a dream that wouldn't go the way you wanted it to," and he is "almost sure he'd died awhile ago" (247). Time, in effect, catches up with him: "When you couldn't run, walk, or stand, it was time to get tired and time to forget" (248).

2. MONEY MONEY MONEY

Charlie Bell may strike us as confused, but Willy Grier, the almost child-like protagonist of *Money Money Money*, appears to be truly asea. He is probably a moron in the technical sense (mentally retarded with a mental age between 7 and 12 and an intelligence quotient between 50 and 75). Much of his confusion and perhaps the retardation itself may be traumatic in origin. We learn from flashbacks that his "aunt," his mother's sister, was his real mother and that his father, who lost an arm in World War I, was bitter all his life about money, particularly after the spurned aunt vengefully left her fortune in trust to Willy. Willy's sexual confusion or immaturity may stem from his aunt's insistence that he "touch" her, but the event that ended his mental development was the violent deaths of his natural parents in 1936 in an apparent murder-suicide. If the novel is intended to be contemporary with the date of its composition or publication (1954 or 1955), Willy would have been born in 1918 or 1919, making him too old for his behavior as it is described on the night of the traumatic episode, which began with an argument over money. He seems to have been much younger then, perhaps ten or eleven. Whatever the case, he has blocked all understanding of money since that moment, despite remembering his aunt's advice that a man can destroy himself either by working too hard or by avoiding work altogether, but that "the best place to be is sitting on top of a pile of money" (152). So it is that we have the premise of a wealthy character who has no sense of money, of its powers or its perils. The result, as Schaefer points out, is "both tragic and comic" (78).

Willy acts with a certain practical economy, however, that excludes money. His life seems somewhat Thoreauvian. He has a voluntary job repairing damaged trees in Pilsudsky Park. He enjoys swimming but regrets that it doesn't "accomplish anything": "Everything ought to be some kind of achievement, even a little one. If you put your hand in water, it ought to be in order to take some out and use it, or else to wash. That was doing something" (4). He rationalizes his recreation by reminding himself that by making himself feel better he is "laying the groundwork for doing another more worthwhile thing." What he likes about children is that they're never "unoccupied for more than two seconds at a time" (20). Life, as Willy sees it, is "made up of pastimes, all very important," but his sense of priorities is unconventional: "The discovery of an itch was more meaningful than a department store" (21). Clearly, he enjoys work for its own sake. His reaction to the body he recovers from the lake is not so much horror or anger over mob violence as it is annoyance over the waste. The murderer should be punished because "[i]t took a long time for a human being to become a man, and there was an awful lot of creative trouble involved. The end product shouldn't just be broken and thrown away" (16).

At the end of the first chapter, Wagoner contrasts Willy's personal sense of economy with that of the money-oriented public when he offers a small one-page drama (18). Since he is known to the city bus driver and his fares are taken care of by his lawyer, Willy rides "free." But a worker who does not know about his arrangement complains. In the world of money one only gets what one pays for, although paying does not necessarily produce satisfaction. Far from feeling good for the fellow who apparently gets by without having to pay, the worker feels envious and bitter. Wagoner presents the scene with a nicely understated touch.

When Willy meets Lena, the murdered man's supposed sister but actually his former mistress, she offers him fifty dollars to claim to have found a packet on the body, but he cannot understand her offer at all. That is, he simply does not comprehend money, either fifty dollars or five cents. Willy does, however, react to Lena's humanity. He sees that she is small, attractive, and frightened, and beyond that, he sees her as childlike, "not completely like a child, but like a mother and a child all mixed together" (29). It is this confusion, particularly the blending of woman and child, that leads Willy to make what he recognizes to be a mistake, for telling a lie is almost alien to his nature. Certainly, it is something he would do only for another, and not to further his own ends. Wagoner closes the second chapter with a small drama that is antithetical to the drama at the end of the first chapter. This time a bus driver does not recognize Willy, and when he fails to pay his fare, he is shown the door (38).

With most of Wagoner's protagonists, Willy shares not only his honesty but also his naiveté about women and love, as we discover when Lena seduces him in her apartment. For her the casual sexual encounter has no significance, but he believes he is in love and wants to marry her. When he asks her "what it meant," she answers frankly that "[i]t meant we needed each other" (81). Lena's use of the past tense here is indicative of her sense of their relationship—it is over, as temporary as everything else in her dangerous and superficial life. "I like money," she says boldly (78), and she openly confesses to Willy her connections with the syndicate, though she does not mention that she is to be engaged to be married to one of the leaders. Money, she explains in an effort to educate Willy, is "the best kind of friend in the world. It doesn't talk back. And if you really need something, it gets it for you" (144–45). Her profession of interest in money prompts Willy to search his memory for anything positive associated with the word, but he comes up only with scenes of bitterness. Nevertheless, he determines to buy Lena's freedom and her love, and it is this Quixotic gesture that propels the remainder of the novel through episodes of alternating comedy and violence.

What Willy discovers is that money will not buy him what he wants, even though, ironically, he must deal with people whose lives are devoted to the acquisition of money at any risk and even though the woman whose love he would gain has the moral sensibility of a prostitute. It is not the discovery that money won't buy happiness that distinguishes this novel thematically, but rather the novel's ironies: money will not buy happiness for those—like Willy—who have no esteem for it, nor will money buy happiness for those—like Lena and the mobsters—who virtually worship it. "Poetry is almost as good as money, but it isn't," Willy's aunt has told him (154). Despite her celebration and manipulation of money, however, Willy's aunt also finds no happiness, only revenge. As Norman O. Brown has observed, pursuit of money leads to devaluation of the human body; accordingly, we should not be surprised that Willy's infatuation for Lena never transcends sensuality, and her attraction for him is the compulsive behavior of a nymphomaniac. The climax of their relationship occurs at the apartment of her mobster boyfriend, when Willy suffers a minor heart attack while they are making love. Eventually, following his rejection by Lena and a subsequent chase, Willy dies while shaking a tree and waiting for something to fall from the branches. The symbolic implications of the last scene vary, but in one sense, for Willy, a man for whom money does grow on trees, the trees are bare.

The nature of Willy's mental retardation is difficult to assess, and some readers will find Wagoner's portrayal of it unconvincing. One problem, for example, is that some of Willy's comments are strikingly clever, even quick-witted. When one of the thugs introduces himself as a "friend" of the drowned mobster, Willy replies, "He needed a few more" (55). And he appears all too suave when, after disarming two thugs, he tells Lena, "Well, I'll think of something. You go sit down. There's a bottle of whisky behind Tennyson on the bookshelves" (60). We should remember, however, that Willy is a special case in a couple of ways. First, his retardation is traumatic rather than congenital in nature. Second, he amuses himself by reading through the encyclopedia; that is, he has some characteristics of the idiot savant. He appears to be slow in many ways, and he recognizes that himself, but his disorder is a product of fiction, not of the clinic. Moreover, Wagoner's metaphoric powers appear several times to be ascribed to Willy's supposedly childlike mind: "He felt as though he'd dropped a key into a puddle and had stirred up clouds of muddy water by grabbing clumsily for it" (54). Or later, "Beyond the short stretch of water he could see more reeds and, far beyond, the hulk of a grim elevator that looked like a dirty Roman temple with columns" (174). Are these analogies intended to be Willy's or the author's? Sometimes it is hard to judge. Willy describes his slowness as the judgment of a man "following behind, who, if he did catch up was always late. And his lack of judgment was like another person sitting in his head, gross and pudgy like a cretin cupid, who invented all terror and complexity" (186).

3. ROCK

Despite his presumably diminished mental capacity, Willy Grier is one of Wagoner's more thoughtful and introspective protagonists. He is far more capable intellectually than Charlie Bell or the twenty-eight-year-old Max Fallon of *Rock* (1958). The origins of Willy's confusion, despite its unusual nature, are fairly clear, but we never discover just what it is that has disoriented Max. Apparently, after a college education in the East, he has been successful in business, but following a painful divorce he returns home to industrial northern Indiana, an extension of Chicago's suburbs. Whatever his problem, though, Max is not a victim, nor is he disabled, in the sense that Charlie and Willy are. Rather, Max's story is a case of the awkward homecoming, of an unwelcome prodigal son, and it has more in common with the later *Baby, Come on Inside* (1968) than it has with Wagoner's two earlier novels or the intervening *The Escape Artist*.

Despite this additional motif, however, *Rock* pivots on the theme of money. Max Fallon is the son who has talent—he is remembered as a star high school athlete—and intelligence enough to have escaped the narrow, ugly confines of his urban, industrial environment. But he returns with no job, no possessions, and no prospects. His father, from whom he is estranged (the missing or estranged father is a near constant in Wagoner's fiction), appears to be something of a ward heeler, but Max is not at all clear about what he does: "He'd never liked his father's job, not understanding it—he'd never been able to tell anyone what it was. . . . A semipolitical middleman between contractors and city officials, a man with contacts. . . ." (13). As usual in Wagoner's fiction, the political world is corrupt, which is to say that the source of power in society is degraded, and the corrupting force is money. When Max says he'll "probably end up at Standard like the rest of them," his father angrily responds, "A kid with a college education doesn't turn pipe handles in a shed" (7). This response capsulizes Max's dilemma. At twenty-eight he finds himself returning home to his boyhood room where he is what he was when he left—a kid. On the streets, however, and at home in the person of his teenaged brother and sister, Max encounters actual kids, and he finds that he is not one of them, nor does he understand them. He does not speak their language or appreciate their music or understand how they spend their time. In these respects the novel provides a critique of the rock generation as it was in the late fifties (the era of Buddy Holly's "Peggy Sue" and Elvis Presley's "All Shook Up!"), though Wagoner does not specify titles of popular hits or names of performers, because Max would not be apt to know such matters. Yet by running away from his job and divorcing his wife, Max has in effect rejected adulthood: "Why was he here? He could feel himself turning into a child: to come back was to go back, to turn around was to turn inside out" (10). Although scriptural echoes of becoming a child again in order to gain the kingdom of heaven may come to mind, it is more likely that Wagoner intends the potentially valuable, psychologically recuperative regressive journey of Roethke's *The Lost Son* poems.

To reenter the adult world, Max must reexperience his teen years. He must become not a child again, but an adolescent. It is ironic that he must begin by finding a job, for he has only recently repudiated the adult world of responsibility by leaving his job. But the culture based upon money—capitalism—dictates work, and after spending four weeks in Pittsburgh trying to sort out his life, Max has neither leisure nor money left for meditation or recuperation. After a bitter exchange with his brother Timmy, who resents both Max's former successes and his present failure, and after an unpleasant moment at a local teen hangout, Max accepts a job as a lifeguard through his father's city hall connections. Almost everything about the job suggests a sort of ritual regression, the end of which will be rebirth into the adult world. As if he were a boy again, Max rides his bike to city hall after a brief flirtation with one of his sister's teenaged friends. At city hall he must play the role of a son again, specifically of a son who relies on his father. But the ultimate insult is the job itself, "a job for a kid," as Max puts it (47). Moreover, it is a job that will place him, for the most part, in the "kids" world where he will be tested and where he must undergo an initiation in order to regain his adulthood.

Max's experiences as a lifeguard underscore his predicament. He meets a middle-aged man named O'Tool, who haunts the beach and makes a fool of himself in an effort to maintain some connection with youth. The results are variously comic and pathetic. Wagoner describes O'Tool as "a sleek-looking, chubby, strutting, greasy-haired near-midget . . . wearing a pair of shiny blue Lastex trunks" (55) whom Max remembers from high school days as a "pin-striped, cigarillo-smoking joke who looked as though he'd been sent the wrong laundry repeatedly" (56). O'Tool might be seen as an admonition to Max for what he has become and as a warning to him against what he might become should he pass up the opportunity to mature.

Max also meets two women, the aggressive teenager, Della Kelso, and the silent, attractive divorcee, Kate Morley, who has a six-year-old daughter. Given his confusion over his identity, it is no surprise that Max pursues both the girl and the woman. His experiences with them reflect his uncertainties about his role, as does his work as a lifeguard, in which he sees himself as "a referee in an unfamiliar game" (59), unsure whether anyone will listen to him if he enforces the rules and in fact unaware of the rules themselves. The implicit irony throughout is that a person so confused about life should be a "lifeguard." An added verbal irony recurs in the teenagers' slang usage of "man." In his confrontation with an arrogant professor who has taken Kate to the beach and who refers to him as "boy," Max replies, "Max Fallon. I'm a man" (67). Later, however, when the adolescent Della refers to him with such phrasing as "What's the matter, man?" Max responds, "Quit calling me *man*" (82). Not far beneath the semantic surface lies Max's genuine confusion as to his manhood.

At first, despite his awkwardness during a date with Kate, Max seems to assert his adulthood, but he moves directly from her bed to a teenagers' dance where he picks up Della. When he awakens the next morning, Max assesses his condition as amphibious: "All his good intentions had seemed to fall away from him piece by piece, or to become absorbed and useless like a tadpole's tail. Yet where were the legs? If he'd been transformed, what was he? He had a right to know. Was it to be gills or lungs? If a creature didn't know that, he'd be stuck at the very edge of the shore forever" (122–23). At "the very edge of the shore" is precisely Max's location, both literally and metaphorically. In an effort to define himself, Max confronts his brother and sister, who have heard about Della, but they both turn from him, in effect rejecting him as a fellow adolescent. An indication of his coming transformation to adulthood occurs soon afterwards, when Max saves O'Tool, who almost drowns in a makeshift diver's outfit designed by one of the teenagers whose approval O'Tool is always seeking.

The moment of metamorphosis itself occurs, appropriately, at the beach, where Max is confronted by a gang of teenagers. After being dragged along the beach by a car, he manages to escape and swim through the darkness to safety after his brother's car breaks down. Symbolically, then, Max passes the test while his brother and his friends are left behind at the shore, still on the border of adulthood. Before the police arrive, the teenagers burn Max's lifeguard stand and rowboat, both representative of his adolescent self. The next morning Max finds that Timmy has thrown out Max's teenage mementos—notebooks, airplanes, and photos. When he shakes Timmy's hand and says "Thanks and nothing" (198), Max expresses both proper gratitude for his education, including what could be called a trial-by-torture, and his intention that the two of them should start their lives afresh. Max then goes to see Kate, who asks if he is ready, not just for their picnic, presumably, but for a mature relationship.

Critics have been divided in their evaluations of *Rock*. Schaefer finds the novel "less successful" (82) than the first two, partly because it "lacks the sharp focus of suspense and terror of the first novels" (83). One critic found it overly "suggestive" (Curley 523). Robert Phelps, however, in his review for the *New York Herald Tribune*, concluded that with *Rock*, Wagoner joined "the dozen or so writers under forty from whom we should expect our most useful novels in the next few decades" (3). Although Phelps's prediction has not been borne out, I think *Rock* is at least among the most successful two or three of Wagoner's serious novels. His characterization of Max Fallon is considerably more thorough than that of Charlie Bell or Willy Grier, and he portrays Max without resorting to far-fetched premises. Moreover, Max's relationships with a range of other characters are more numerous and more complex than those of Charlie or Willy, who are both loners. It is as if Wagoner isolated the two earlier protagonists until he could figure out how to handle character interaction. Willy interacts much more than Charlie, and Max more than either of them. Unlike Charlie and Willy, Max is not on the run, so he is able to resolve his dilemma, and in that respect the novel anticipates the more positive thrust of Wagoner's subsequent fiction. Max's earnest search for self-identity succeeds, and Wagoner asserts the potential of love to heal and renew.

Rock is also more mature thematically than Wagoner's other early fiction. The undercurrent of warning against the corruption of money and the debasement of life in the industrial city are fused with a well-developed angle on the maturation motif. Finally, Wagoner fully orchestrates the symbolic and semantic strata of this novel. It is no accident, for example, that the verb "know" recurs throughout this narrative of a quest for self-discovery and self-knowledge. When Max tells his mother he doesn't "know anybody in Pittsburgh except bartenders," she replies, "You know we all love you" (16). But love is what Max really does not know. The phrase "you know" is used frequently in the novel, often with an added nuance, but from Max we most often hear what he tells one belligerent teenager at the beach: "I don't know. Trouble with me is, I just don't know" (62). A favorite colloquial usage in the novel is "I know you" (e.g., pages 75, 78, 114), often said with a sneer, and generally not true. By the novel's end, however, Max has escaped the redundancy of "I don't know": "He lay on his back and knew the rocking motion came from his own center" (195).

4. BABY, COME ON INSIDE

"Knowing" is also a problem for the aging (just turning fifty, and not gracefully) pop singer of *Baby, Come on Inside* (1968): "There wasn't any of that stuff about wondering where he was when he woke up: Popsy Meadows *knew* he didn't know" (3). Like Max Fallon, Popsy Meadows has come home to what turns out to be a mixed welcome, and like Max he has come home, apparently, for a cure of sorts. Just which midwestern city Popsy calls home is never indicated, but it is considerably smaller than Chicago, and it is in an agricultural rather than an industrial area. If Max Fallon suffers from financial hardship, Popsy Meadows might be said to suffer from fiscal surfeit. Like Willy Grier, Popsy has plenty of money, but unlike Willy he knows how to use it, at least after a certain reckless fashion. Willy must learn what money can and cannot buy, and in some ways Popsy needs to learn the same lesson. But Willy has been unexposed to money, whereas Popsy has been overexposed to it.

Ten or more years separate *Baby, Come on Inside* from the three novels just examined. In the interim Wagoner had two more books of poems published, *The Nesting Ground* (1963) and *Staying Alive* (1966) (both the subject of the next chapter) and another novel, *The Escape Artist* (1965), which largely altered his course as a novelist along lines signaled by the positive tone at the end of *Rock*. Thematically, *Baby, Come on Inside* has much in common with the earlier three novels, but its tone is comic, although it has touches of the pathetic throughout, which may parallel the tragic aspects of the first two novels. Schaefer refers to the early novels as comedies of the absurd (72), and certainly we encounter in *Baby* an aimless irrationality and a blend of anguish and humor that might justify his description. One reviewer referred to the novel as a "comic nightmare" (Powers 26).

Popsy, characterized by one reviewer as "gross, flamboyant, and quite often anything but engaging" (Powers 26), spends his time avoiding the adulation of sycophants, camp followers, groupies, and hometown admirers, even as he resents his declining popularity and bemoans his fading voice. He also telephones three former wives, living respectively in New York, Miami, and Pasadena, and sends them to various cities for rendezvous with him that he has no intention of keeping. It is the behavior of a man in pain, and though his actions are cruel, they are also pathetic. Such pathetic gestures, however, do not win much sympathy for Popsy any more than his drunken bar-hopping or his mistreatment of such faithful retainers as his accompanist, Sport. Popsy is Wagoner's most unsympathetic protagonist and in some ways his most opaque. The fact that he awakens in a hotel room in his hometown but has no recollection of how he got there suggests that he has some sort of instinctive need to be where he is. He is not consciously aware of a good reason to be back in the boondocks he has not visited for thirty years. Sport says he "blanked out again" (10) in Los Angeles, and he adds that Popsy has already called his friends and invited them to a party to celebrate his fiftieth birthday.

Temporarily escaping the party that he himself arranged, Popsy visits the sort of small-city nightclub in which young performers begin their careers. Already slipping into the role of elder statesman and teacher, Popsy listens closely to the amateurish singers, thinking of how he might advise them. Although the novel cannot record the poor quality of the singing, Wagoner suggests it through Popsy's comments and by creating some of the most dreadful lyrics imaginable. At fifty, however, Popsy appears to be headed in a new direction. Living up to his name, he offers himself as a sort of father figure to the young male and female vocalists, and to the young man he tries to pass on some fatherly advice along with a self-portrait intended to correct the glamorous image the young singer has of the life of a star.

I float on a big plastic sea horse full of self-esteem, kid. I decide
which of my twenty-five agents and managers is going to be the
human sacrifice of the afternoon, and I sing a little for him. No
matter what he says, I can him. Then I call up two or three dames
and knock a couple of them down, saving one for the middle of
the night—like raiding the icebox, you know?—and in-between
times I work on books, rehash arrangements, straighten out all my
confused friends, spend lots of money, or try to keep the top of my
head from blowing off and hurting somebody, and if there's any
time left over, I drink. As soon as I figure I've drunk too much, I
eat too much. (68)

This accurate self-portrayal suggests that Popsy may not be as confused as
he first appears, but it also indicates that he can do little to control his
compulsive nature. He is the popular star who is forced by circumstances,
largely his own fame, to call upon resources he does not possess.

Later in the evening Popsy listens to Rachel Corey, a singer who does
apparently have talent. Wagoner's lyrics are distinctively those of pop music, but one of the passages includes the line from which the novel's title is
drawn, and it also reflects the loneliness of Popsy's life, which he is constantly and hopelessly seeking to remedy.

> *Baby, come on inside.*
> *Let's go for a joy ride.*
> *We don't need streets*
> *Or those old red lights,*
> *Just a room*
> *Where it's warm*
> *And nothing else can get in.* (78)

It is Popsy's inability to discover more than a "joy ride" in life that is destroying him, along with booze, age, the loss of his voice, and his inability
also to find a "room" where "nothing else can get in." Ironically, in fact, he
creates in his hotel suite a room where anybody else can get in. Even as he
turns on his old stand-up comedian's cleverness for the hometown fans at
the nightclub, he senses the shallowness and dishonesty of his act. The
reader knows when Popsy tells the "hometowners" he loves them and
makes a "big gesture with both empty arms" (86) that his arms are empty
not just because he has let go of Rachel. He leaves the stage inviting every-

one to a party at the fairgrounds, but like his invitations to his former wives, the invitation is insincere.

Near the middle of the novel, after attending his party and awarding a series of ribbons along a sort of best-of-breed line to the partyers, Popsy blacks out and awakens in an amnesiac state, this time to find himself in bed with an old friend and fellow performer, the obese Mary-Mary. He has scarcely pieced together the events that led to that comic catastrophe when the mayor, his former high school football coach, nicknamed "Gut," shows up to blackmail him into serving as grand marshal of the Cornflower Festival parade. The comedy becomes almost frenetic as Popsy gets involved in the speeches, is presented the key to the city, suffers through a reunion with his former music teacher, and crowns the Cornflower princess. His speech to the assembly leads him to serious self-revelation, similar in nature to his advice to Rachel, the nightclub singer. He concludes: "Ever try to open somebody else's fist? And then finally it opens and there's nothing in it. Just the palm of my hand" (154). But like the young singer, the hometown audience is unaware of what he is saying; Wagoner describes them as "listening like machines" (154). Popsy then gives a large check to the Community Chest and accepts the keys to a pickup truck, which he drives to the edge of town where his parents run a shabby bar and grill.

Popsy's reunion with his father parallels Max Fallon's reunion in several ways. Popsy's mother is somewhat less warm in her greeting than Max's, but his father resents his return quite openly, just as Max's does. These reversals of the prodigal son motif may reflect some strain in the relationship between Wagoner and his own father, who appears in some of the poems, like "Our Father," to be an object of some trepidation (*Through the Forest* 62). The wandering son is not welcome home whether, as in Max's case, he has failed or, as in Popsy's case, he has succeeded. That he has sent money home periodically does not purchase Popsy so much as a welcome mat. Moreover, he discovers that he has acquired a twenty-year-old adoptive brother; in effect, his parents have simply replaced him with a newer, more suitable model.

He leaves their place as if deserting the sound stage of a movie set and drives back to the hotel, where he encounters one of his former wives and the two singers he met before the party. The singers have vague plans to marry, but Popsy intervenes and, accompanied by a *Time* photographer, marries Rachel himself. The wedding, the typical ending of a Shakespearian romantic comedy, provides a positive note, but the reader is not convinced that Popsy and his young bride will live happily ever after. At best we are offered another of Popsy's temporary solutions to the loneliness and emptiness of his life, another joy ride with a hotel room at the end. The problem for the reader is that Popsy Meadows remains an unendearing protagonist who uses people as readily as they use him. He is a victim, like other protagonists in the urban novels, but he is also a victimizer, capable of dealing out at least as much pain as he receives. He is perhaps Wagoner's best example of Norman O. Brown's "alienated consciousness" (237).

5. THE ESCAPE ARTIST

The protagonist of *The Escape Artist*, Wagoner's fifth urban novel, published three years before *Baby, Come on Inside*, offers a happy alternative to those who are destroyed by the materialistic world, Charlie Bell and Willy Grier, and to those who are injured by it in varying degrees, Max Fallon and Popsy Meadows. Danny Masters, a sixteen-year-old magician on his own in a city rife with political corruption, deals with money more skillfully than any of the other four characters, even though they are adults. That is to say, he has a proper lack of respect for it, though he is far from naive about it. Popsy is controlled by his wealth and success to such an extent that he cannot sustain normal relations with anyone. Max, having lost his first bout as a businessman, is starting all over. Willy never does genuinely understand the nature of money or its dangers. And Charlie is a victim of wealthy and powerful men who do not even regard him as human.

Danny Masters, a fast-talking orphan who was raised by his grandmother, comes to the city (probably Chicago) in search of his Uncle Burke, whose show business career as a magician he has emulated. Like so many of Wagoner's protagonists, Danny is also seeking a father figure. After showing off at a magic shop, he runs afoul of "Stu" Stukovich, the forty-five-year-old neurotic son of the corrupt mayor. To put Stukovich in his place, Danny steals his wallet, which he discovers is filled with hundred-dollar bills. Sensing that it is illicit money, Danny cleverly contrives a plan to find out for certain and to discover what is behind it. His procedures are similar to those of a private detective, and he also provides a sophisticated rationale regarding his own theft.

> Maybe just having the money had made the man [Stukovich]
> loud, but he himself didn't feel loud with it in his pocket. The
> money hadn't kept the man from being obnoxious, therefore it
> wasn't necessary to him, therefore it would be no loss to him,
> therefore Danny could keep it and see whether it did *him* any
> good. (32)

This line of chop logic does not mean that Danny is, as one reviewer characterized him, a "rotten egg" (Frankel 66). Recognizing that the money
belongs to the man only more-or-less and that it was "probably produced
by some kind of manipulation," Danny concludes that a magician is indeed
"a kind of thief," but that he is not truly a thief because he is not "trying to
hog it all" (33). Danny is scrupulously honest, in fact, paying for what he
needs with his own money and later using money he has earned to pay
back a musician whose coat he has borrowed. Realizing the evil he has
chanced upon, Danny proceeds to reveal and destroy it, an act which is beyond the capacity of either Charlie Bell or Willy Grier, or for that matter
Max Fallon, who does not destroy the evil he detects in the teenaged rock-
and-rollers but merely fulminates against it and refuses to succumb to it.

One reason that Wagoner describes *The Escape Artist* as his favorite
among the "contemporary-scene" novels (McFarland, "Interview" 17) is
that it has been filmed—produced in 1982 by Francis Ford Coppola but
not a box office success—and another reason is that he himself is an amateur magician. Mona Van Duyn has noted the parallel between the young
magician in the novel and the young artist or writer (332). Like the artist or
poet, the magician differs from what a reporter in the novel calls "just
plain folks" because, Danny says, "[h]e does what others wish they could
do, and even if he can't, he makes them think he can." "Sometimes," he
adds, a magician "does what people dream about. . . . Sometimes he's like
he's dreaming himself" (163). Earlier he notes that "almost all people
hated magicians" (56). The public, like the people in Kafka's "The Hunger
Artist," never fully understands or appreciates what is going on, and implicitly this refers not just to the art of fasting, or of magic, but to art in
general.

In his poem entitled "The Escape Artist," first published in 1966, a year
after the novel appeared, Wagoner depicts the "artist" escaping from a
straitjacket while hanging upside down from a crane as a sort of *alter* human, man's other or would-be self. He hangs from his feet "[l]ike some-

thing restless dreaming about flying" (*New and Selected Poems*). Sweat flows into his eyes like "tears coming backward" and "his smile is wrong side up." At the end of his act, the crane lowers the escape artist, "[p]utting him back where he was, among us" (146). The artist's or magician's escape is at best temporary and illusory. Eventually, he or she must deal with the real—that is, ordinary—world on its own terms, or else risk the fate of Kafka's hunger artist: ridicule, followed by oblivion and death.

Danny Masters, as William Schaefer has observed, successfully resists being "sucked into the sordidness of here-and-now reality" (85) with all its corruption. As his name implies, he *is* a "master" of his art, for he achieves the magician-artist's dream of transforming reality. In order to attract attention to himself and to his act, as advised by a theatrical agent, Danny arranges a publicity stunt whereby he will escape from the city jail, in the meantime freeing Stukovich and unmasking the corruption at city hall. Prior to his escape Danny speculates on the impact of his magic on the unsympathetic, materialistic world:

> They wanted to be sure where *everything* was. They had it all counted: the money, the split seconds, the assistant people, the candy, the cigarette butts, and if anything was missing or put back crooked they could always tell. That's why making something out of nothing bothered them so much. That's why making something disappear threw them for a loss. And that's why pretending to have everything, and even being funny about it, made them mad because it showed them what they loved most and sweated for was unimportant. (167)

In a way, Danny has described the role of the poet and artist—to make something out of nothing, to create, prompting the great pretense of the imagination that one has everything, which leads in turn to humor or insanity on the part of the poet and to admiration or envy on the part of the public.

Confronting and threatening Danny's youthful idealism, however, is the has-been show biz act of his aunt and uncle, a pathetic pair for whom all magic is a bag of worn-out tricks. The alcoholic Uncle Burke is so far gone that he cannot recognize either Danny's genuine talent or his wife's clairvoyance, which he takes to be just part of the act. Uncle Burke is the antitype of the master magician or sorcerer who would pass on the mysterious lore to a worthy apprentice. He is burned out, defeated by the quotidian, by the item counters of the world. Wagoner's novel is in part a *Bildungsroman* and in part a *Kunstlerroman*, but Danny Masters has no teachers or worthy companions. Although his name suggests he is already master of his art, throughout the novel it is clear that Danny is searching for guidance, for a father, in the form of his uncle or perhaps even in the form of his adversary, Stu Stukovich. He attaches himself to Stu and to his muddle-headed sidekick, Mud. Much of the ample comedy, in fact, comes in scenes in which Danny dupes the inept Mud. By the middle of the book Danny senses that he is somehow "changed" (109), but only near the end does he see himself as "a man now" (195).

Danny's initiation into manhood involves not only the recognition that his former father figure, Uncle Burke, represents a false or tarnished image, but also the resolution of a set of dilemmas. He must decide whether Stu provides a better model than his uncle, and for a while he appears to be tempted, despite Stu's vicious streak, by his quick wit and engaging manner. In most respects, Stu is a far more worthy opponent or antagonist than others Wagoner sets against his main characters. After he frees Stu from jail, however, Danny ingeniously breaks the combinations of the mayor's and the city treasurer's safes, plants the wallet full of marked currency, and calls the FBI. When Stu realizes what has happened, he goes berserk and pursues Danny with a butcher knife. Danny hides in a mailbox while the police arrest the deranged and outraged Stukovich. Danny discovers, then, that Stu has been too close to the corruption of his father's money to avoid being tarnished.

Danny also makes a last effort to reestablish his uncle and aunt as surrogate parents, but it fails. His emergence from the mailbox, therefore, represents Danny's passage from the idealized, boyish fantasies into the world of hard realities. There may even be something womblike about the dark enclosure and Danny's "deliverance." Throughout the novel Danny has successfully escaped or mocked the unpleasant aspects of genuine corruption, both in the political world and in the more specialized world of his art. His aunt, however, he finds has shut herself up in a locker in the dressing room, unable at last to cope with reality even though she has joined with her husband in debasing their art and her own gift. Danny perceives that he must compromise his own sense of magic in accordance with the demands of the public. The agent who earlier demanded such tricks as levitation and sawing a lady in half speaks for the public, and Danny intends to succeed.

[H]e needed a few calm days recruiting an assistant with a smile
that could reach the back of the balcony, who wasn't afraid to float
or wake up in half, who wouldn't disappear at the wrong time or
let the rabbit out of the bag, and he'd find her if he had to try
every waitress and movie cashier in town. (220)

Danny's successful publicity stunt may have transformed the world in a
way, but the cost has been high and the result is not a new respect for escape artistry any more than the hunger artist's record-breaking fast revives
enthusiasm for professional fasting in Kafka's fable. The last sentence in
the novel suggests, perhaps, that Danny is leaving the castle of romance,
via the drawbridge, and entering the world as it is: "The door fell down flat
like a drawbridge, and he put his legs out into the pale morning" (220).

William Schaefer describes Danny Masters as "immensely intelligent"
(85), an "articulate hero" (87) who is "self-sufficient" (88) to the extent of
being able to maintain his "imaginative integrity" (87). In *The Escape
Artist* Wagoner himself escapes the brooding environs of what Schaefer (à
la William Blake) calls the "mills of Satan" (71). In the four comic Western
novels that follow *Baby, Come on Inside*, where the industrial midwestern
city is replaced by an agricultural city, Wagoner returns to the youthful
protagonist who is characteristically quick-witted, fast talking, wisecrack-
ing, resourceful, and honest. The scene shifts to Nebraska and beyond, the
time period shifts to the nineteenth century, and the dark images of urban
decay are shed, as are the soot and grime of modern society. One thing
that does not change, however, is the avid pursuit of money, which threat-
ens always to undermine human values. In the Western novels, all narrated from a first-person point of view, the young protagonists, age
seventeen to twenty, are seeking their fortunes, and they are generally
successful, but their attitudes toward money contrast sharply with those of
their greed-driven antagonists.

WORDS AT PLAY:

The Nesting Ground, Staying Alive, and
New and Selected Poems

ALTHOUGH IN HIS AUTOBIOGRAPHICAL essay David Wagoner expresses considerable ambivalence about his marriage to Patt Parrott in 1961, a marriage which collapsed and ended in a traumatic divorce nearly twenty years later, he recognizes that year as a "clear demarcation point" in his poems. "The rhythms are frequently more open," he reports, but more important, "a whole new area of personal experience becomes available. . . . I came out of hiding" (*Contemporary Authors* 407). The three collections of the 1960's, *The Nesting Ground* (1963), *Staying Alive* (1966), and *New and Selected Poems* (1969), move from the self-questioning of *A Place to Stand* to self-discovery and self-revelation. The poems are distinguished by an expanding exuberance of language and an increasingly playful tone and comic manner. James Dickey acclaimed Wagoner's "curious, sardonic and often authentically wild comic imagination" in his review of *The Nesting Ground* in the *New York Times Book Review*, adding that some of the poems have the effect of the "high-speed jottings of a man who envisions the world as a complicated joke" (4).

A brief stint with the Seattle *Post-Intelligencer* in 1962 convinced Wagoner that his preference was for teaching, and a 1965 Ford Fellowship in drama, spent with the Seattle Repertory Theatre, temporarily ended his flirtation with the stage, which had included a few acting jobs in 1953. Of his several attempts at playwriting, only the one-act comedy, *The Song of Songs Which is Sheba's*, produced at the University of Washington in 1973, has seen print, in a special issue of the *Slackwater Review* (1981). A number of his poems, however, possess dramatic qualities such as narrative, dialogue, setting, character interaction, and even dramatic structure and dramatic irony. "A Guide to Dungeness Spit," certainly the best known poem from *The Nesting Ground*, exemplifies most of those qualities, as does "The Skate's Egg" (not one of his more endearing efforts), "The First Day of a Search," and "That Old Gang of Mine."

With his fourth and perhaps his most successful novel, *The Escape Artist* (1965) and his fourth collection of poems, *Staying Alive* (1966), Wagoner was tenured and promoted to full professor at the University of Washington. His friend and mentor, Theodore Roethke, had died in 1963, leaving his ghost to haunt the creative writing program at the university. More than anyone, Wagoner realized that Roethke could be neither replaced nor imitated. It would be sufficient if he could just keep himself from being overshadowed by that lingering presence. By 1966 Carolyn Kizer had left for a position with the National Endowment for the Arts in Washington, D.C., and Wagoner was named to succeed her as editor of *Poetry Northwest*, a position he has now held for some thirty years. He credits his experiences as an editor and teacher for improving his writing. In an interview with the editors of *Yes* magazine in 1973, Wagoner commented, "Right now, I feel about editing the way I feel about teaching: it is the other half of some mysterious process which, for me, is largely beneficial, rewarding me with as much as I give to it" ("Conversation" 22). In 1968 Wagoner turned out his fifth novel, *Baby, Come on Inside*, and the next year marked something of a milestone, the appearance of his *New and Selected Poems*, which he describes as "more widely and favorably reviewed than any of my previous work" (*Contemporary Authors* 408).

1. THE NESTING GROUND

Asked for a contribution to Paul Engle and Joseph Langland's *Poet's Choice* in the fall of 1961, Wagoner selected what was to be the title poem of his next collection, "The Nesting Ground," which he modestly described as "one of my least disappointing poems" (Engle and Langland 251). Robert Cording describes "A Guide to Dungeness Spit" as "a kind of prototype for Wagoner's best poems" (350), but that poem was not written till several months later. Perhaps it would prove most instructive to examine the two poems in tandem, for they embody significant similarities and differences. In his comments on "The Nesting Ground" in Engle and Langland's book, Wagoner claimed to dislike poets who "swarm around their matter . . . like a lesser Victorian who has discovered a spring flower and treats it like an all-day sucker" (250). Of his preferences he wrote:

> The poems I most admire are simultaneously free and controlled;
> they have no padding, yet aren't jammed together; the lines tend

to be "open" most of the time, without knotted syntax, or metaphors at cross-purposes visually. The rhythm is related to the subject matter and doesn't simply drone. The poems tend to be dramatic presentations which have to account for themselves with as little author comment as possible. (250)

With few exceptions, this statement applies well to all of Wagoner's poems, especially to those written after 1961.

Both "Nesting Ground" and "Guide to Dungeness Spit" are such "dramatic presentations," in which we encounter a distinct cast of characters enacting a scene of sorts in a specific setting. In "The Nesting Ground" (12–13) a couple come upon a killdeer nest, and the drama revolves around the efforts of the parent birds to distract their attention from the nest by pretending to be injured. In effect, there is a play within the play, the embedded drama of the killdeer whose ploy amounts to a sacrificial gesture. The birds succeed in distracting the couple, who realize what has gone on only after they have been led from the nest. They turn at the end to observe through their "strongest glass" the nestlings, now safe, springing from cover, "[p]iping one death was over."

Beneath the serious life-and-death game of the killdeer is a subtle story of love and discovery involving the humans. They walk "straight to the spot" of the nest, presumably because of their need "to stir what we love." They have come to a source of life in nature, but when they kneel down and look in the "sparse grass," they find nothing, for the birds have carefully camouflaged their nest: "We flattened disbelief / With the four palms of our hands." Only at the end of the poem, when they turn "as the birds turned," do they recognize the nest, looking back at "the source," the place "[w]here we had touched our knees." The language suggests both the reverence of their kneeling and the romantic touching of knee to knee. Above all, however, the poem celebrates the couple's recognition of love and sacrifice and their realization that such love and sacrifice can, in a sense, conquer even death.

"A Guide to Dungeness Spit" (*The Nesting Ground* 10–11) also focuses on a pair of lovers on a nature walk, and it also involves a turning back to the source, but the poem is more complex and richer in a number of ways, aside from the obvious fact that it is thirteen lines longer than "The Nesting Ground." Sanford Pinsker identifies the woman in the poem as Patt Parrott and notes that she and Wagoner married soon after it was written

(*Northwest Poets* 107). Written in the present tense, "A Guide" portrays a more directly dramatic moment, which perhaps prompted Richard Howard to detect the "new adequacy of scene to agent and of agent to action" (630). Unlike "The Nesting Ground," "A Guide" is located in a specific place, Dungeness Spit, a National Wildlife Refuge on the Olympic Peninsula. Wagoner's locales have, in fact, remained fairly evenly divided over the years, with some poems like "A Guide" seemingly distinctive in their regional orientation, while others, like "Nesting Ground," might be situated wherever the wide-ranging killdeer breed. Regionalists who wish to insist upon Wagoner's "northwesternness" might cite, from *Staying Alive* (1966), an obvious title like "Water Music for the Progress of Love in a Life-Raft down the Sammamish Slough" (22–23), while those who find such tags to be too limiting might find an exception in the very next poem, "The Poets Agree to be Quiet by the Swamp" (24).

The first seven lines of "A Guide to Dungeness Spit" set the scene: the couple step down from the "switching road" and wild roses to "an arm of land washed from the sea," where they encounter cormorants, "their wings held out like skysails." The exposition is then interrupted by a question: "Where shall we walk?" In effect, the remainder of the poem answers this question, alternating passages of exposition, which establish the identity of their surroundings, with imperatives, which both propel the poem and subtly pressure the "you," who is identified as the speaker's lover at the end. The careful use of the second person contributes to the intimate tone of this poem, in which the reader becomes part of the "we" and eventually one of the lovers, and presumably of the world which the speaker defines.

The goal of "our" excursion, appropriately enough, is the lighthouse, seven miles away. Some might object that the symbolism is overly obvious, but it should be credited to his account that Wagoner's introduction of the lighthouse early in the poem seems so natural a part of the landscape as to attract little suspicion, at least on a first reading. After the speaker's command to "put your prints to the sea" and "pause there," he directs us past the kelp, geese, loons, pipers, and other flora and fauna for the next fourteen lines. But Wagoner does not merely catalog the items of the seashore. One of his techniques is the use of puns, some of which, as Howard has observed, are "brilliant," while others are "outrageous" (630). In a way, the pun in line thirteen is both: "And we must go afoot when the tide is heeling." The tide "heels" or leans away, ebbs, providing a dry passage and a playful association with the prospect of going "afoot." But the tide is also, as it turns out, "healing," for it fosters the moment of revelation and community that is about to occur.

The birds seem to be ordered in their appearance from the most distant Canada geese overhead to the Bonaparte's gulls perched nearby. From the gulls, he directs our attention to sponges, and then casually, as if it were to be expected in the natural scheme of things, he says, "Those are the ends of bones." But he does not elaborate. Instead, he suggests that if we cross the "inner shore," we will find grebes and goldeneyes fishing. Then he points to some cockleshells. There appears to be no logical transition operating from one observation to the next, though we might detect an up-and-down, distant-to-near inner rhythm here and elsewhere in the poem. Karl Malkoff suggests that the poem "operates effectively out of the contrast between the narrator's explicit assumption that he is simply pointing out what happens to be there and the implication in the poem that he is attempting to put the universe in order" (314). Other readers have likened the speaker to Adam in the Garden of Eden giving names to the beasts.

From the cockleshells, as after his reference to the sponges five lines earlier, the speaker again turns away from a simple catalog: "And these are the dead. I said we would come to these." Again his observation seems casual, as death is among creatures who cannot conceive of their own deaths. For the sentient reader, however, the terse sentences have considerable impact. They echo rhythmically the previous allusions to sponges and bones, and they vary dramatically from the previous sentence, which runs three and a half lines. Furthermore, the speaker's voice immediately shifts from exposition to command: "Stoop to the stones." The action picks up as, ordered to turn over one of the stones, we discover a colony of small crabs lifting their pincers "[t]o defend the dark." Again the speaker attempts to make very little of this, his own, pregnant observation. Instead, he invites us to "step this way," and he leads us past snowy plovers feeding on sand fleas, without commenting on what must be obvious to us about the wildlife community. He says simply, "The air grows dense."

Then he turns to his companion, and to us if only by implication, and confronts her with a pair of decisions which may appear incompatible. The first one seems simple enough: "You must now decide whether we shall walk for miles and miles." Shall we keep on going? But clearly the speaker is suggesting a journey much farther than the day's excursion. The second decision is more complex: You must also decide "whether all birds are the young of other creatures / Or their own young ones, / Or simply their old selves because they die." He explains that when a bird falls, the others "touch him webfoot or with claws / Treading him for the ocean." "This," he adds, "is called sanctuary," apparently referring to the community of birds and their instinctive unity with their surroundings. Of course, Dungeness Spit is also literally a bird sanctuary.

The couple are then enshrouded with fog, and the speaker issues another command: "Wait." He then directs our attention to the last of the birds in the poem, a "snowy owl / Facing the sea," whose "flashing yellow eyes" act as a beacon, in effect a natural lighthouse leading us "through the shallows," as if we were ships, to the manmade lighthouse. The passage also suggests a transition from the superficial to the profound. Emerging from what might be regarded as a sort of mystical dark night of the soul, the "you" of the poem is weeping. At the literal level, of course, the tears the speaker calls to our attention are caused by the wind.

In the concluding nine lines, the speaker gives his final command, "look," in a passage that triumphantly asserts the visionary experience:

> *Those are tears. Those are called houses, and those*
>   *are people.*
> *Here is a stairway past the whites of our eyes.*
> *All our distance has ended in the light. We climb to the*
>   *light in spirals,*
> *And look, between us we have come all the way,*
> *And it never ends*
> *In that ocean, the spit and image of our guided travels.*
> *Those are called ships. We are called lovers.*
> *There lie the mountains.* (11)

As Hyatt Waggoner has asserted in his study of American visionary poetry, "A Guide to Dungeness Spit" is "a major poem by any standard" (185). Only after confronting life and death, from the height of a passing flight of Canada geese to the depth of inch-long crabs under a stone, are the couple prepared to understand what it is to be human. In his review of Wagoner's *New and Selected Poems*, John T. Irwin describes this perspective as a variant of "Roethke's later poems celebrating the material world and man's continuity with that world," that variant being Wagoner's "acknowledgment of man's animality and its consequences" (168). Returning from the animal to the human world, distance dissolves into light, the seven miles to the lighthouse yields to eternity, and "we" become worthy "lovers." The concluding image reminds us not only that the poem began in descent, the familiar mystical journey backward in order to go forward, but also that images of ascent have dominated the poem throughout, ever since the cormorants in line six "floating on trees / In a blue cove," stretched "to a point above us."

While the conceptual and thematic power of "A Guide to Dungeness Spit" distinguishes it significantly from "The Nesting Ground," we should not overlook the technical differences between the two poems. Both poems exemplify Wagoner's preference, stated in Engle and Langland's book, for poems that are "simultaneously free and controlled" (250). In "The Nesting Ground" he adheres to a three-stress accentual line. Scansion of the accentual line is tricky because it is more subject to individual nuances of stress than the accentual-syllabic line, but the stress markings below of the concluding nine lines provide a fair indication of the poem's pulse:

> ⌣ / ⌣ / ⌣ /
> We kept on walking led
>
> ⌣ ⌣ / ⌣ / ⌣ /
> By pretended injuries
>
> ⌣ / ⌣ / ⌣ /
> Till we were far away,
>
> ⌣ / ⌣ ⌣ / /
> Then turned, as the birds turned
>
> ⌣ / / ⌣ ⌣ /
> To sail back to the source
>
> ⌣ / ⌣ / ⌣ /
> Where we had touched our knees,
>
> ⌣ / ⌣ ⌣ / ⌣ /
> And saw through our strongest glass
>
> ⌣ / / / ⌣ / ⌣
> The young spring out of cover,
>
> / ⌣ / / ⌣ / ⌣
> Piping one death was over. (13)

Of these lines, five have six syllables and four have seven. At least five lines, including the first through third, could be measured as conventional iambic trimeter, but the effect of the passage is of free verse. Free, that is, but not unconstrained. Throughout the poem the reader is reined in by the terse lines carefully arranged in three scenes, the first two running twelve lines each and the last seventeen.

With respect to form, "A Guide to Dungeness Spit," with its alternating long and short lines, is more open and rambling. The poems might be aptly described as formally antithetical to each other. The restraint of the lovers in "The Nesting Ground," who have come upon the birds' nest in "sparse grass," seems reflected in the clipped lines. The ambling seaside stroll of the couple at Dungeness Spit, on the other hand, seems to call for a looser sort of line. Perhaps their experience resists the compartmental-ization into scenes that frames "The Nesting Ground." Or the difference might be described as that between an insight and a vision. The 54 ebbing and flowing lines of "A Guide," however, are by no means haphazard. Wagoner has described the ternary form in this poem as a "6–beat, 5–beat, 3– or 2–beat sequence," which "has some sort of sine-curve or expansion-contraction pulsation" (McFarland, "Dynamic Form" 41, 45). He has returned to this form again and again in some of his most effective poems, including the title poems from *Staying Alive, Sleeping in the Woods,* and *Landfall.* He uses the form in all nine poems of the "Travelling Light" sequence (*Collected Poems* 249–61) and in the six poems of the "Sea Change" sequence (*Landfall* 101–10). The form or some adaptation of it, including a binary form, appears in 20 of the 63 poems that make up the volume, *In Broken Country.*

Even an experienced reader of Wagoner's poems would be hard put to anticipate where the lines might break in this highly flexible, dynamic form, which I have elsewhere called a "combination of line and stanza" (*David Wagoner* 26). Wagoner suggests that the form works best "where I'm trying to be alternately matter-of-fact seeming (or even flat) and lyri-cal" (McFarland, "Dynamic Form" 46). The following passage illustrates the visual as well as rhythmic effects of Wagoner's ternary form (I have marked the accentual stress):

> ⏑ / ⏑ / ⏑ / ⏑ ⏑ /   ⏑ ⏑ / ⏑ / ⏑
> *And we must go afoot at a time when the tide is heeling.*
> / / ⏑ / ⏑ / ⏑ / ⏑ ⏑ /
> *Those whistling overhead are Canada geese;*
> / ⏑ ⏑ / ⏑ /
> *Some on the waves are loons,*

⌣　/　⌣　⌣　/　⌣　/　⌣　　/　　/　⌣　⌣　　/
And more on the sand are pipers. There, Bonaparte's gulls
/　⌣　⌣　/　⌣　/　　/　⌣　/　⌣
Settle a single perch. Those are sponges.
　/　　⌣　⌣　/　⌣　/
Those are the ends of bones. (20)

Syntax behaves independently of both stanza and line in the ternary form, and the shortened third line is variable in its function. For example, in the passage above, the first short line simply offers information, while the second introduces intimations of mortality. In the final analysis, the effect of Wagoner's ternary form is spatial. Elsewhere, I have likened it to a painter's use of foreshortening to create an illusion of three-dimensionality, particularly in the last lines of "A Guide," where words like "distance" and "never ends" are placed at the ends of short lines instead of long ones, causing the "ideas of distance and infinity to draw inward," to be internalized ("Dynamic Form" 44).

There is probably no way to account adequately for a book of poems, short of examining each poem in the collection. But even to comment briefly on the twenty-six poems from *The Nesting Ground* that Wagoner included in his *Collected Poems* is impracticable, and his more recent collections are often twice the size of his earlier ones. *First light* (1983), for example, comprises eighty-seven poems. Of the forty-one poems in *The Nesting Ground*, perhaps seventeen, including the two just examined, could be considered nature poems. The remainder are quite varied in subject, theme, and voice. Throughout the collection, for example, are poems pertaining to the urban business world, the world of *negotium*—which Wagoner enjoys depicting in humorous, generally satirical counterpoint to the world of *otium*, the immensely more serious and more important leisure world of poems like "The Nesting Ground" and "A Guide to Dungeness Spit."

In the first poem of *The Nesting Ground*, "Diary" (9), the first person speaker gets the best of the quotidian from the opening stanza:

> *At Monday dawn, I climbed into my skin*
> *And went to see the money. There were the shills:*
> *I conned them—oh, the coins fell out of their mouths,*
> *And paint peeled from the walls like dollar bills.*
> *Below their money-belts, I did them in. (9)*

Throughout the days of the week, the speaker gradually acquires his clothes, only to be encircled and smothered by an overcoat on Thursday. On Friday he strips back to his skin and is naked on Saturday "for love." On Sunday, the poem concludes, "I wrote this." "A Guide" and "The Nesting Ground" follow "Diary," as if to remind the reader that the real work is not done at the office or in the workaday world.

Other poems that make light of the business world include "Offertory" (25) and "After Consulting My Yellow Pages" (15), in which we are assured that "[a]ll went well today in the barber college," and "[b]usiness came flying out of the horse-meat market." In "No Sale" (32–33) the first-person speaker, "after pounding weeks / Through showers and heat-waves" and talking to "all the wives / Who leaned on shaky walls," gives up on selling siding. The concluding stanza typifies Wagoner's wordplay:

> *Swindled by someone else,*
> *They sat in curls all day,*
> *Waiting to be let down,*
> *Waiting to fall straight*
> *And stringy at midnight.*
> *So I went straight, and quit.* (33)

In "Writing to Order" (52–53), the speaker finds himself set apart from "[o]ther men elsewhere" who "[a]re plugging what they know." These are "The good buyers and sellers . . . Who all know what to do / With blanks and fountain pens." The speaker, however, is a poet standing "beside furniture / Which even death-cells use / To prop a prisoner— / A table and a chair." His dilemma is summed up in the following lines, the latter two of which might pass for a cynical aphorism on poetry itself:

> *I face what I don't know,*
> *Can't follow or wait for,*
> *The private enterprise*
> *For which there's no demand.* (53)

Obviously, the first-person speaker in these poems assumes many personalities. In "Homage" (16), an almost pure nature lyric which addresses the phenomenon, a pair of hummingbirds, as perceived but not really received or responded to, the "I" is present throughout, but the reader acquires scarcely any sense of his personality. The poem is nearly voiceless.

In the next poem though, "The Emergency Maker" (17–18), the speaker projects a distinct personality and voice.

> *"Still alive—" the message ran,*
> *Tapped on a broken rail—*
> *"The air is somewhere else, the shaft*
> *Is blacker than the coal.*
> *Lower a light and break the rock*
> *That plugged this bloody hole."*
>
> *But I, who had tossed the dynamite,*
> *Had better things to do*
> *Than juggle stones from here to there*
> *Or bring the dark to day.*
> Go shovel yourself and hold your nose:
> The diggers have to die. (17)

The poem develops in three stanzas, the second pertaining to an engineered disaster at sea and the third to one involving mountain climbers. In each case, the speaker surfaces as a devious sort of gremlin who, at the end of the poem, ironically joins the victims in the line, "We *climbers have to die*" (18).

The speaker in "Free Passage" (19) is a reckless seafaring lover whose breezy wordplay suggests the influence of Dylan Thomas as he urges his beloved to take some risks and join him for "a crack at the sky."

> *Oh my snifter, my tumble-rick, sweet crank of the stars,*
> *My banjo-bottomed, fretful girl,*
> *Tear off those swatches of silk, your hems and haws, and*
> *   coil them up like streamers—*
> *Get set to toss them over the bounding rail.* (19)

The speaker in the next poem, however, "The Calculation" (20–21), is a playful academic reminiscing on a confusing problem in calculus. The final stanza represents a sort of formalism which may be appropriate to the poem but which seems almost a repudiation of the free verse of the lines cited above, in which the syllable count varies from eight to eighteen.

> *But I was late because my shadow was*
> *Pointing toward nothing like the cess of light,*

> *Sir, and bearing your cold hypotenuse—*
> *That cutter of corners, jaywalker of angles—*
> *On top of my head, I walked the rest of the night.* (21)

Tracking the first-person speaker in a volume of Wagoner's poems, in short, is no simple matter. If the reader expects consistency, he or she is likely to be frustrated, perhaps even annoyed. But for readers who enjoy the unexpected, Wagoner's poems supply surprises time after time. In "Standing Halfway Home" (60), the speaker finds himself standing utterly still on a trail, "central and inert," until a "hiss of feathers parts the silence": "At my arm's length a seedy, burr-sized wren, / As if I were a stalk, bursts into song." It is the sort of quiet epiphany one finds so often in poems by James Wright, Robert Bly, and Gary Snyder, among others. Such moments, in fact, have become fairly common in American poetry since Robert Frost. What makes that sort of poem surprising, and not just another well-written poem of its type, is its context. In this instance it follows "A Day in the City" (58–59), in which the speaker rambunctiously leads an imagined wild bunch through town:

> *And the city is ours. See, the bridges all give up, the arcades*
> *Rattle their silver shops,*
> *Buildings chip in, the sidewalks roll over like dogs, hotels*
> *Chime their fire-escapes.* (58)

Then, directly after the quiet, self-effacing speaker of "Standing Halfway Home," comes the self-teasing speaker who examines an x-ray of his head and calls it a "madcap, catch-all rattlepot" (61). Near the end of *The Nesting Ground*, in "Every Good Boy Does Fine" (62) and "Filling Out a Blank" (63), the first-person speaker is unabashedly autobiographical: Wagoner himself recalling cornet practice and his first basketball game, for which he forgot his uniform, and his job preferences when in high school—chemist, magician, or ———.

What *The Nesting Ground* demonstrates most importantly for Wagoner, then, are his confidence in the language and his versatility. The multiple voices, modes, and forms attempted in this collection are indicative of Wagoner's work as a whole. It is not that he lacks a distinctive voice, but rather that he has several distinctive voices, though clearly the critics have tended to prefer one or two of those to all the others, and "A Guide to Dungeness Spit" most clearly anticipates those voices for which he has been most admired. In his next collection, *Staying Alive* (1966), Wagoner's poetry began to receive the attention it deserved, though in at least one instance, in a review by Robert Boyers of *New and Selected Poems* (1969), the achievement of *Staying Alive* led to an unfortunate underestimation of *The Nesting Ground*.

2. STAYING ALIVE

Boyers praised the poems of *Staying Alive* for their "solidity and intensity" (181), and Sanford Pinsker has echoed him in hailing the volume as "the breakthrough to a firm voice" ("The Achievement" 43). Richard Howard described the collection as "his finest achievement to date" (634). Most frequently cited by the commentators is the title poem, which, as Robert Cording has ably demonstrated, "begins Wagoner's search for the 'pathway' that leads out of the 'wilderness.' . . . It presents us with Wagoner's most characteristic stance and voice: 'we' are instructed in a voice that is, at once, matter-of-fact, self-mocking, witty, and quietly reverential to accommodate the most negative and disintegrative aspects of life, balancing the good against the bad" (352). Wagoner appears to have agreed with the critics, for of the forty-one poems in *Staying Alive*, he included all but six in his *New and Selected Poems* and later in *Collected Poems* (1976).

In the seashore at Dungeness Spit, Wagoner developed one of the fundamental, universal elemental symbols: the sea as the source of life and transformation and as eternity. From *The Odyssey* and the story of Noah to Arnold's "Dover Beach" and Frost's "Neither Out Far Nor In Deep," the seashore has been a place of returning and recognition. At the seashore or at sea, humankind contemplates itself and realizes what it is and what it will become. In the title poem, "Staying Alive" (12–14), Wagoner makes use of an elemental symbol with a comparable pedigree: the wilderness as a place of trial, representative of the mysteries, uncertainties, and dangers of life. In the forest, humankind—Jesus, Natty Bumppo, Hester Prynne, Nick Adams—is tested, and there humankind confronts its inner self.

The speaker in "Staying Alive" comes across as one who has been tested, knows the challenges, and performs now as an instructor or master in the Way. The via in Wagoner's poems is distinctly Western, not a Tao or a Zen koan, though there are similarities with some aspects of Taoism. Simplicity and the maintenance of a serene mind and spirit, for example, are at the heart of Wagoner's poem, as are the insistence on integrity of the self and respect for all nature. The speaker's first lesson is that "Staying alive in the woods is a matter of calming down." Later he advises, "It may be best to learn what you have to learn without a gun, / Not killing but watching birds and animals go / In and out of shelter." He adds that we should follow their example and "build for a whole season." He also warns that in the wilderness we are on our own: "If you hurt yourself, no one will comfort you." The initial thirty-seven lines of the poem pertain to the first of two alternatives: either "wait for rescue, / Trusting to others" or "start walking and walking in one direction / Till you come out"—or something happens to stop you. Under the circumstances, the "safer choice" is to "settle down where you are, and try to make a living / Off the land." Not just coincidentally, this advice corresponds to what might variously be termed a Taoist, Stoic, or American pioneer ethic and at the same time to standard lessons in search-and-rescue manuals.

The remarkable achievement of "Staying Alive" is Wagoner's ability to sustain a voice which is both commonsensical and profound. The literal, ordinary, "Eat no white berries," is transformed into the moral, aphoristic, "Spit out all bitterness." Offering advice about the fear of freezing to death, the speaker begins with a simple, prosaic assertion: "Don't try to stay awake through the night, afraid of freezing." He appears to be lapsing into textbook prose. But against the flatness, Wagoner balances the loaded rhetoric of, "The bottom of your mind knows all about zero."

The first part of the poem concerns fear, whether of starving, freezing, or being attacked by wild animals. At line 38, however, the speaker turns to the second alternative for survival:

> But if you decide, at last, you must break through
> In spite of all danger
> Think of yourself by time and not by distance, counting
> Wherever you're going by how long it takes you.

Again, the advice makes sense with respect to the practical aspects of surviving in the wilds, but it also directs us to another dimension of our lives, shifting our attention from place to time. By this point in the poem, such simple statements as "Remember the stars" resonate with meaning. In the poem's climactic passage, the speaker announces:

> There may even come, on some uncanny evening,
> A time when you're warm and dry, well fed, not thirsty,
> Uninjured, without fear,

> *When nothing, either good or bad, is happening.*
> *This is called staying alive. It's temporary.*
> *What occurs after*
> *Is doubtful. . . . (13)*

What we must be prepared for, the speaker continues, is our discovery: "Here you are face to face with the problem of recognition." What we acquire from the trial in the wilderness, after all, is a new sense of self, the result either of renewal or of an evolution in self-awareness. The speaker, sustaining his metaphor, suggests "You should have a mirror," a signal mirror, "to show the way you suffer." The new or renewed self is attained only through an ordeal.

But in the wilderness, there is no guarantee of survival. The poem concludes with the speaker's terse reflection on the possibility that we might not be rescued: "Then, chances are, you should be prepared to burrow / Deep for a deep winter." In the varied worlds of Wagoner's poems, we are occasionally offered reassurances, but not often. If we follow the speaker's advice in "Staying Alive," we might survive by remaining calm and living off the land, adapting to nature. Or we might survive by walking out, provided we go in one direction and follow other sensible suggestions, like retracing fences or wheel ruts. But all the advice might fail, rescuers might not appear, and in that case we must prepare for "deep winter," for that death which the poem promised in its title would not happen.

It takes a distant, almost cold-blooded sort of speaker to confront the reader as Wagoner does in "Staying Alive" and other poems in the volume. For example, in "The Shooting of John Dillinger Outside the Biograph Theater, July 22, 1934" (17–20), the speaker is both a relentless interrogator and an omniscient witness. For this 106–line poem narrating the final hours and the funeral of the notorious gangster, Wagoner contrived a flexible form composed of brief one-line questions and three long-line responses. The four lines in each stanza end with the same sound, but the rhymes are often weak, as in the following passage.

> *Why was Johnny frantic?*
> *Because he couldn't take a walk or sit down in a movie*
> *Without being afraid he'd run smack into somebody*
> *Who'd point at his rearranged face and holler, "Johnny!"*
> *Was Johnny ugly? (18)*

The first line is structurally part of the previous three lines, rhyming with "back," "Kodak," and "automatic," but is conceptually joined to the three lines that follow it as an answer. The word "ugly" rhymes weakly with the three previous lines, but it connects functionally to the next three lines.

Throughout the poem, the speaker moves between apparent sympathy for Dillinger's plight and overt ridicule. For example, in responding to the question, "Was Johnny a thinker?" the speaker seems sympathetic: "No, but he was thinking more or less of Billie Frechette / Who was lost in prison for longer than he could possibly wait, / And then it was suddenly too hard to think around a bullet." But the response to the question, "Did Johnny have a soul?" is teasing, even comical: "Yes, and it was climbing his slippery wind-pipe like a trapped burglar. / It was beating the inside of his ribcage, hollering, 'Let me out of here!'" The speaker, in fact, appears to deplore the morbid curiosity seekers who pay a quarter each to see the corpse and to commend Dillinger's "old hard-nosed dad," who "refused to sell / The quick-drawing corpse for $10,000 to somebody in a carnival." But he will not let the maudlin preacher get away with the platitude that Dillinger could have been a minister: ". . . up the sleeve of his oversized gray suit, Johnny twitched a finger." In the concluding lines, the speaker establishes his ironic perspective in answering the question, "Does anyone remember?"

> *Everyone still alive. And some dead ones. It was a new*
>   *kind of holiday*
> *With hot and cold drinks and hot and cold tears. They*
>   *planted him in a cemetery*
> *With three unknown vice presidents, Benjamin Harrison,*
>   *and James Whitcomb Riley,*
> *Who never held up anybody.* (20)

Ironically, in death Dillinger moves into a respectable neighborhood, and ironically again, in death he acquires fame.

"The Shooting of John Dillinger," despite a certain pathos in places and despite the grim subject matter, is one of David Wagoner's most broadly humorous poems. The form itself, with its consciously forced rhymes and mocking questions (for example, "Was Johnny a fourflusher?") is playful. William Studebaker has described Wagoner's poems as "often metaphoric . . . and sometimes symbolic observations stretched over a rack of irony—most frequently irony of situation" (100). In this poem the ironies are

sometimes established by history; for example, Dillinger did watch a Clark
Gable gangster movie, *Manhattan Melodrama*, just before he was killed.
But most of the humor derives from Wagoner's play with language; for example, he describes Dillinger's "new profile," a result of plastic surgery, as
giving him "a baggy jawline and squint eyes and an erased dimple / With
kangaroo-tendon cheekbones and a gigolo's mustache that should've been
illegal." Of the two women with Dillinger, one, we are told, "looked
sweet," while the other "looked like J. Edgar Hoover." And of course Wagoner cannot resist a pun: Dillinger kicking a bank vice president "in the
bum checks."

"Staying Alive" and "The Shooting of John Dillinger" constitute an-
tipodes of a sort for the collection. Seventeen of the forty-one poems in
Staying Alive might be classified as nature poems, including two short poems about poetry which are themselves antipodal in ways. In the first
poem of the book, "The Words," he writes:

> Wind, bird, and tree
> Water, grass, and light:
> In half of what I write
> Roughly or smoothly
> Year by impatient year,
> The same six words recur.

The poem is flat and simple, the diction predominantly monosyllabic, the
lines short. "I take what is," he insists, sounding as though he were about
to announce a phenomenologist's manifesto.

But as Wagoner points out, this Spartan diet applies at best to only half
of what he writes. Moreover, the suggestion in "The Words" that the same
six elemental nouns recur should not mislead a reader into assuming that
Wagoner embraces a poetic that would promote flat, generalized diction.
In "The Poets Agree to be Quiet by the Swamp" (24) both water and light
appear, but as usual, Wagoner specifies the birds—herons. This nine-line
poem is as playful as "The Words" is plain.

> They hold their hands over their mouths
> And stare at the stretch of water.
> What can be said has been said before:
> Strokes of light like herons' legs in the cattails,
> Mud underneath, frogs lying even deeper.

> *Therefore, the poets may keep quiet.*
> *But the corners of their mouths grin past their hands.*
> *They stick their elbows out into the evening,*
> *Stoop, and begin the ancient croaking.*

The poets recognize that they have nothing new to say about what they see, so they attempt to say nothing. The line, "Therefore, the poets may keep quiet," may be read in two ways. Because it has all been said before, they can be silent. Or, the poets may or may not be silent. What prompts them to "croak" is sheer delight; poets can no more stop writing poems than frogs can stop croaking.

More than half of the poems in *Staying Alive* feature a first-person speaker, sometimes clearly autobiographical, as in "The Circuit" (47), in which Wagoner retells an anecdote about his great-grandfather, a Methodist circuit rider, and sometimes not, as in "Speech from a Comedy" (48–50), in which the speaker is a petulant God, out of sorts with humankind. One of his most effective poems in the autobiographical first-person voice is "A Valedictory to Standard Oil of Indiana" (44–45), a poem offered as the self-appointed "Laureate of the Class of '44." With "refined regrets," Wagoner puns, "Standard Oil is canning my high school classmates." "What should they do," he asks

> *gassed up in their Tempests and Comets, raring to go . . .*
> *trying to find the beaches*
> *But blocked by freights for hours, stopped dead in their tracks*
> *Where the rails, as thick as thieves along the lakefront,*
> *Lower their crossing gates to shut the frontier?*

Much of the effectiveness of this poem stems from Wagoner's use of colloquialisms like "raring to go" and supposedly dead metaphors in novel contexts, like the rails, related to the oil barons, "as thick as thieves." He selects the models of his classmates' automobiles with care: the Tempests and Comets reflect the high velocity of their hopes. And Wagoner relishes wordplay of the sort that exists between "lakefront" and "frontier." Near the end of the poem, he detects "two towns now . . . One pampered and cared for like pillboxes and cathedrals. / The other vanishing overnight in the dumps and swamps like a struck sideshow." It is the metaphorical comparison of the "other" town to a sideshow that provides the springboard for Wagoner's conclusion, in which he offers his advice to his classmates: "like Barnum's 'This Way to the Egress,' / Which moved the suckers when they'd seen enough. Get out of town."

In "Working Against Time" (57), the first-person speaker is more militant in his defiance of industries that threaten people's well-being or the environment. Coming across fallen hemlocks near a "newly bulldozed logging road," he climbs over the tangled trees "squeezing as many as I could into my car." Although he sees himself as "no tree surgeon" and recognizes that it is "against the law to dig up trees," he is "Working against / Time and across laws" as he steers his "ambulance" home and plants the hemlocks in the dark. Those driving by might have seen:

> *A fool with a shovel searching for worms or treasure.*
> *Both buried behind the sweat on his forehead. Two green survivors*
> *Are tangled under the biting rain as I say this.* (57)

This poem anticipates the later, more overtly political poems directed at Weyerhaeuser forest products company, and with his "Valedictory to Standard Oil of Indiana," it demonstrates that his social commentaries have not been limited to his urban Midwest novels.

One other first-person voice which recurs increasingly in the poems after *The Nesting Ground* is that of the lover. "Water Music for the Progress of Love in a Life-Raft down the Sammamish Slough" (23–24) offers an elaborate, eighteenth-century-style title, beginning with echoes of Handel and Georgian England and ending with a distinctively American episode and setting. Instead of palaces or great houses, the couple begin their journey waving to an empty house with a crumbling chimney and a sagging gate, and instead of a royal barge, they glide the slough in a blue and yellow life raft. As in other lovers' excursions, such as those to Dungeness Spit and the nesting ground of the killdeer, the speaker identifies the local fauna—mallards, kingfishers, salmon. And once again, the excursion involves a "lesson":

> *We begin our lesson here, our slight slow progress,*
>   *Sitting face to face,*
> *Able to touch our hands or soaking feet*
>   *But not to kiss*
> *As long as we must wait at opposite ends,*
>   *Keeping our balance,*
> *Our spirits cold as the Sammamish mud,*

> *Our tempers rising*
> *Among the drifts like the last of the rainbows rising*
> *Through the remaining hours*
> *Till the sun goes out. What have I done to us?* (23–24)

Obviously this "progress" has begun in discord, the positions of the lovers in the raft being not only distant, but also as unsteady as the vessel itself. In answer to his own question, the speaker offers these "unromantic strains," with very likely a pun (straining his muscles in rowing as well as strains of music). But although he can give neither "horns on the Thames" nor "bronze bells on the Nile" nor even "the pipes of goatmen," the lovers do achieve a "confluence," a "bridge," albeit an "awkward passage . . . [o]ver love's divisions."

The poem ends as night falls and the lovers regain their unity by "letting the air out / Of what constrained us." This metaphor applies literally to deflating the life raft, the unsteadiness of which has sustained their separation, and figuratively to airing their grievances:

> *We fold it together, crossing stem to stern,*
> *Search for our eyes,*
> *And reach for ourselves, in time, to wake again*
> *This music from silence.* (24)

As in the earlier poems, the excursion leads to a new vision, a new insight into the self, implicit here in the "[s]earch for our eyes," and a new awakening, a new awareness, accompanied by "music," in effect, this poem.

3. NEW AND SELECTED POEMS

Of the thirty-five new poems included in his *New and Selected Poems* (1969), the most effective may be "In the Open Season" (154–55), which is also a love poem. In it a pair of lovers find themselves in the forest during hunting season. The poem follows two strongly imagistic poems, "Tumbleweed" (147) and "The Soles" (148), in which the visual thing itself is established in its concrete reality, not as metaphor or as setting for some human drama. Following these are two love poems, "Recollection" (149) and "Getting Above Ourselves on Sunday" (150–51), the latter involving yet another excursion of lovers, this one onto a cliff during a mountain thunderstorm. A third love poem, "Fire by the River" (152) also places the lovers in the out-of-doors; then comes the powerful "Nine

Charms Against the Hunter" (153), which works as a companion piece to "In the Open Season." John T. Irwin's suggestion that in Wagoner's poems there is a "psychoanalytic motif" involving "the acknowledgment of man's animality and its consequences" (168) applies particularly to this poem. In effect, we must grant our own animal nature and cease our "overestimation of man's worth" (168). This being the case, Wagoner perceives the hunting and killing of animals, particularly as it is done by the modern American sportsman, to be reprehensible, and a number of his poems reflect that conviction. "Nine Charms Against the Hunter" begins:

> *In the last bar on the way to your wild game,*
> *May the last beer tilt you over among friends*
> *And keep you there till sundown—failing that,*
> *A breakdown on the road, ditching you gently*
> *Where you may hunt for lights and a telephone.* (153)

The poem ends with a graphic vision of "[d]azed animals sprawling forward on dead leaves," "imaginary skinning," "unraveling guts," and "[b]eheading trophies to your heart's content." The poem is hardly one to ingratiate Wagoner as a writer with what one might feature as a typical northwesterner.

"In the Open Season" begins with a question to which the rest of the poem may be read in answer:

> *By what stretch of the mind had we come there, lurching*
>   *and crackling*
> *Mile after mile uphill through the ruts and ice-lidded*
>   *chuckholes*
> *On the logging road, the pine boughs switching across our*
>   *windows?* (154)

When their vehicle stalls, they climb on foot until they hear guns sounding in the valley below. At that point, they behave like the hunted animals, zigzagging through the stumps and snow, then "lying down as if breathing our last." Out of their pain, cold, and fear comes an illumination:

> *And the light broke out*
> *Of everything we touched in bristling spectrums,*
> *And we felt the day break over again*
> *And again, snow blowing across the sun*
> *To dazzle our half-crossed eyes.* (154)

But below them, "the earth shivered with guns" and the animals are "bleeding toward sundown." The deaths of the animals, now fully perceived, drive the lovers closer to one another as they recognize each other's wounds. Wagoner concludes the poem with an allusion to *Romeo and Juliet*, followed by a wordplay, which suggests that the lovers need the "open season" announced in the title, though of course in a very different way: "We touched each other's wounds / Like star-crossed, stir-crazed lovers / Dying again and again." Karl Malkoff has suggested, in fact, that Wagoner also intends "the traditional pun on dying as orgasm, which brings to the poem another mode of experience in which the self is both lost and affirmed at the same time" (316).

In his review essay on *New and Selected Poems* for the *Kenyon Review*, Robert Boyers hailed Wagoner as "one of our best poets, perhaps one of the best we have ever had in this country" (176). The opening poem of the section entitled "New Poems," though not representative of the work for which Wagoner is most often admired, shows his power, as Boyers phrased it, to "transfigure through language" (178). In "At St. Vincent DePaul's" (123), rows of free shoes outside the used clothing outlet come to life, "Rocking on round heels / Or turning up at the toes / As if to jump for joy." This poem is an appropriate introduction to what in many ways is Wagoner's most playful collection. In "Getting Out of Jail on Monday" (137–139), the first-person speaker accompanies a "husky, bowlegged, upright, sockless Indian" on an all-day tour of the bars. The sun follows their progress in egg fashion, from "sunnyside up" early in the morning, to "over easy," and finally to the point that it is "scrambling off." Along the way, the sun becomes "a raw egg in a beer." As they pass the world of serious business (*negotium*), the speaker notes that the secretaries are "sharpening the corners of their eyes" and that "good signatures / Are flourishing at the business-ends of letters." All over town, as the city awakens, "the time-vaults are yawning open," but time for the poet is traditionally at odds with time for the businessman. In Donne's "Breake of Day," love can admit the poor, the foul, and the false, but "not the busied man" (36), and in "The Sunne Rising," hours, days, and months become "the rags of time" (72). For the speaker in Wagoner's poem, "trying to see Friday west of Monday / Takes an Indian's eyes. It's over the brow of the hill / Like the U.S. Cavalry with its spit and tarnish."

Part of the playfulness of *New and Selected Poems* derives from Wagoner's creation of a more varied cast of characters than in his previous collections. In addition to the Indian from "Getting Out of Jail on Monday," he offers several amateur magicians, himself included, in "Magic Night at the Reformatory" (124–25), wandering hobos in "Bums at Breakfast" (126–27), and the "general" and his "gimp-legged and tatterdemalion" (130–35) mob in the long historical poem, "The March of Coxey's Army," which follows the mode of "The Shooting of John Dillinger." In "The Burglar" (140–41) and "The Visiting Hour" (144–45), Wagoner's use of second person strikes an identity between the reader and the criminal, but his use of third person for "The Shoplifter" (142) and "The Escape Artist" (146) locates us, like the speaker, outside the character. In "The Shoplifter" we join the speaker watching the apprehended woman as she climbs the stairs: "Rising along the stairways, looking back. / She smiles serenely against the light. / The shop is lifting, lifting itself with her." We are relieved not to be identified with the victim of "The Hold-Up," who watches as "My shoes and money are running away in the dark" (143).

At least a third of the poems in the new section of this book demonstrate what Sanford Pinsker has called an "oblique angle we recognize as wit," but, as he observes, "the gentle sense of verbal play always teeters toward a transposed key" ("The Achievement" 362). Stephen Dobyns notes, "Superficially, Wagoner seems to walk through the world, always looking in faint surprise at his surroundings. But the quiet tone is deceptive" (397). There is also something deceptive about the comedy in his poems. They can be very funny, yet they are rarely what one could call "light." The poems are frequently playful, but they are not mere *jeux d'esprit* not, that is, simply intellectual or witty gewgaws. In effect, it is serious humor. "Nine Charms Against the Hunter," for instance, contains many funny passages, but the speaker's attitude toward hunting (and Wagoner's) is best expressed in the grim final lines: "Or if these charms have failed and the death is real. / May it fatten you, hour by hour, for the trapped hunter / Whose dull knife beats the inside of your chest" (153).

Probably the best example of Wagoner's serious humor in *New and Selected Poems* is the last poem in the collection, "The Apotheosis of the Garbagemen" (175–76), the first twenty-eight lines of which he forces into a single sentence. I say "forces" because at several points in the rambling syntactic unit he could—and conventionally speaking, should—have placed periods and started new sentences. In several of the latter poems of the book, Wagoner also runs out a rambling sentence pattern that was to become more common in subsequent work. "The Warbler" (159), for example, has a twelve-and-a-half-line sentence near the end and "Crossing Half a River" (166–67) includes a sentence that rambles over 15 lines, while "Stretching" (168), appropriately enough, ends with a 17–line sentence. For "The Apotheosis of the Garbagemen" Wagoner also fabricated a form unlike anything he had used previously. As John Irwin has observed, Wagoner "never wholly abandons regular surface structures," though those that survive are "always diluted, often amounting only to a stanza of a fixed number of lines without [rhyme] or meter" (166). Elsewhere, I have written in some detail on his accentual meter and ternary "stanza" form, which has something of the effect of a stanza break without using a gap between the lines ("Dynamic Form"). "The Apotheosis," however, appears to repudiate form altogether, for in this poem Wagoner creates no stanza breaks, and he staggers the lines back and forth between the margins. Only his capitalization of the first word in each line follows conventional formal structure. One needs only to leaf through *Collected Poems* (1976) to see how much of a formal departure this poem is from his usual practice, which is to walk a tightrope of sorts between freedom and control. The flush margin and homostrophic form predominate, even as Wagoner teases meter and jumps sentences across stanzas.

The first eleven lines will give some impression of how the open form works in this poem:

> And they come back in the night through alleys to find us
> By the clashing of raised lids,
> By garage doors' lifted heads, the swung gates, the bottomless
> Galvanized cans on their shoulders,
> In luminous coveralls
> They follow the easy directions on boxes, scattering
> Bushels of brown grass and apple cores,
> Old candy wrappers folded around sweet nothings,
> And sacks with their stains on fire,
> They are coming through hedges, dragging geometry
> In a dark clutch of rainbows, . . . (175)

This typesetter's nightmare constitutes what I would call an artful disarrangement of line. The garbagemen come back in the dark to discover "us" in the chaotic rubble of our detritus. The clatter and confusion of the scene are mirrored in the sprawl of both line and syntax on the one hand and of images on the other. Against clichés like following "easy directions on boxes" and "sweet nothings," Wagoner establishes not only fresh and appropriate contexts, but also a rich euphony. Consider, for example, the short *a* sounds between "scattering" and "sacks," the alliteration of boxes/bushels/brown, the near rhymes (assonances) of apple/wrappers and old/folded. The garbagemen are associated with light ("luminous coveralls," "sacks with their stains on fire," "a dark clutch of rainbows"), and in the next passage, which grammatically speaking should start a new sentence, the smashed jars they come upon are "[p]rinked out with light."

But against such evocative images as "a dark clutch of rainbows," Wagoner offers us a slapstick view of the garbagemen's feet: "As solid as six-packs on the lawn." The garbagemen deal with our wishes and dreams, "the marrow whistling / Out of the wishbones of turkeys" and "The coupons filled out / With our last names for all the startling offers." Beneath the apparent playfulness and fun of the poem, then, is that persistently quiet yet disturbing tone which Stephen Dobyns describes as "frightening," a voice always "whispering, 'Fire!'" (397, 398). As the poem ends, we see the garbagemen "singing / To the dump" in the "sea of decay where our foundering fathers / Rubbled their lives." Ironically, the garbagemen have "found the way / Back to God's plenty, to rags and riches," and that way is not through acquisition, but through relinquishment. They will come back to us, in our darkness, "with all we could wish for . . . singing love and wild appetite, / The good rats and roaches, / The beautiful hogs and billygoats dancing around them." The vision is reminiscent of Yeats's "foul rag-and-bone shop of the heart."

Again, as in "A Guide to Dungeness Spit" and "Staying Alive," but from a very different angle, Wagoner reminds us that enlightenment and vision come from unexpected sources. Even the most trivial or most commonplace event or item can spark our perception, can give us an awareness of what we are. That recognition of self often is painful or humbling, if not humiliating. Another poet might draw this self-recognition in dark nights of the soul, in ascetic endurance of suffering, or in excoriations administered by love and war. But Wagoner's perspective is much less familiar and much more palatable, for while he is arguably a "religious visionary poet," as Hyatt Waggoner has demonstrated, he is also "consistently empirical and skeptical" (180). He is a visionary comedian. I mean this, of course, in the most positive sense of the phrase: Wagoner's comic vision is not superimposed upon a religious vision; rather, it is part of that vision. He is the true comedian in the Elizabethan sense of the term, for like

Marlowe and Shakespeare he rarely perceives only the pain or tragedy of the human condition. We may rubble our lives as we will, and ashes may rain on our heads, but "[a]s the skeletons of lampshades catch at the first light," we will sing and dance with the apotheosized garbagemen. We may even laugh.

THE COMIC WESTERNS

FOLLOWING A NOVELLA AND FIVE urban novels, which included *The Escape Artist* (1965), filmed in 1982, David Wagoner wrote four comic Westerns: *Where is My Wandering Boy Tonight?* (1970), *The Road to Many a Wonder* (1974), *Tracker* (1975) and *Whole Hog* (1976). William J. Schaefer, writing in 1966 of Wagoner's first novels and the novella, "The Spinning Ladies" (1962), found Wagoner "oddly unacclaimed" and judged him "one of the most gifted novelists of the past fifteen years" (73). Time has not upheld Schaefer's critical judgment, apparently. At present, none of his ten novels are in print, but Schaefer's comments on Wagoner's "essentially tragicomic" novels, set in Chicago and the nearby "suburban industrial complex" (71), offer a useful perspective from which to examine his Westerns, which may eventually prove Wagoner's best efforts in the genre.

As I discussed in chapter 2, Schaefer's paradigm for "Wagoner's basic story" is "an innocent man, in some way disabled or incomplete and out of touch with his society... involved unwillingly or accidentally with corruption (in the form of organized crime); he is pursued relentlessly by evil forces, becomes himself corrupt (falls from 'ethical grace') and is therefore damaged or destroyed" (71–72). The protagonists of his early novels, and of course the settings, would seem to bear little similarity with those of the Westerns. For example, Charlie Bell, of *The Man in the Middle* (1954), is in his early forties and Willy Grier, of *Money Money Money* (1955), is thirty-six, while the protagonists of the Westerns are all at some stage of late adolescence. It is the adolescent Danny Masters of *The Escape Artist*, then, who appears to be a pivotal or transitional character between the tragicomic, contemporary, urban novels and the comic, nineteenth-century, Western novels. Schaefer characterizes Danny as "immensely intelligent" and "physically adroit" (85), "articulate" and capable of maintaining his "imaginative integrity" (87). He notes that "Danny is the first Wagoner protagonist to control his fate in the end" (87), but as we shall see, he is actually the first of several such protagonists—and, at sixteen, the youngest.

For the Westerns, of course, Schaefer's paradigm requires some alterations. Wagoner regards the best feature of his fiction to be "humor" and has described most of his novels as "serious farces" (McFarland, "Interview" 15). Despite occasional surreal moments, the Westerns are best described as conventional comic novels with strongly picaresque elements. The protagonists are ages seventeen (*Where is My Wandering Boy Tonight?* and *Tracker*), nineteen (*The Road to Many a Wonder*), and twenty (*Whole Hog*). With the exception of *Whole Hog*, the titles themselves suggest the journey motif which fuses with the picaresque mode, and the ages of the protagonists place them at that crossroads between adolescence and adulthood which almost necessarily makes these novels types of the *Bildungsroman*. Various reviewers, among them novelist Edward Abbey, have observed resemblances between Wagoner's protagonists and Huck Finn; that is, they are wisely innocent—only apparently naive—despite their lack of wide experience or formal education. They may have lessons to learn in the proverbial school of hard knocks, but they are invariably either equal or superior to the crises confronting them. Schaefer's innocent and disabled or incomplete man, therefore, might be modified to "clever youth." In this respect Wagoner's wandering protagonists are Odyssean, never at a loss. The "incompleteness" of the protagonists in the Westerns parallels that of Danny in *The Escape Artist* in that it involves parents. Like Danny Masters, Ike Bender of *The Road to Many a Wonder* leaves home; Junior Holcomb (*Wandering Boy*) is motherless; Eli (*Tracker*) is an orphan; and Zeke Hunt (*Whole Hog*) is orphaned early in the novel. In general, however, these protagonists are in quest of self-identity or self-understanding rather than a parent substitute of any sort.

In fact, it might be more accurate to say that Wagoner's adolescent protagonists are searching for self-confirmation and self-fulfillment, for they are so quick-witted, sharp-tongued, and physically adept that we come across few moments of serious self-interrogation or self-doubt. The characters may indeed seem so self-confident as to cause some readers to challenge their credibility. They rarely struggle; rather, they confront and overcome. Reviewers like John Gardner and Roger Sale, who have panned Wagoner's novels with almost suspicious glee, have largely contented themselves with catcalls. It may well be, however, that Wagoner's protagonists lack what might be called "innerness," by which I do not mean simply that they are not very thoughtful or introspective. Arguably, and perhaps ironically, we rarely glimpse the inner depths of Wagoner's protagonists in the Westerns, because the first person limited point of view, which one might suppose would provide for direct insight into the character's mind, in fact keeps the reader at some distance.

While the subject of the first element of Schaefer's paradigm must be revised, substituting "clever youth" for "innocent man," the predicate may be left pretty much unaltered. As in the first four novels, the protagonists in the Westerns are "involved unwillingly or accidentally with corruption." But as I have suggested, the protagonists in these novels take that corruption in stride. The second element of Schaefer's paradigm details the protagonist's relentless pursuit by "evil forces," an element which is often reversed in the Westerns, where we find the protagonists pursuing those evil forces at least as often as they are themselves pursued. Schaefer's description of the gangsters from *The Man in the Middle* as "fumbling all-too-human thugs who bungle one task after another" (74), might be applied, at least generally, to the adversaries in the Western novels. Certainly "Colonel" Stull in *Whole Hog* is a sufficiently deranged and sinister villain to be taken seriously, but he is served by a crew of louts, and his own delusions make his viciousness so hyperbolic as to be comical. One might argue, of course, that genuinely threatening adversaries in the mode of Cormac McCarthy's *Blood Meridian* do not properly belong in the comic novel.

Schaefer concludes that Wagoner's protagonist "becomes himself corrupt" and is therefore "damaged or destroyed." *The Escape Artist*, however, Schaefer considers to be an "evolution" in Wagoner's treatment of the individual in his confrontation with "the power of industrialized mass society" (88), for Danny Masters is able to escape "into imaginative freedom, into a creative present and future" (89). The protagonists in the Westerns follow in this new direction. They are not corrupted by experience, though they do learn from it, and they certainly are not "damaged" in any severe sense, despite the murder of Zeke Hunt's parents, nor are they "destroyed." In *Whole Hog*, Wagoner arranges the apparent murder of Zeke's mother and father so that it occurs off stage, while Zeke is suffering from a concussion, and he never locates their bodies. While he feels certain that they are dead, Zeke is too much beset by the challenge of survival to spend much time pondering their fate. This suggests not so much that he is insensitive, but rather, like the other protagonists in the Western novels, that he is preeminently practical. The revised paradigm, then, might read like this: A clever youth is involved unwillingly or accidentally with corruption; he alternately is pursued by and pursues evil forces, which he survives and over which he prevails.

Lacking experience and formal education, these protagonists succeed thanks to their pragmatic outlook, their ingenuity, and their integrity. Searching for everything from gold to instruction in the lore of tracking, the protagonists are usually ahead of their adversaries simply because they use common sense. All of the protagonists speak roughly the same dialect, which Wagoner whittles out of Mark Twain, common misusages, midwestern colloquialisms, and wisecracks, so it is not surprising that all of them, from Zeke Hunt in 1850s Nebraska to Junior Holcomb in 1890s Wyoming, refer to a range of citizenry, from desperadoes to idle bystanders, as "lunkheads." In effect, these are people who are not with it. While conniving appears to be within reach of the various crooks and murderers—all of whom are obsessed with greed—common sense and ingenuity turn out to be their short suits. They are, in a word, lunkheads. Most of the villains are not overcome violently, for Wagoner's protagonists are essentially non-violent, non-gun-toting young men; rather, the villains are outwitted.

It is perhaps in their moral superiority, however, that Wagoner's protagonists most thoroughly confound both their adversaries in the novels and the reviewers on the outside. They do not (as one might expect of the picaro) lie, cheat, steal, curse, or fornicate. "I was never no good at lying," Ike Bender declares flatly (*Wonder* 31). Their adversaries, who represent the fallen world, do all of the above. The reviewers have reacted variously to this state of affairs, some of them choosing simply to consign Wagoner's Westerns to the juvenile or young adult shelves, which is where they belong only if one places them alongside *Huckleberry Finn*, *The Catcher in the Rye*, and *Goodbye, Columbus*. Wagoner's protagonists, however, are not just simple-minded do-gooders, not just so many boy scouts afield on a nature hike. Discovering his father in bed with a "soiled dove" (*Wandering Boy* 56), Junior Holcomb is not cowed. His father, a smalltown judge, asks if he hasn't read the law on breaking and entering. Junior replies, "No, but I'm pretty well up on fornication in the Old Testament" (64). After a crazed gold seeker attempts to ram him, Ike Bender reflects: "I vowed then and there I wasn't going to do nothing like that, but do my work and take my turn and prepare for the worst and hope for the best and manage with what come along" (*Wonder* 82). Such are the simple ethics of Wagoner's roving young stoics.

Unlike Odysseus or Tom Jones, Wagoner's protagonists do not face the hostile world alone. Junior Holcomb and his friend Fred Haskell, a minister's son, thrown in with a wise old cowhand, Greasy Brown, and his partner "Kid" Lassiter; Ike Bender is joined by his clever and resourceful hometown girlfriend, Millie Slaughter; Eli joins up with the old part-Arapaho, Tracker Boyd; Zeke Hunt is rescued more than once by Casper, the "whiskey man." All of the youthful protagonists need mentors, and Millie Slaughter becomes distinguished among these mentors by virtue of her age and sex. What the mentors have in common is a certain wisdom, variously based: Greasy Brown's and Tracker Boyd's sources are similar—hard work in the out-of-doors, living the simple life off the land, and maintaining a skeptical attitude toward anyone who works or lives otherwise; Casper is a student of human nature, the bartender in effect, on the road; Millie possesses a fascinating combination of book learning, one-room schoolhouse style, and common sense which appears to be founded rather on intuition than on experience.

1. WHERE IS MY WANDERING BOY TONIGHT?

Where is My Wandering Boy Tonight? (1970) was generously reviewed by Edward Abbey, who praised it as "a good piece of entertainment, sly, witty, vernacular and true" (58). The story takes place in Slope, Wyoming, during the 1890s as the West is being civilized, modernized, and exploited, notably by the fathers of the protagonist, Junior Holcomb (a judge's son), and his friend, Fred Haskell (a preacher's son). The judge and the minister are forced to hire a pair of crooks, Mauger and Pinkus, apparently business partners who are blackmailing them, to "educate" their sons in law and theology, but when the heat gets too intense, Judge Holcomb absconds. Upheld by Flint, an honest banker through whom the judge has set up a trust fund, Junior experiences a day as a wealthy, respected citizen before Mauger and Pinkus realize what's going on. Since he dreams of becoming a cowboy, Junior charges up a considerable bill, buying a saddle even though he has no horse and has not yet learned to ride. In a confrontation at the Checker Casino, scene of several "lessons" in his induction into the adult world, Junior meets the old cowboy, Greasy Brown, a partner of Junior's new-found friend, Kid Lassiter. Meanwhile, Mauger arranges to marry the judge's housekeeper and, aided by a crooked lawyer, to adopt Junior. Flint helps rescue Junior from this swindle, provides him with a thousand dollars in trust money, and sends him out of town. Greasy and the Kid find Junior and Fred, and Junior proposes to pay Greasy for cowboy lessons. Headed toward the ranch, they stop at the town of Sideslip where they encounter Fred's father, Reverend Haskell, with Lulu, former owner of the casino and brothel, who has been rechristened "Mary Magdalene Morehouse," appropriately enough. Reverend Haskell, who burned his house to the ground before leaving town, has divorced his wife, changed his name to "Reverend Oxymoron Morehouse," and married Lulu. Junior also encounters his father in Sideslip with a "soiled dove" and a broken ankle. Here the crucial comic revelation occurs: Mauger and Pinkus are actually illegitimate half-brothers of Junior and Fred respectively. All the principal characters are gathered in the final comic scene, but in a reversal of conventions, in which justice is not imposed, Junior yields the "family business" (various forms of larceny) to the greedy judge and the unscrupulous Mauger, while Junior himself rides off to fulfill his dream of becoming a cowboy, taking a reluctant Fred Haskell with him, at least for a year: "and we headed out west of town to start scraping the green off our horns" (247).

Guns are drawn a number of times in the novel, but scarcely a shot is fired, and Junior Holcomb never resorts to violence. His best weapon is always his quick tongue. The following passage, from the episode in which lawyer Shanklin informs Junior that he has been adopted by Mauger, is representative of Wagoner's skill with dialogue and repartee:

> "What happened to my old man?" I says, crowding forward a little and aiming it right at Rev. Haskell. I wasn't scairt of him no more. His face looked like a boiled potato.
>
> "I don't know," he says. "You must try to take your loss with Christian fortitude, boy."
>
> "You've got a *new* paw," Shanklin says. "Try to get it through your head."
>
> "If you don't tell me where my old man is," I says to Rev. Haskell, "I'm going to foreclose on your church and your house, and you'll have to go to the Checker Casino permanent instead of part-time."
>
> That shocked him to life a little, and he give Shanklin a glance. "He can't do that, can he?" he says.
>
> "Try to take your loss with Christian fortitude," I says.
> (136–37)

Despite his clever tongue and an occasional fast escape, though, Junior must rely on the know-how and courage of old Greasy Brown, who brashly disarms various lunkheads.

2. THE ROAD TO MANY A WONDER

The level of violence increases somewhat in *The Road to Many a Wonder* (1974), which Wagoner has described as his favorite among the Western novels "because its shape and its lore and its speech and its characters and its general atmosphere come closest to fulfilling my original intentions" (McFarland, "Interview" 17). The setting for this novel is along the Platte River in the Nebraska Territory and near the Denver gold fields during the 1859 Pike's Peak gold rush. Although the protagonist, Ike Bender, is out to make his fortune, his attitude remains at odds with that of other gold seekers he encounters, who are consumed with greed and covetousness. Ike has spent time digging wells for neighboring farmers so that he will be prepared for the hard life in the gold fields, and he has a brother in Colorado, Kit, who has already staked a claim. That is to say, he does not proceed from gold lust so much as he does from a sense of wonder, and he is willing to work. For transport Ike fashions a sturdy wheelbarrow, and he sets off with full confidence and what he calls a "Vision of the Future" (11). In addition to their sense of destiny, Wagoner's protagonists may be said to possess certain classical virtues, self-knowledge and moderation being chief among them. Before he leaves, Ike imparts an important secret to his girlfriend: "I ain't the same as anybody else that ever lived in the whole world" (23–24). I take that to be not youthful naiveté, but honest self-assertion.

Like Junior Holcomb, Ike Bender is a "happy man" in the *beatus vir* tradition, but Wagoner might prefer an epigraph not from a Horatian ode, but from his mentor's, Theodore Roethke's, villanelle, "The Right Thing":

> *Let others probe the mystery if they can.*
> *Time-harried prisoners of* Shall *and* Will—
> *The right thing happens to the happy man.*
> (Collected Poems, 1975, 242)

Ike admires some birds on the prairie wading in a mud puddle, and in them he detects a lesson:

> [T]hey was drawing their life out of it [the puddle] that evening,
> just like me, and happy to have it and know how to use it, finding
> things down in that muck nobody or nothing else knew how to
> find. . . . And maybe not even finding much, or maybe finding
> nothing till tomorrow but still happy to be there, now, doing what
> they liked to do. (30)

All is a wonder to this pilgrim, including mirages and the silty river Platte
itself, which seems to Ike to be filled with gold. Different readers will associate Wagoner's optimistic protagonists with various literary counterparts, but I would suggest Dickens' buoyant Mark Tapley, from *Martin
Chuzzlewit*, who acts always with "great alacrity."

Ike's self-possession manifests itself throughout the novel, but especially when he confronts the many unhappy travelers who are either former gold seekers or would-be gold seekers. Early in the novel he is
jumped by a pair of bushwhackers, one of whom accidentally kills the
other in attempting to shoot Ike. Ike's reasoning as to the disposition of the
body in the morning typifies his mode of moralizing and his self-awareness:

> And I come to the conclusion I couldn't do everything right in a
> problem like this here, so I had to pick what had the least wrongs
> in it: I just left the body laying there and everything like it was,
> come what may. What was the sense in being innocent if you
> wasn't going to act like it? (52–53)

The happiness and innocence asserted in the two passages above appear
to be fundamental to all the protagonists in Wagoner's Westerns. But Ike's
innocence and happiness, his integrity and self-understanding do not pro-
tect him from some degree of uncertainty, and after yet another confrontation with a roadside crook, Ike finds himself wanting to "keep clear
of people": "I figured I could keep liking them and maybe even keep a
charitable thought in my head if I wasn't running up against them all the
time" (75).

While this moment in Ike Bender's pilgrimage does not constitute anything like a Slough of Despond or Cave of Despair, it does indicate a potentially dangerous inclination on his part to avoid human community with
its risk of conflict and confrontation. But communal happiness, the well-
being of the social order rather than simply that of the individual, is the

aim of the adult world, and it demands that people take risks, confront one another, and resolve issues. It is at this crucial moment, then, that Wagoner reintroduces Millie Slaughter into the story. An odd combination of hard-headed intelligence, storybook romance, and Victorian propriety, Millie points out that she has read of young men leaving their ladies behind while they go out to make their fortunes, and "[t]hose stories mostly have happy endings, but they take too long in coming" (87). Equipped with some savings and five pounds of valuable quicksilver (for use in separating gold), Millie asserts her role immediately. Somewhat domineering by nature, she will be the strong but loving mother figure Ike has never had, his actual mother being a pathetic woman under the thumb of an irascible husband. When Ike objects that "it wouldn't be fittin'" for her to accompany him, since she is a girl, Millie's response illustrates both her pluck and Wagoner's good sense of comedy: "'I have no intention of being a sister to you, Mr. Bender,' she says with slumgullion on her chin" (89).

After their marriage at Fort Kearny, Ike discovers that Millie is "the greatest wonder I'd found or was yet to find, on that road to many a wonder" (108), and hereafter his view of things is colored by her sensibility. "You should cultivate a more romantic nature" (116) she informs Ike when they come across an abandoned cherrywood chest of drawers on the trail. It probably goes without saying that Ike had perceived the chest as firewood and little else before Millie altered his perspective. In one of the funniest moments in the novel, Ike and Millie save themselves from an Indian war party through a ruse that Ike conceives, perhaps because Millie's presence inspires him, for the stratagem seems very much in her domain. Recalling his teacher, Miss Wilkerson's, recitations, Ike launches into a passage from the conclusion to Tennyson's "The May Queen" (1842), a maudlin poem in which the speaker is a girl near death. He then recites four more lugubrious lines, not from the same poem (nor could I locate the source), and Millie joins in with a hymn. The impromptu performance saves their scalps.

Further trials and tribulations await the pair at the gold fields, where they find Kit's partners at the Collywobble Mining Company none too hospitable, with the exception of the senior member, an old prospector named Zack. But Ike and Millie share a common sense of their future: "I have always believed I was destined to be happy" (156), Millie says, and Ike agrees. Kit, as it happens, has been prospecting in the mountains on his own, and when he returns he has lost most of his fingers and toes to frostbite and is every bit as frustrated and despondent as the other gold seekers they have encountered. The emotional pitch of those who lust for gold appears to be a combination of self-pity and anger, both of which are understandably exacerbated by the appearance of this pair of overtly happy, benevolent newcomers.

Millie takes control of the situation almost at once. She accompanies Ike to town where she runs a subtle sting operation to convince the gold-hungry citizenry that she and Ike have made a big strike. She operates, for the most part, without her husband's connivance, or even awareness, but she has read up on mining; in effect, she has prepared her mind for the gold fields just as Ike has prepared his body. It only remains for Ike to dig a well, as Millie directs, in an improbable spot on their claim, for the Hearthstone Mining Company to be born and the gold-grubbing banker and speculator to be hooked. Clearly, however, this state of affairs causes problems for the immovably honest Ike—not quite a moral dilemma, perhaps, but pangs of conscience nonetheless. Their fortunate destiny, however, saves Ike from any lost sleep on that account. In a delightfully farcical scene, Ike does strike it rich, after which he and Millie sell their claim, take care of Kit and their other needy relatives, and retire to a life of modest wealth, preferring in the end not to prolong their pursuit of riches, pretty much as Junior Holcomb turned his back on an inherited fortune in *Wandering Boy*.

3. TRACKER

In both of his first Western novels, then, Wagoner depicts young people acquiring a fortune but settling for a simpler life that will provide them what they desire implicitly without the risk of corruption through luxury. One is reminded, almost, of medieval allegory. A similar opportunity for riches is offered in *Tracker* (1975), which begins in mid-July 1889 in Sheepshank, Colorado, when Eli, an orphaned seventeen-year-old stable boy, witnesses a bank robbery. This novel, the shortest of the four Westerns, bears some comparison with *Where is My Wandering Boy Tonight?*, which it resembles more nearly than it does *The Road to Many a Wonder* or *Whole Hog*. Early in *Wandering Boy* Junior Holcomb is handed a copy of *What a Young Man Ought to Know*, from the Sex and Self series by Sylvanus Stall, D.D. The epigraph to *Tracker* is a quotation from that volume, to the effect that a Bible, "a few well-chosen books," and a pair of dumbbells augur that "that young man's future is full of hope and promise." Since Stall's books were not published till 1897, Wagoner is anachronistic, though the spirit of his references is certainly to the point. Stall's volumes (he wrote two others for the series, one for young husbands and one for men of forty-five) are pious exhortations to the pure and physically fit life. Published by his own Vir Publishing Company in Philadelphia, the volumes sold over a million copies, so the former Lutheran minister claimed, in at least eight foreign languages. Stall's advice avails the protagonists of Wagoner's novels very little, though, except to remind them at certain critical moments that indeed they are having impure and dangerous thoughts.

Eli immediately recognizes the bank robbers as Lud and Sooger Worley, but he does not report them, and most of the citizens are more enthusiastic about chasing down the coins scattered all over town by the explosion of the vault than they are about joining Sheriff Spitzer's posse. For Eli, the opportunity to learn how to cut for sign from old Tracker Boyd, and thereby to "Amount to Something" (13), is more important than turning in the thieves of the gold bullion. "My joy was too good to waste," Eli observes, "and the day was a better gold mine than Mr. Bastion's [the mine owner's] kind" (27). Lud and Sooger soon join the posse and lead a portion of it astray while Tracker and Eli go their own way. Since he wants the education, Eli does not inform Tracker of what he knows, but when Mr. Bastion rides up with Lud and Sooger to report that the two robbers were shot down in Crockville, he realizes the implications, as does the reader.

In the process of trailing the robbers, Eli learns Indian lore from Tracker in equal doses with tracking techniques; for example, he learns to ask permission before entering a gulch so that the rocks will speak to him. Here they are ambushed and Tracker is wounded, so they head for Crockville where Eli meets Bastion's beautiful and imperious daughter, Cherry, who provides him with a brief lesson in flirtation. In the parlor of the Bastion residence, Cherry is confronted by her father, who accuses her of involvement in the bank robbery, but she brazens it out. When she sees that Eli has the robbery figured out, Cherry has him clapped in jail, and the sheriff attempts to get him to perjure himself about the robbery, but he escapes. On the prairie at night, Eli and his mount are pursued by a ghostly wild horse, until an even ghostlier Arapaho appears from nowhere to club it into submission. The Indian leads Eli to Tracker, who reveals his "real name" means "He Is Turning into a Bird" (170), and as Tracker falls asleep the medicine man performs a healing ritual for him. In the morning, Tracker gives Eli an Indian name meaning "He-Wants-to-Win" (174), and Eli adds it to his own, in effect adopting Tracker as his father, even as he earlier, in his sympathy over her condition, adopted the demented Mrs. Bastion as surrogate mother.

Tracker and Eli trail Sooger and Lud to an abandoned mine which they are salting with gold at Cherry's request in order to swindle her father, who has gypped her out of a productive mine and left her with this worthless one. Her plan is to use the mine as a cover for the bullion she has had the Worley brothers steal from the bank. Cherry rides up to warn them that her father has figured out the ruse and is coming after them. While the four of them argue, Eli steals the saddlebags of bullion. As he and Tracker escape, Lud murders Bastion with his shotgun, still appropriately filled with golden pellets, and then Cherry avenges her father by killing Lud. The novel ends in a flurry of accommodations, which typifies the conclusions of these Westerns. Sooger and Cherry concoct an elaborate lie and get married, so the greedy retain their wealth, or in this case, acquire it. Eli and Tracker, in possession of some thirty thousand dollars worth of bullion, ride off together "headed for Denver or Cheyenne or wherever we decided to track ourselves, not needing no crock of gold at the end of a rainbow but holding up one end of it our own selfs and taking it along" (216).

As the conclusion to *Tracker* suggests, Wagoner's protagonists are not heroes whose task it is, traditionally, to reestablish or establish moral order in the universe. Avarice will continue to exist in the world, Wagoner appears to be saying, and the innocent will be affected by it. In fact, one might argue that Eli loses his innocence more dramatically than any of Wagoner's protagonists, actually resorting to theft in the process. But in these Westerns the "right thing" does happen to the "happy man," and whether Tracker and Eli go to Cheyenne, Denver, or elsewhere, we sense that they will not submit to a life of idle luxury and greed.

4. WHOLE HOG

Through the first three novels Wagoner gradually escalates the violence from *Wandering Boy*, in which nobody gets hurt, to the single homicide of *Wonder*, to the four murders of *Tracker*. Violence and threatened violence increase until, in *Whole Hog* (1976), the comedy verges throughout on catastrophe. Zeke Hunt, age twenty, is herding hogs along the Platte River in 1852, accompanying his mother and his abusive father to California

from a farm in Missouri. Early in the novel we meet the man who will become Zeke's sinister adversary, the "buckskin man" (23), who introduces
himself pompously as Arthur Shadwell Parkhurst (the first of many names
he provides himself—two pages later he refers to himself as Stanhurst
Parkman Postbody). Among the three bullies with him is the "tattery,
blue-bearded, schoolteachery-looking" man whom Zeke refers to as the
"moonhead" (25). Threatened, Zeke gives a hog call which causes the
horse of the buckskin man—called Stull by his henchmen—to rear, and
when Stull draws a gun, Zeke disarms him with his staff (perhaps a parody
of the epic weapon). Despite his comical identification with the hogs,
therefore, Zeke comes off in the initial encounter rather as an epic hero
than as a buffoon.

In a second altercation, Zeke is knocked out, but when he comes to he
successfully unhorses the buckskin man, who spouts a confused stream of
quotations from the Bible, Shakespeare, and other literary sources. The
moonhead then reports that Zeke's father has killed one of their band, and
soon afterward he shoots Zeke, grazing his head. When he awakens, Zeke
finds the wagon overturned in the river, but no trace of his parents. Remaining alive are only four, but eventually seven, of his precious herd of
hogs, which once numbered twenty-seven. At this point he is assisted by
Casper, a man who claims to sell "the best whiskey west of the Mississippi"
(68) and whose perspective on life is summed up in a fairly simple creed:
"I believe in human nature all right, but I don't like it much" (67). Casper
will become the father figure for Zeke, just as Tracker Boyd and Greasy
Brown serve Eli and Junior.

While selling whiskey for Casper, Zeke comes across the first of another
brood of villains, the so-called "pockmarked man"—or the "pockmarker"(110)—one of the "crows" or scavengers working for Cole Selfridge. Zeke and Casper are forced at gunpoint to set up a still for Selfridge
in the treacherously steep hollow that claims emigrants' wagons. There
Selfridge has set up a store and tavern, and there Zeke meets Peggy, a pathetic young prostitute whose honor he intends to defend in the Don
Quixote-Dulcinea tradition (though unlike Quixote, he has no illusions
about his lady love—he simply considers her "misfortunate" [218]). Hard-
ened by her struggle to survive in this harsh land, Peggy nevertheless pos-
sesses a clichéd romantic strain. If Selfridge bothers her again, Peggy says,
speaking Frontier, "I'll lop off his butt and paint it purple and hang it out
for the horseflies" (154). But when Zeke asks her surname, she responds

in Harlequin: "I won't say it. . . . Never again will it cross my ruby lips" (154). Not surprisingly, she claims to be the daughter of a deposed queen.

Peggy is the last in a line of strong, hard-soft, female characters in Wagoner's Westerns, beginning with Lulu, the independent, high-spirited casino manager and madame in *Wandering Boy*. Cherry Bastion, the headstrong, spoiled beauty of *Tracker*, is the least thoroughly developed of these characters, while the most fully developed and most appealing is Millie Slaughter of *The Road to Many a Wonder*. Cherry and Lulu harbor few illusions about themselves or their circumstances, nor does Millie, for all her schoolgirlish notions of rectitude and propriety. All of these women appear to know the world and its deceptions better than the male protagonists. Peggy, however, plays at self-deception for as long as she can, but yields always to the temptation of her baser, that is, materialistic, ambitions. What the female supporting cast teaches the male protagonists varies, but sexual awareness is inevitably some part of the lesson. The protagonists do not get closely involved with Lulu (*Wandering Boy*) or Cherry (*Tracker*), Ike and Millie succeed in their relationship, while Zeke and Peggy part company, not without pain.

Trying to escape from Selfridge, Zeke runs into "Colonel" Stull's raiding party of "Territorial Pacifiers" (244) at work on a small Sioux camp. He witnesses the death of one Sioux and comes across the body of a raider disguised as an Indian, but actually one of the party that had attacked Zeke and his family. One at a time, it appears, Zeke is being avenged. When he returns from the scene of this violence, Peggy takes Zeke to what she calls an "Enchanted Valley" (215), actually the site of some fossilized bones, including a mammoth's tusk. During this peculiar interlude, reality and romance clash almost constantly as Zeke attempts to create an imaginative world for Peggy, an acceptable myth, one in which she will appear in a silver gown on a sunny June day in a luxuriant forest. When Peggy demands an imaginary treasure, however, her actual self emerges. She wants no rainbow gold or dragon hoard, but the Selfridges' cash and jewels. Zeke informs her that he is "no kind of robber" (223), and he quickly comes to grips with the hard realities of the situation:

> By that time, I was so far from being in a spellbind, I couldn't hardly bear to look at the sky I'd been drinking in earlier, and the gully was looking bleak and dingy and scrabbly and nothing enchanted about it whatsoever. (223)

Despite this gloomy vision, they do make love, but upon returning to the Selfridge place, Zeke runs straight into the deadly actuality of the buckskin man and the moonhead.

At the tavern, Stull's Territorial Pacifiers take bloody control of the operation, killing three of Selfridge's crows outside and the Selfridges themselves within. Then Stull turns on Zeke and holds a mock trial and parodic wedding, intending to execute him the next morning. Casper, however, saves the day by gunning down the moonhead and slipping a mickey to Stull's men. But in the scuffle, the empire-crazed Stull, who represents mankind thoroughly insane with avarice, makes off with Zeke as his prisoner and turns up at a Sioux camp, where he sells whiskey and where, apparently, he intends to have Zeke executed. If what Stull is doing appears foolish, perhaps we should remember that his rapacity has filled him with utter contempt for his fellow man, especially for the "salvages" whom he wishes to exterminate. Stull's luck runs out as the Indians begin to pass out from the drugged liquor and an Indian leader recognizes him from one of his murderous raids. He is promptly tomahawked and scalped while Zeke, having given a desperation hog call to save his favorite pig from the dinner menu, is released, presumably because the Sioux recognize his special powers.

Back on the trail, Zeke meets Casper and Peggy, who has stolen the Selfridge treasure and is being pursued by the pockmarker. Although Casper offers her room in his wagon along with Zeke, Peggy refuses to leave her treasure, and when the crows catch up with them she decides to go back and take over Mrs. Selfridge's position. Zeke, of course, emerges sadder but wiser from the experience, vowing to find a girl "half-hog" like himself and together be whole, "because all people wanted to do was kill hogs and each other and raise more and then kill the next ones, and I wanted to try it some different way" (298–99).

A "different way," of course, is what each of Wagoner's protagonists seeks, and some aspects of that way are constant. It will be non-violent and it will involve a new relationship with another person or persons. It will be founded on optimism and on confidence in one's self and the future. Above all, perhaps, the new way will entail a special attitude toward material gain. Wagoner's protagonists are ambitious young men, but they are never depraved or corrupted by greed as are their adversaries. Moreover, the protagonists clearly acknowledge "wonders" other than gold or jewels. On the other hand, Wagoner's Westerns are not simply conventionalized sermons against materialism. The line between healthy ambition and diseased lust for luxury is always clearly drawn. His Westerns are not mere farces or empty comedies, but moral comedies, and that in the best sense—not cloying, or sentimental, or preachy, but fun.

CELEBRATING THE UNPREDICTABLE:

The Poems of the Seventies

IN A SHORT ESSAY ON THE PAINTINGS of Oregon artist Carl Morris, printed in the *Malahat Review* in 1974, David Wagoner describes the works as "dramatic threats against the safe place where we think we have found sure footing and a sensory place to stand" (6). But if such titles as *A Place to Stand, The Nesting Ground*, and *Riverbed* support the contention that Wagoner was in the process of discovering just such a "safe place," a refuge of sorts, the titles of subsequent volumes would refute such a premise. Beginning with the sequence *Travelling Light*, published handsomely in 1976 by Scott Walker at Graywolf Press in Port Townsend, Washington, Wagoner's titles begin to reflect his sense that "the closer we look, the less certainty we have that we're seeing a universe where physical principles can be depended on" (6). He is speaking here of Morris's paintings, but the statement applies well to much of Wagoner's own poetry. All is in a state of change, flux, mutation, metamorphosis. Like the viewer of Morris's acrylics and oils, what the reader of Wagoner's poems derives is "not the meditative reassurance of geometry, but the geophysics of the psyche" (6). After *Collected Poems* (1976), followed *Who Shall Be the Sun?* (1978), and *In Broken Country* (1979), where we are warned that "The shortest distance between two points doesn't exist" (91). "Dramatic threats" against the safe places we think we have discovered is a very apt description of Wagoner's own poems during the seventies, and in fact throughout most of his career. His is rarely a voice of assurance and confidence.

Yet few writers could have entered the decade of the seventies with better cause for self-confidence than Wagoner. His position at the University of Washington was secure, and he could reflect on five collections of poems, five novels, and growing critical acclaim. But confidence is dangerous. Its twin is complacency and its firstborn child is that smug spoiled brat, overconfidence. To ward off such perils, the poet who had already assumed so many voices would have to find others, or else elaborate those that were already in his repertoire. As a novelist, Wagoner had a wider range of unexplored territories, and he set about the expedition with the first of four comic Westerns, *Where is My Wandering Boy Tonight?*, in 1970. These are set on the frontier in the mid to late nineteenth century, and they include his most enjoyable fiction, notably *The Road to Many a Wonder* (1974). Wagoner reports that the Westerns earned him "money in movie options over the years," but his only excursion to Hollywood to date has been with *The Escape Artist*, released in 1982, which he describes as "a disappointment to everyone involved." He has indicated that he has no plans to return to the comic Western mode (*Contemporary Authors* 408). Wagoner also undertook the task of editing Theodore Roethke's notebooks for the University of Washington Press; these appeared in 1972 under the title, *Straw for the Fire*.

Following the publication of a London edition drawn from *New and Selected Poems* in 1970, Wagoner embarked on a tour of the Middle East under the auspices of the U.S. Information Agency. The high point of the tour, which involved readings and dialogues with internationally prominent writers, was his stay in Istanbul, but after six weeks, just as he was about to leave for Pakistan from Beirut, skirmishes broke out between India and Pakistan, and he returned to the United States. In his autobiographical essay, Wagoner represents himself as prepared to speak out against the war in Vietnam whenever the occasion might arise, but he adds that the literary people he met "simply took it for granted that no American writer could support such lunacy" (*Contemporary Authors* 409). Readers who turn to Wagoner's poems from the late sixties and early seventies in search of antiwar diatribes and activist political outcries, however, will be disappointed. From one perspective at least, Wagoner was out of step with the times. Poets like Robert Bly, Denise Levertov, and W.S. Merwin participated in antiwar rallies and penned protests that marked such volumes respectively as *The Light Around the Body* (1967), *Relearning the Alphabet* (1970), and *The Lice* (1967). Wagoner's books from the Vietnam era contain no mention of the war and the domestic disturbances over it.

Given the broad range of voices among his poems, Wagoner's disinclination to find a voice or persona to reflect his sentiments on the war in Vietnam may seem peculiar to some readers. But Wagoner's political expressions have remained more implicit than explicit and more private than public. A consistent political sentiment can certainly be derived, for example, from poems like "The Breathing Lesson," "A Valedictory to Standard Oil of Indiana," "Working Against Time," "The March of Coxey's Army," and "Getting Out of Jail on Monday," all of which are included in *Collected Poems, 1956–1976*. Wagoner's sympathies are with the social outcast—Indian, radical, burglar, bum—and the manual laborer, like his steelworker father. His antipathies are toward exploitative, environmentally threatening big business and industry (Standard Oil, Weyerhaeuser). More broadly stated, as we see time and again in his novels, Wagoner's is the political voice of the private individual, and his major foe is the corrupting influence of materialism. In his review of *Riverbed* (1972) in the *Saturday Review*, John W. Hughes calls for "more of Wagoner's socially conscious, 'impure' poetry precisely because his obvious distrust of bourgeois values, like his sympathy for the uprooted and the underdog, derives from his knowledge of the authentic bases for community that can be uncovered by means of nature and our link to nature, the Word" (62). To some extent, Wagoner was to comply with this request.

Wagoner has described himself as a man who, at the time, seemed from all appearances to be "extremely fortunate": "good income . . . handsome house . . . loving wife . . . good health . . . prolific" (*Contemporary Authors* 409). "Behind the surfaces," however, Wagoner asserts, in his "private life everything occurred in a different shade of light" (409). His wife, Patt, to whom so many volumes of poetry had been lovingly dedicated, was a lifelong hypochondriac, and she was on occasion hysterical, suicidal, and addicted to prescribed drugs and alcohol. In 1974 she was found to have breast cancer. Following the deaths of her grandmother and mother in 1977 and 1978, she became estranged from other members of her family, and her relations with her husband worsened until their divorce in 1980. The "flaws" in his own personality, to which Wagoner candidly pleads guilty in his account of their breakup, may explain in some ways his silence amid the political turbulence of the seventies. Principally among these he lists his "reclusiveness," a "desire for a calm surface to domestic life at almost any cost," and a "reluctance to give time to friendships" (410).

Wagoner is a self-professed loner. Though he is an able reader of his poems and though his readings are well attended, he hasn't the extroverted, even exhibitionistic, flair or showmanship of a Robert Bly or a Gary Snyder, and arguably this lack of a public presence, of either an easy conviviality or charisma on the one hand or a cantankerous waspishness on the other hand, has damaged his popularity. In the world of campus readings and workshops, and particularly in the arena of the political "happenings" of the late sixties and early seventies, the charismatic poets had a decided edge. Bly and Snyder have sung, chanted, strummed dulcimers, donned masks, paced the stage, and ranted and ommed their way to notoriety. This is not to say that their work is of lesser quality or that their renown is simply a matter of performance, but certainly their dramatic self-presentation has assisted them to their National Book Awards and Pulitzer Prizes, while Wagoner's more reserved ways have led him to be better known among poets and professors than among undergraduates and whatever general readership exists for poetry. Wagoner also lacks the personable, low-key affability or warmth that assisted fellow northwesterner, William Stafford, in building a following. Wagoner is neither a rabblerouser, nor a guru, nor a father figure. He is a difficult man to know well, sustaining his ironic detachment and a certain personal security, not without some cost to his popularity.

In 1974 his seventh volume of poems, *Sleeping in the Woods*, was nominated for the National Book Award, and his *Collected Poems* (1976) was also nominated, but neither volume won. *Collected Poems* includes among the new contents the superb nine-poem sequence entitled "Travelling Light." In 1978 a collection of poems appeared that is singular among his works, *Who Shall Be the Sun?*, songs and narratives of the Northwest and Plains Indians, which Wagoner offers not as translations but as "retellings" (Author's Note n. p.). Twenty-seven of these poems had comprised one section of *Collected Poems* and fifty-one were new additions. That same year Wagoner received a three-year appointment as editor of the Princeton University Contemporary Poetry Series and was elected a chancellor of the Academy of American Poets. The decade of the seventies ended for Wagoner with what Harold Bloom, on the book cover, has called his "best work."

1. RIVERBED

In his comments on the poems in *Riverbed* (1972), Sanford Pinsker reiterates his pleasure in what he calls the "quiet astonishment" ("On David Wagoner" 361, 365, 368) of Wagoner's persona, when his voice is most in tune. More than half of the forty-eight poems involve a first person speaker, and more than a third concern animals, including the first eight poems in the book (salmon, trout, a killer whale, vultures, a parrot, a horse, birds, ants). In the title poem, the speaker, presumably with his paramour, watches the salmon returning past gill nets, fishermen, and pulp mills to "the one true holding place" (1). The "we" of the poem wait at the nesting area, hoping to find that place. In effect, the movement of the poem is back to the source, as in "A Guide to Dungeness Spit" and "The Nesting Ground" (*Collected Poems* 20–21, 22–23): "The river turns its stones like a nesting bird / From hollow to hollow" (2). As the gulls and ravens set upon the spawning and dying salmon, the lovers "lie down all day beside them" (2). The flat expression in this last phrase of the poem, as the lovers take on the role of the salmon, typifies the quietly understated moment of recognition that dawns on Wagoner's persona in many of his poems.

"The Middle of Nowhere" (35–36), on the other hand, begins in astonishment of a sort: "To be here, in the first place, is sufficiently amazing." In the rugged, weedy terrain we find ourselves following directions "Not yet invented-north / By south, upright by easterly, northwest by nothing." The sun, we discover, is "too high, too rigorous, too downright for measuring." Located in the middle of the collection, this poem might be regarded as an appropriate fulcrum between the opening poem, "Riverbed," in which the "one true holding place," the spawning grounds of the salmon, is as much a place of death as of life, and the last two poems, "Lost" and "Fog," in which the "you" is instructed to let the forest find you and in which the fog is said to "wrap all love and fear in a beautiful blindness" (75, 76). In "The Middle of Nowhere" we are warned that "the problem of being / Here is not deducible." The line break here is significant. Wagoner is concerned not simply with the problem of being lost in the wilderness, the problem of "being here," but also with the dilemma of "being." That is, the speaker goes on to say, the problem is not "deducible" through the senses or through such man-made contrivances as maps and compasses. With "perfect eyesight" and a "feeling for surfaces," he concedes, a "balancing / Act of a kind may be carried out against / The odds for a moment," but "the curvature of the earth and the curvature of the spine" have little real connection. Our confidence is only momentary, and it is based on superficial grounds at that. "The middle of nowhere," the speaker reminds us, is "the hole in all the assembled data / Through which we look" into the "heart of our matter," only to discover that it is "neither logical nor ecological." The concluding lines of the poem sum up very well what might be described as man's existential crisis:

This is the place where we must be ready to take
The truths or consequences
Of which there are none to be filched or mastered or depended on,
Not even, as it was in the beginning, the Word
Or, here, the squawk of a magpie. (36)

The structural parallel between the Biblical "Word" and the "squawk of the magpie" at the end of "The Middle of Nowhere" reasserts the close, mysterious relationship between human and animal worlds celebrated in the title poem of this collection. Humans are frustrated everywhere in Wagoner's poems, especially when they perceive a dichotomy between their world and the natural world or when they seek to manipulate or exploit nature. As Wagoner phrases it in "The Makers of Rain," "We are masters of nothing we survey" (69). In "The Survivor" (52) a couple comes upon a dying salmon, and although the speaker is able to coax the fish into the current, it is obvious that its life is "wavering" and its existence is limited to "the cold time being."

In the human world, however, Wagoner's personae fare somewhat better. The speaker and his lover in "The Doves of Merida" buy five mourning doves and set them free, hoping for "peace" or "hope" (70). The first one joins the "lean gray city pigeons" (71) in the Plaza de la Independencia. The second flies into a chicken coop, where it is destined to end up on the plate with other domestic fowl, and the third does even worse, falling into a gutter where it will feed the vultures. The fourth, however, defying the tortoiseshell shop, the dogs at the butcher's shop, and the zoo, flaps to rest beyond the Pyramid of the Magician at the Casa de las Palomas. And the fifth dove circles upwards, "groping for distance / Turning half gold" and disappearing before the couple can "Tell it apart / From what was beyond it" (72).

The "quiet astonishment" to which Pinsker refers is well illustrated in the last two poems of the volume, "Lost" and "Fog." In "Lost" we hear the familiar imperative voice of the teacher:

Stand still. The trees ahead and bushes beside you
Are not lost. Wherever you are is called Here,
And you must treat it as a powerful stranger,
Must ask permission to know it and be known.

Though people may be lost in the world, their condition is far from hope-
less. The sentient forest answers:

> *I have made this place for you.*
> *If you leave it, you may come back again, saying Here.*
> *No two trees are the same to Raven.*
> *No two branches are the same to Wren.*
> *If what a tree or a bush does is lost on you,*
> *You are surely lost. Stand still. The forest knows*
> *Where you are. You must let it find you.* (75)

The lessons of this poem are reiterated throughout Wagoner's poems. Being lost does not imply a hostile world, but rather human arrogance (we
must not demand, but must "ask permission") or lack of attention to details (no two trees or branches are the same to the raven or the wren,
though all seem alike to humans). What the lost individual must do is be
humble and patient and open, receptive to the world, in order to be found.

In the last poem from *Riverbed*, "Fog," the imperative voice of the
master addresses, in a literal sense, an Indian youth who has awakened
from his vision quest, which will establish his adult name and identity, to
discover not a fox, a bear, or a snake, but "only Fog as the eye of your heart
opened" (76). The idea is intrinsically humorous, and it also might suggest
the obscurity of man's place in nature. But Wagoner takes the poem in a
different direction. "You" will not become engulfed or confused by the
fog, nor will you become simply a part of the natural environment, as you
would have been had your vision been of a fox or a bear, but you will become the whole of that world. I sustain Wagoner's second person pronoun
here because I think he intends that the reader be enveloped as fully as
the imagined character in the poem.

> *You will become trees by holding them inside you,*
> *And tall stones, become a whole valley*
> *Where birds fall still, where men stay close to fires.*
> *You without wings or hands will gleam against them,*
> *They will breathe you, they will be lost in you,*
> *Your song will be the silence between their songs,*
> *Your white darkness will teach them,*
> *You will wrap all love and fear in a beautiful blindness.*

Placed last as it is in the volume, and directed via the second person to the reader, "Fog" encompasses both the reader and the various personae of the book. The inability to deal effectively with the material and animal world and the feeling of being lost and of alienation are peculiarly countered in this poem by a sort of magic, a metamorphosis that assures we will not be left stranded in the middle of nowhere, unable to live meaningfully in the universe.

2. SLEEPING IN THE WOODS

Nevertheless, as the title of Wagoner's next volume, *Sleeping in the Woods* (1974), implies, we are not "out of the woods" yet. The "you" of the title poem is "Looking for somewhere to bed down at nightfall / Though you have nothing / But parts of yourself to lie on" (62), or "to rely on," he might equally well have said. The title poem is the climactic part of a four-poem sequence, beginning with "Report from a Forest Logged by the Weyerhaeuser Company" (56–57) and including "The Lesson" (58–59) and "Elegy for a Forest Clear-cut by the Weyerhaeuser Company" (60–61). "Sleeping in the Woods" was published a year before the Weyerhaeuser poems and it does not concern a clear-cut forest, but it does function well in the sequence Wagoner arranges.

In "Report" (56–57) the first-person speaker, finding "[t]hree square miles clear-cut" on a sunny April morning, states grimly:

> *Now only the facts matter:*
> *The heaps of gray-splintered rubble,*
> *The churned-up duff, the roots, the bulldozed slash,*
> *The silence.* (56)

The speaker offers an accounting. Among the living are "bent huckleberry," a "patch of salal," "a wasp," and two butterflies that, in Wagoner's understated irony, mistake the speaker for an item of the natural environment. Among the dead are "thousands of fir seedlings" planted by the company as part of its reforestation project but doomed "for lack of the usual free rain," two "buckshot beercans," and a vulture. The speaker mocks the concept of "selective logging" in the penultimate stanza, in which Wagoner's rhetoric is strident, even sarcastic, a rare lowering of the mask in his poems.

Selective logging, they say, we'll take three miles,
It's good for the bears and deer, they say,
More brush and berries sooner or later,
We're thinking about the future—if you're in it
With us, they say. . . . (57)

The poem ends with the focus shifting to the speaker himself: "But staying with the facts, / I mourn with my back against a stump" (57).

The next poem, "The Lesson" (58–59), appears to be a reflection on the same "promising morning," shifting the time to the moments before the speaker came upon the clear-cut. "Driving beside the river," he comments on a pair of newborn lambs and a colt, "Three staggering new lives / Above the fingerlings / From a thousand salmon nests." Buoyed by these signs of new life, he sings as he drives up the logging road until he comes upon "a fresh two thousand acres / Of a familiar forest / Clear-cut and left for dead / By sawtoothed Weyerhaeuser." He haunts the area for hours, haunted himself by the emptiness and the realization that

the salmon will die
In gillnets and crude oil,
The colt be broken and broken,
And the lambs leap to their slaughter. (58)

The speaker is brought out of his rage, however, by a rufous hummingbird, "Exulting in wild dives . . . / Making me crouch and cringe / In his fiery honor." In the midst of the desolation, then, the speaker is soothed by the minimals of nature, the butterflies and the hummingbird, in a way reminiscent of similar moments in poems from Roethke's North American Sequence, which had been published ten years earlier.

In "Elegy" (60–61) the speaker returns to the clear-cut five months later to lament its passing and to calculate the costs. From the shadows of ninety-year-old trees, reduced to "slash and stumps," only nettles, groundsel, fireweed, and fern "come to light." Only one in ten fir seedlings have survived the summer drought, and "[b]elow the small green struggle of the weeds," grasshoppers provide the only music after what he describes as the "immoral equivalent of a forest fire." He concludes in anger, lashing out against the hypocrisy of what the timber companies refer to as "selective logging," the euphemism by which the industry seeks to justify its practice of clear-cutting:

> *I sit with my anger. The creek will move again,*
> *Come rain and snow, gnawing raw defiles,*
> *Clear-cutting its own gullies.*
> *As selective as reapers stalking through wheatfields,*
> *Selective loggers go where the roots go.* (61)

The unremedied pain and anger at the end of "Elegy for a Forest Clear-cut by the Weyerhaeuser Company" cries out for some sort of treatment or resolution. "Sleeping in the Woods" (62–63) provides the medication, as Wagoner must have realized when he placed it after the bitter elegy. The speaker uses what Richard Howard describes as "a voice mildly expostulating, gently instructing, lightly dismissing" (637). Although Wagoner uses the second person point of view, the context suggests that the speaker is addressing himself, his inner self, as much as he is the reader. Caught in the woods at night, the individual must come to terms with his animal nature ("You must help yourself like any animal"). At the almost incantatory heart of this poem, Wagoner's persona goes to sleep:

> *For the first time without walls, not falling asleep, not losing*
> *Anything under you to the imponderable*
> *Dead and living*
> *Earth, your countervailing bed, but settling down*
> *Beside it across the slackening threshold*
> *Of the place where it is always*
> *Light. . . .* (62)

These six lines (and the first word from the seventh) are a fragment of an immense sentence that runs some twenty-three lines, expanding and contracting, inhaling and exhaling, as if following either the rhythm of the heart or the measured breathing of a sleeper. The persona half awakens in a green dawn and sees his "cupped hand lying open . . . like a flower":

> *Making light of it,*
> *You have forgotten why you came, have served your purpose, and*
> *   simply*
> *By being here have found the right way out.*
> *Now you may waken.* (63)

The healing process has begun, or at least that is the impression created by this poem, given Wagoner's placement of it in the collection.

Not every poem is lined up sequentially in *Sleeping in the Woods*, or in any of Wagoner's books, but as subsequent collections demonstrate, beginning with the chapbook, *Travelling Light* (1976), he is very fond of such sequences, as popularized by Roethke in 1948 with the "Lost Son" poems. Moreover, Wagoner carefully arranges the poems in his collections, as do most poets, so that they resonate with each other in various ways. The next two poems after "Sleeping in the Woods," for example, clearly do not fit in the sequence which starts with "Report from a Forest Logged by the Weyerhaeuser Company." "For a Winter Wren" (64) is a nearly pure, eleven-line nature lyric, and "Bonsai" (65) moves us from the forest to the cultivated garden. That is to say, as Wagoner leaves the powerful Weyerhaeuser sequence, in which he makes as strong a political statement as anywhere in his work, he does not immediately confront the reader with a poem out of tune with the sequence, but he offers a sort of transition to poems in which the voices and attitudes are quite different. Following "Bonsai," for instance, is "The Lost Street" (66), one of the playful-but-serious poems which Wagoner builds on a foundation of wordplay (in this case, an ambiguous passage in a pamphlet distributed by the Auto Dealers Traffic Safety Committee).

Each of the four sections of *Sleeping in the Woods* is prefaced by a poem about the poetry. The first, which acts as a prefatory poem to the whole collection, is "The Singing Lesson" (15), in which "you" are instructed to "stand erect but at your ease, a posture / Demanding a compromise." What applies to singing applies equally well to writing poems, and the "martyred beggar" that Wagoner metaphorizes in the poem as "[a] flightless bird on the nest dreaming of flying" could well stand as his fanciful definition of the poet. Learning "measures," the voice instructor tells us, will require both "labor and luck," but if we succeed, we will find ourselves some day "before an audience / Singing into the light, / Transforming the air" we breathe "[i]nto deathless music." Many poets would be satisfied with the latter phrase as an ideal conclusion for the poem, but Wagoner rarely embraces the idyll of the easy and obvious out. As Richard Howard notes, "What is remarkable about Wagoner's ongoing lessons . . . is that they do not pretend to presume to teach us what we could learn" (637). No sooner has the instructor suggested "deathless music" than he cautions, "But remember . . . / Some men will wonder / When they look at you without listening, whether / You're singing or dying." The singer/poet, then, must "[t]ake care to be heard," but that may not be enough, for even "singing alone, / Singing for nothing," he must "[k]eep time." On the one hand the teacher refers to tempo or rhythm, but the phrasing also suggests that only time will tell whether the performance wins "tacit approval."

Most of the poems of the first section concern love and are perhaps autobiographical. Following "The Singing Lesson" is "Beginning," a Roethkean sort of nature poem which concludes,

> *I came to a stand of alders*
> *As pale as my bones*
> *And waited a dead hour*
> *In the thawing dirt of their roots*
> *Like them to begin.* (17)

Even the motif of the journey backward in order to go ahead is reminiscent of Roethke, but in a more personal sense, this preoccupation in the love poems to follow may reflect Wagoner's efforts to reconstruct his disintegrating marriage. Following "The Bad Fisherman" and "Talking to Barr Creek," which also involve a first-person speaker in close communion with nature, Wagoner offers five love poems, all of which pertain to a quest for origins.

In "The Bad Fisherman" the speaker goes home "in the dark with nothing" (18). Since then he has been left waiting and watching at the river's edge like a heron, a solitary bird often evoked as a symbol of loneness. In "Talking to Barr Creek" the speaker admires the oneness and wholeness of the stream, and he ends with something of a prayer: "Teach me your spirit, going yet staying, being / Born, vanishing, enduring" (20). "The First Place" (21–22), the most fully developed of the love poems, moves easily from "Talking to Barr Creek" because it locates the lovers on a stream in which specific images from the three previous poems are gathered— ferns, rainbow trout, alders. The poem is infused with an understated sensuality: "Among the touching ferns, by our touching fingers, / And led by wren-song through alders felled by beavers, / We came to a pool flowing deep." The deep pool here, as elsewhere in poetry, amounts to a sort of abyss of potentiality, the love that might be. "While the rainbows leaped," the speaker narrates (relishing his pun, no doubt), his beloved "opened / The gift of her nakedness" and stepped into the icy stream "singing, welcoming the wonder / Of the river that held her light as her beauty." As the scene is bathed in sunlight, the two see "the beginning . . . / And we put our lives in our hands on a morning / That had no ending." But at this point the poem takes a sudden turn. The speaker plunges into the cold stream, as if fighting the love he has just celebrated. "Numb as a half-man," he struggles to a sandbar, and his beloved wades out to him "out of mercy," after which they swim together (*"not alone,"* he insists), "Upstream to spawn in the last place on earth / We could have hoped for: the first place."

A poem like "The First Place" does not have to be read autobiographically in order to be effective, but the poem may reflect in some ways Wagoner's deepening marital problems. Here, he plays with the prospect of his beloved coming to his aid, meeting him halfway, so to speak, before they join and are transformed into a pair of fertile salmon. The next poem, "The Vow" (23), is a somewhat playful naturalist's oath to love, as experienced by every animal from the snowy owl and the skate's egg to the harbor seal and the salmon, all of which have been subjects of Wagoner's poems. The poem after that, "Slow Country" (24–25), urges the beloved to stay when she arrives at that "permanent kingdom," for

> you will have time
> Between the dream of embracing and the full embrace
> To find your love
> Lying beneath you like the willing earth,
> Neither turning nor falling. (25)

The first section ends with "An Offering for Dungeness Bay" (30–31), a poem which must inevitably remind anyone familiar with Wagoner's work of the more renowned "A Guide to Dungeness Spit" from *The Nesting Ground* (1963). The poems do not bear close comparison, although they have in common a pair of lovers in the same setting and a number of images, particularly those referring to birds. "A Guide" is a hopeful poem, perhaps even more than that—a celebratory poem. The instructor's voice exudes a sort of confidence as it leads upwards, into the light, and quietly insists, "We are called lovers." "An Offering," while it is certainly no ode to dejection, is more tentative. The tern in the opening section of the poem dives into his own reflection, "Trailing silver / Falling to meet itself over and over." The opening image itself, then, suggests a self-probing, reflexive attitude. In the second section, as the moon rises, the plover calls out *"Begin"* and is answered in echoes, *"Again, again, again."* In the third section, the sanderlings announce, *"Here is the place."* Finally, in the fourth section, geese "at the brim of darkness" rise up and fly away "Lifting, beginning again, going on and on." The poem is an urgent plea both for starting over, for renewal of love, and for continuing that love. The poet who performed as a guide at Dungeness Spit ten years earlier now makes a humble offering.

The second section of *Sleeping in the Woods* opens with the vividly comical, six-line description and evocation, "Muse":

> *Cackling, smelling of camphor, crumbs of pink icing*
> *Clinging to her lips, her lipstick smeared*
> *Halfway around her neck, her cracked teeth bristling*
> *With bloody splinters, she leans over my shoulder.*
> *Oh my only hope, my lost dumfounding baggage,*
> *My gristle-breasted, slack-jawed zealot, kiss me again.* (33)

Courting *this* muse, as the cliché would have it, could be unpleasant, even dangerous. Appropriately, Wagoner's mock evocation opens the most playful section of the book, a collection of fourteen poems marked by some of his most outrageous yet most effective punning. Wagoner's puns are quite self-conscious tours de force. Readers may either embrace them or reject them out of hand, but they cannot simply ignore them. In his seventy-line modernized version of the Beauty and the Beast fable, for example, the Beast tells Beauty:

> *You'd be a sweet relief. I'd gorge on you.*
> *I'm sick of retching my time with hags and gorgons.*
> *You're gorgeous. Put down my rising gorge forever.*
>   ("Beauty and the Beast" 38)

The wordplay is either funny, or it's awful. In Wagoner's version of the tale, the beast does not change into a handsome Prince Charming, but remains his own bestial self. Beauty, however, bored with the charms of conventional princes, embraces the monster and walks away with him into the "bewitching forest" (39).

In "Elegy for a Woman Who Remembered Everything," Wagoner's punning reaches another crescendo:

> *Her ears were as perfectly pitched as a piano-tuner's.*
> *In the maze of total recall, she met with amazement*
> *The data of each new day, absorbed the absorbing facts and the*
>   *absorbent*
> *Fictions of everyone's life but her own. . . .* (45)

It may well be, in fact, that Wagoner will emerge as a most unusual phenomenon: a genuine visionary poet who is also an accomplished clown, not
the "joyous visionary" but the "playful visionary." Ronald Wallace has detected something of this "fusion of voices" in his study, *God Be With the
Clown* (1984), in Wagoner and a wide range of other contemporary poets
(206–10). In "The Man Who Spilled Light" (46), Wagoner toys with the visionary premise of the prophet who would enlighten a benighted civilization. But when the people discover that "[t]here was nothing they couldn't
see," they start to squint, and the bringer of light is compelled to take back
the light.

> *They should have been looking at everything, and everything*
> *Should have been perfectly clear, and everyone*
> *Should have seemed perfectly brilliant, there was so much*
> *Dazzle: people were dazzled, they were dazzling,*
> *But they were squinting, trying to make darkness*
> *All over again in the cracks between their eyelids.*
>
> *So he swept up all the broken light*
> *For pity's sake and put it back where it came from.* (46)

Certain visionary poets, perhaps Robert Bly and many of his followers
among them, would not be likely to tolerate this sort of playful irrever-
ence, but the element of play is by no means inconsistent with visionary
poetry, at least in recent times. We would hardly expect playfulness in
William Blake or Maria Rainer Rilke, but we encounter it frequently in
the poems of James Wright and Pablo Neruda. Play, then, seems to be a le-
gitimate expression of the joy felt by many visionaries.

Other poems in the second section vary in nature from the powerfully
sinister "Snake Hunt" (41) to the thoroughly comical "Note to a Literary
Club" (48) and "The Boy of the House" (49), but the dominant tone of the
section is playful, and Wagoner sustains that tone in the prefatory poem to
the third section, "This is a Wonderful Poem" (53). Like his poem to the
muse, Wagoner's introduction to this poem is cautionary and eccentric.
The poem, he informs us, is not a "thing of beauty and a joy forever," but
an untrustworthy imposter, unwashed and "wearing stolen rags." Its
breath "[w]ould look moss-green if it were really breathing," and like
Robert Lowell's skunk, "[i]t won't get out of the way." Like a confused
thief, the poem confronts us, wanting "something," but not sure whether

to request it or take it by force. It is a "[t]hing standing between you and
the place you were headed." Wagoner's playful contempt for the poem in
this definition is reminiscent of Marianne Moore's reductive dismissal of
"all this fiddle" without her open affirmation of poetry as "a place for the
genuine." But Wagoner, instead of offering the reader a positive assertion
about poetry or a line of reassurance, poses a question, perhaps even a
challenge: "Now, what do you want to do about it?"

After the Weyerhaeuser sequence and other poems, Wagoner begins
the fourth and final section of the book, entitled "Seven Songs for an Old
Voice," with "Fire Song" (73), which also performs a prefatory role. The
speaker, an American Indian, is starting a fire and addressing the fire spirit
as he blows into the sparks. The fire lies inherent in the wood where the
speaker twirls his stick, and the warm breath he blows into the sparks is
kindred to the spirit of fire itself. It is the animating spirit. The speaker
only asks for the temporary company of fire through the night, and at
dawn, he promises, "you may lie down slowly . . . / To sleep again at the
cold point of my spirit." While "Fire Song" does not so obviously pertain to
poetry as do the other prefatory poems, it does celebrate the poetic spirit,
the life-giving light and heat which are symbolically related to poetry. The
poems which follow are collected again in *Who Shall Be the Sun?* (1978),
which shall be discussed hereafter.

3. COLLECTED POEMS

Collected Poems 1956–1976 was timed to coincide with Wagoner's fiftieth
birthday and added four sets of new poems (42 poems in all) to the seven
previously published books. All of the new poems were anticipated in
some way in *Sleeping in the Woods*. The magnificent, nine-poem sequence, "Travelling Light," which surely features Wagoner at his best in a
sustained effort to that date, had appeared earlier in the year as a chapbook. These poems are similar in tone and texture to "Sleeping in the
Woods," the title poem of the 1974 collection. The fifteen poems in the
second section of the "New Poems" constitute what might be called a
"Wagoner miscellany." The eighteen poems that make up the last two sections make use of the "Indian cosmology," as Robert Cording calls it (353),
and are included in *Who Shall Be the Sun?* (1978).

Although most of Wagoner's poems have not been subjected to close
analysis, the "Travelling Light" sequence has been ably examined by poet

and critic Laurence Lieberman in an essay entitled "The Cold Speech of the Earth," which runs nearly thirty pages in his book, *Unassigned Frequencies* (1977). Lieberman sees the poems as dramas of survival, operating on three levels: literally, the poems concern survival in the woods, but at the same time they "resonate in all the best images" the survival tactics necessary to sustain both love and the craft of poetry (154).

The nine poems in the sequence vary in length and complexity from the disarmingly simple, 18–line introductory poem, "Breaking Camp," to the sublimely visionary, 48–line finale, "Travelling Light," which is anticipated in the penultimate line of "Breaking Camp." Although, as Lieberman notes, Wagoner writes in a "lean style" without "[e]xcess freightage" (155), the poems in this sequence are not appreciably more spare than poems like "A Guide to Dungeness Spit," "Slow Country," or "Report from a Forest Logged by the Weyerhaeuser Company." That is, they do not involve a major departure from Wagoner's prevailing vision. His love of wordplay is sustained in "Breaking Camp" (249) as the instructor's voice advises us to "break camp" at the "break of day." We are told that the next campsite may be no nearer our destination, but it will be "deeply, starkly appealing / Like a lost home." The conclusion of the poem prepares us for the title poem when the instructor reminds us that the new campsite must have "the makings of a fire" because we will be "travelling light" (249).

Nothing in "Breaking Camp" indicates that "you" might refer to more than one person, and in fact the title poem of the sequence, in which the instructor assumes a more companionable "we," clearly involves a major departure in voice and circumstances from the other poems of the sequence. Moreover, only after reading "Travelling Light" might we be inclined to interpret at least some moments in the earlier poems as survival lessons in love, as Lieberman suggests. But virtually all the poems of the sequence may be said to contribute to a guidebook on the craft of writing poems.

The next two poems of the sequence, "Meeting a Bear" and "Walking in a Swamp," concern on the literal level the natural impediments to our progress through the wilderness, life, or the craft of poetry, or whatever association the reader brings to the central metaphor. Few motifs in literature are as universal as the individual wandering in the wilderness. The intimidating bear in "Meeting a Bear" (250–51) might be read as a literal danger confronting a backpacker, or as any particular adversary facing us in life, or more narrowly as the unwilling reader or hostile critic who, like the bear in the poem, would prefer to avoid us and our poems. Such a narrow reading might be more allegorical than what Wagoner had in mind, but the poem is playful and suggests an openness to interpretation. Lieberman, who considers this the weakest poem in the sequence complains justly that Wagoner offers no "palpable actuality of bear" (156). If my suspicions are correct, however, Wagoner is after different game in this poem and in "Walking in the Swamp" as well.

Face to face with the bear, the would-be poet's future depends on "what he makes of you / And your upright posture." In this confrontation a direct assault is as risky as retreat:

> *Gaping and staring directly are as risky as running:*
> *To try for dominance or moral authority*
> *Is an empty gesture.* . . . (250)

Certainly if we read these lines as they reflect on Wagoner's poetics, they fit strikingly well. The direct stare and the bid for "moral authority" are alien to his perspective. Informing the poet ("you") about the audience ("he"), Wagoner conceives of the audience as it is in reality, at least in the contemporary United States outside the comfortable confines of academe: "He doesn't *care* what you think or calculate; your disapproval / Leaves him as cold as the opinions of salmon." Under the circumstances, the speaker advises, "You would do well to try your meekest behavior." (The advice is reminiscent of that urged by another instructor in the craft, William Carlos Williams, in "Tract" [1920], where I take the driver of the "rough plain hearse" [the poem] to refer to the poet, who is ordered to take off his formal silk hat "and walk at the side / and inconspicuously too!" [13].) The speaker in "Meeting a Bear" suggests standing still "[a]s long as you're not mauled or hugged," and "if you must stir, do everything sidelong, / Gently and naturally, / Vaguely oblique." One could hardly do better by way of defining how many of David Wagoner's best poems work: gently, naturally, obliquely. What can the poet say, after all, but that which "softly," even "monotonously," "comes to mind"? To plead or appeal to the hostile reader's "better feelings" is of course a waste of time: "He has none, only a harder life than yours." Moreover, as the speaker insists, "There's no use singing / National anthems or battle hymns or alma maters / Or any other charming or beastly music." The most plain, even dull or bland, "most colorless, undemonstrative speech you can think of" is what affects the contemporary audience: "Bears, for good reason, find it embarrassing." Wagoner *will* have his pun. And as the perplexed bears "cover their eyeteeth as in answer," the poet may slip away unscathed.

Lieberman detects a "false note" in "Meeting a Bear"—"Wagoner posturing as social commentator" (157)—but the sustained playfulness keeps the potentially programmatic element in the poem from getting out of hand. Between the cold opinions of the salmon and the embarrassed bears, the poem maintains its humor so ably that the reader could not care less about what Liberman calls the "palpable actuality of bear" (156). The same might be said for the companion poem in the sequence, "Walking in the Swamp" (252), which can be read as advice to the poet who gets bogged down. The first advice the speaker gives to those who feel the ground getting "soft and uncertain" is to "start running," but if we do not escape "in those few scampering seconds," he asserts, "It's time to reconsider / Your favorite postures, textures, and means of moving." Just as the correct response to the hostile audience (the bear) was "yielding the forest floor," so the proper response to the poet's uncertainty is not to struggle, but to "lie down . . . / Be seated gently, / Lie back, open your arms, and dream of floating." The worst response would be to insist upon your human dignity by staying "vertical." The best response would be to "slither / Spread-ottered casually backwards out of trouble." Beneath the wordplay, which assumes that the reader will expect to read "spread-eagled," lies serious advice: the way out of this dilemma is not the arrogant assertion of one's "uprightness" any more than an "upright posture" would be a satisfactory response to a bear, who would read it as "a standing offer to fight for territory." As Lieberman observes, survival in the wilderness "requires that a man dredge up lost or forgotten animal skills" (159–60). But Wagoner leaves us stranded in the muck at the end of the poem, in it over our heads, "[a]s upright as ever."

By this stage of the sequence, Wagoner's *modus operandi* should be clear. He intends to pose dilemmas—or to impose them—that might occur when we cut ourselves loose from home, our base camp in life. Such risky journeys are precisely what the poet or any serious artist undertakes. But what this instructor teaches cannot really be called solutions. At the end of "Breaking Camp" we are left with the admonition that we must always search for the "makings of a fire" (249). In "Meeting a Bear" the best we can hope for is a strategic withdrawal, and in "Walking in a Swamp" we are left "in it" (252) over our heads. Most of the poems in this sequence were published in 1975, just one year after Wagoner, in his review of Carl

Morris's painting warned that reliance on conventional "physical principles" in our universe is folly ("Carl Morris" 6). This sequence, then, is constructed on a foundation of irony that ensnares the reader, who naturally
identifies with the "you," by offering a teacher whose lessons are always
north-by-northwest instead of true north. What we are offered in these
poems are not axioms and theorems, though the voice may suggest that,
but what might be called a state of mind, a proper attitude, given the nature of our universe, which will prepare us for the sort of enlightenment
that is being reserved for the last poem in the sequence.

In "Tracking" (253), the fourth of the sequence, Wagoner shifts the focus from natural hazards (lack of firewood, a bear, quicksand) to human
conflict. Given the dilemmas of the previous poems, the reader probably
expects himself or herself to be cast in the role of the quarry, but instead
the reader—"you"—is the tracker in this poem. Or, to resume the
metaphor, the poet is the stalker, and the quarry is revealed only in the last
few lines of the poem, and even then only in the most ambiguous terms.
The "man ahead," as the quarry appears in the first line, is unaware of being followed, so he leaves many signs, but now he is wary, so we must
"learn to read" what we have never read before: "the minute language / Of
moss and lichen, / The signals of bent grass, the speech of sand, / The gestures of dust." We might read these lines as advice, that to understand the
human condition, we must first be able to interpret the world, nature itself, or as Wagoner playfully suggests, "the natural disorder." But the pursuit of the human appears to lead us not to a comfortable understanding of
the "man" we've been after; instead, the "unwelcome meeting" is with
"the other," who (or which) now stares back at our "dead-set" faces to discover our intentions. Did we mean, in our pursuit of the elusive "other," to
destroy it, to join it, or "simply to blunder past"? Typically, Wagoner does
not answer this implied question, but offers it as a quandary. At the end of
the tracking experience, apparently staring success in the face, we are left
uncertain as to our own motives. The poem comes off as the antithesis of
the conventional pursuit story, for here the confrontation of the quarry
raises new issues instead of providing resolutions.

The identity of the quarry in "Tracking" is by no means obvious. If we
approach the poem as literally as possible, we are following a "man" for no
particular reason, a man who never assumes an identity. Nothing in the
poem, for example, would associate the man with an escaped convict any
more than it would associate "you" with a law officer. The man might be

taken to represent humankind in general, a sort of Everyman, the object, perhaps, of all literary and philosophical inquiry. Lieberman, on the other hand, suggests "two antithetical sides of the same man" (163), a double—in effect, the alter-ego of "you." I associate the quarry with a personification of the unknown, based upon what I see as a play on words in line 32, where "the other" may refer to the person being tracked or to the preternatural being that suddenly confronts the speaker.

With Professor Lieberman, I think "Tracking" is closely associated with "Being Shot," probably the most striking poem of the sequence with the exception of the title poem, but two poems separate "Tracking" and "Being Shot." "Missing the Trail" (254) begins, "Only a moment ago you were thinking of something / Different." But now the "you" of the poem has taken a wrong turn and finds himself or herself (the sexual identity will vary comfortably with the reader) alone and lost, a common dilemma for a Wagoner character and one that might relate to his own early experience on the Olympic Peninsula (*Contemporary Authors* 406). For poets, the bewilderment and the uncertainty over whether "to turn back, bear left or right, or flounder ahead" often occurs when they contemplate taking a new direction with their work. We are advised to come to our senses, all six of them, to be patient, and to stand in one spot. But the bulk of the speaker's advice is offered in the last fourteen and a half lines of the poem, which comprise a single sentence. We are advised to "memorize" everything around us, to become thoroughly familiar with the new terrain, looking for "landmarks" or "some ragged signal" that can "reestablish" our eyes—our vision—while we "branch out from there," metaphorically establishing an identity with the new environment, in "all directions." The destination here is, predictably, ambiguous. It is a place "You may now (having been lost and found) barely remember / Wanting to get to, past the middle of nowhere, / Toward your wit's end." Arguably, this is the true poet's destination, beyond conventional place, though through it, and past the limits of reason.

The next poem in the sequence, "From Here to There" (255–56), is a sort of antithetical companion to "Missing the Trail." The "you" in this poem "can see in the distance, outlined precisely / With speechless clarity, the place you must go" (255). Finding the right language, however, remains the pivotal problem. In "Missing the Trail" there was "fear that screaming is the only universal language" (254), hardly the proper voice for a serious poet; in "From Here to There" the clarity of the destination is "speechless." Between us and our "place" are mirages, shifting light, loose stones, and no clear pathway. The instruction here is to avoid illusions and "to rap with your knuckles / Against the reality / Of those unlikely rocks you've stared at." Lieberman speaks of the "writer lurking within the backpacker persona" as stripping away the "ornaments and excesses of his style" (167) and turning to the "irreducible language of substance" (168). The poem ends with one of Wagoner's finest puns:

> *But to find yourself*
> *In the Land Behind the Wind where nothing is the matter*
> *But you, brought to your knees, an infirm believer*
> *Asking one more lesson.* (256)

This virtually metaphysical pun works three ways: first, the conventional, colloquial meaning: nothing is wrong; second, the ontological inference: there is no matter, no material or substance, where we are headed; third, as we move to the next line, an ethical assertion: only we are in the wrong here, for we lack strong conviction.

The "one more lesson" we have requested is offered in the next poem, "Being Shot" (257–58). The poet's search for self, for resolution of the human mystery, necessarily leads him or her to confront death. It is perhaps Wagoner's skill as a novelist that prompted him to delay this shocking meeting with human nature and death by isolating the "you" of the sequence for two poems after leading us to the brink of confrontation in "Tracking." "Being Shot" appears to be a natural companion piece to "Tracking," but its placement in the sequence is clearly intentional. Only after we have faced natural dangers, established our own response to "everything human" ("Tracking" 253), and been pushed to our "wit's end" ("Missing the Trail" 254) in our quest are we prepared for "seeing things / In a new light," which is the aim of the sequence in which "Being Shot" is the climactic poem.

Ironically, we no sooner discover our identity than it is violated, the private self invaded in the most violent way. Moreover, the intrusion into this inner and implicitly spiritual self is decidedly material. The shot is presented as a "loud afterthought" which we will hear unless we are

> *Too strongly preoccupied*
> *With absorbing the impact of this bullet, in sharp contrast*
> *With your soft flesh and blood, your unwilling sinew,*
> *Your tractable bones.* (257)

The speaker's voice throughout is aloof, sometimes clinical in a sinister way, even mocking, and it offers no comfort, no lessons in evasion or compromise. Near the end of "From Here to There" we are told that our "hope should be . . . to find yourself" (255–56); in "Being Shot" we are told that the "new light" in which we are seeing things "doesn't come from the sky but from all loose ends / Of all your hopes, your dissolving endeavors / To keep close track / Of who you are." The stranger leans over us with a "disarming smile," a comical pun which reminds us that the speaker is not necessarily a friend. The speaker can make light of our predicament, as the concluding lines demonstrate:

> *Not wishing to make yourself conspicuous*
> *By your endless absence*
> *And having meant no harm by moving quietly, searching*
> *Among this second growth of your own nature*
> *For its first wildness,*
> *You may offer him your empty hands, now red as his hat,*
> *And he may grant mercy or, on the other hand,*
> *Give you as gracefully*
> *As time permits, as lack of witnesses will allow*
> *Or your punctured integrity will stand for,*
> *A graceful* coup de grace. (257–58)

In this return to our animal nature—in which the "you," instead of becoming all spirit, becomes one with the fallen deer—human nature turns on us mercilessly. Only the speaker's wordplay, which seems absurdly comical under the circumstances, keeps the poem from being morbid or despairing.

But "Being Shot" is less an invitation to lament the human condition or human violence than it is a dramatic obliteration of self-concern and egocentricity. It is tantamount, in effect, to the mystical death of the self that precedes enlightenment. In this process the powerful, 18-line "Waiting in a Rain Forest" (259), all a single torrential sentence, works as a poem of healing and restorative quietness. The rain does not fall, but stands in the air "drifting from time to time like breath" (259). The "you" now rests "under a green sky" reminiscent perhaps of Marvell's "green thought in a green shade" in "The Garden." We are left with "nothing to do but watch the unbroken / Promises of the earth" in this "wild garden" where all is "[f]lourishing in silence." It is from this fertility and quiescence that the enlightenment for the finest creative work will come. At the heart of that work is metamorphosis, the poetic transformation implicit in the simile which likens "you" to a "fallen nurse-log" which will nurture "the deepest longing of young hemlocks."

Lieberman describes "Travelling Light" (260–61) the final poem of the sequence, as an "exhaustive vision of transfiguration by cold" (174). In "Breaking Camp" the phrase "travelling light" is clearly intended only in the colloquial sense of being unencumbered, though we are also informed that we must search for the "makings of fire" (249), implying our need for illumination in the literal sense. The most immediately obvious transformation in "Travelling Light," however, is in the speaker's voice. We have heard the speaker address us as a fairly conventional guide, particularly in "Breaking Camp," and we have followed his voice as it becomes increasingly ironic and occasionally mocking from "Meeting a Bear" to "Being Shot." In "Waiting in a Rain Forest" the teacher's voice turns quiet and gentle as it urges us to "learn without fear or favor" (259). In "Travelling Light" the teacher joins us, dropping "you," which establishes a sort of distance elsewhere in the sequence, for the communal "we." As Arthur Oberg notes in his review of Collected Poems, "Wagoner is always certain to help create the reader he wants for his poetry" (162). This Wagoner does essentially by establishing a "you" who is "the reader as well as the important self of the poet" (162). Moreover, the language of romantic love near the middle of the poem ("We will make fire, then turn in each other's arms, / Embracing once more" [260]) brings a genuine intimacy into the sequence. Whether "Travelling Light" qualifies as a love poem, however, is debatable; it is more importantly a celebration of the unified self—of the speaker and of the poet and the reader—and of poetry.

The "most difficult country" which had been perceived as "a cross-grained hummocky bog-strewn jumble of brambles" has been transformed by "blizzard and sunlight" to a "rolling parkland" of "brittle whiteness." No longer distracted or detained by flowers, berries, and bird-songs, we hurry smoothly on snowshoes traveling so light-footedly that our feet seem not even to touch the earth, and we are "disembodied by the cold." The "cold-spelled morning" will bring the vision

> Of the place we were always looking for: so full of light,
> So full of flying light, it is all feathers
> Which we must wear

> As we had dreamed we would, not putting frostbitten hands
> Into the freshly slaughtered breasts of birds
> But snowblindly reaching
> Into this dazzling white-out, finding where we began,
> Not naming the wonder yet but remembering
> The simply amazing
> World of our first selves where believing is once more seeing
> The cold speech of the earth in the colder air
> And knowing it by heart. (260–61)

In this visionary conclusion to the poem, the speaker anticipates our meta-morphosis into birds, perhaps the grouse mentioned earlier in the poem, which are capable of perching in the fir tree "through a whole winter," so well attuned are they to the world. Most important, this vision of flight will not sustain our nightmare of frostbite and violence, but will bring us back to our "first selves" as it takes us into the light.

Lieberman finds in this poem an "unwavering and astonishing eleva-tion of . . . language": "The very crux of major poetry is the successful im-provising of an experimental language, the finding of a vital new idiom with roots in common speech" (174). If other poems in the sequence offer instruction in the craft of poetry, "Travelling Light" is the product, the poem itself. Moreover, as might be expected, this poem moves to a firm resolution, a knowledge that, after the sidestepping of bears and the mi-rages, is thoroughly satisfying.

After the spectacular impact of the "Travelling Light" sequence, the fif-teen-poem miscellany that makes up the second part of "New Poems" (*CP* 1976) seems anticlimactic. The poems are sound, though, and they repre-sent familiar voices. The first and last poems in that section, "The First Trick" (263) and "The Uncanny Illusion of the Headless Lady" (279), reflect Wagoner's continuing infatuation with magic, with the magician who, like the poet, can "produce something from nothing" while the audi-ence sits in "chairs screwed to the floor . . . staring through darkness" (263). Poems like "The Return of Icarus" (264–65) and "The Death of Paul Bunyan" (268–69) are in the mode of "The Labors of Thor" from *Sleeping in the Woods* (1974) and " 'Tan Ta Ra, Cries Mars . . .'" from *A Place to Stand* (1958), playfully serious returns to myth and folklore. "Roles" (266) and "Getting Somewhere" (267) are in the autobiographical vein that goes back to "Every Good Boy Does Fine" and "Filling Out a

Blank" from *Nesting Ground* (1963) and that anticipates poems in the first section of *In Broken Country* (1979). Several poems in the second section of "New Poems" focus on love, including "At Low Tide" (275), which is reminiscent in setting and tone of other more ambitious seaside romances by Wagoner. Here, the lovers see "Our love once more in the salt brimming over our eyelids / Where nothing is lost, where the tide turns over and over."

Collected Poems was well reviewed. While John Gardner, in the *New York Times Book Review*, panned Wagoner's recent novel, *Whole Hog*, he praised the poems "about things directly experienced" as "magnificent creations, partly because of the precision of Wagoner's eye and language as he recreates the experienced moment . . . and partly because of the *way* he seeks to realize the moment. His purpose, always, is to become one with the world by empathy" (7). In a review essay for *Poetry* magazine, Arthur Oberg comments on Wagoner's increasing "respect for that absolute otherness of things which can never be fully known, yet which can be approached as we possess enough reverence and awe" (163). He admires the range in Wagoner's voice "from the loudly exuberant to the movingly quiet" (162) and the turn to "real ground, local ground, American ground" (165) in the poems after *Riverbed*. Oberg finds Wagoner moving toward a "styleless" style, a "simplicity and an authority which allow us momentarily to forget from whose mouth the words come," and he concludes that there is "something creatively rebellious" (166) about Wagoner, whom he hails as a "straight-faced, lovingly ironic, major poet" (167). Not surprisingly, *Collected Poems* was nominated for a National Book Award in 1977, but Wagoner was thwarted in this bid for greater national prominence when the award went to Richard Eberhart for his *Collected Poems 1936–1976*. The Pulitzer Prize in poetry for 1977 went to James Merrill's *Divine Comedies*.

4. WHO SHALL BE THE SUN?

The eighteen poems that make up the third and fourth sections of "New Poems" were included, with two exceptions, among the 78 poems in *Who Shall Be the Sun?* (1978). Subtitled "Poems Based on the Lore, Legends, and Myths of Northwest Coast and Plateau Indians," this collection constitutes a new perspective for Wagoner, but one that had been evolving for a number of years. In fact, Wagoner's poems show from the start his kinship with a people whose animistic views he finds so "admirable and worthy of imitation": "they did not place themselves above their organic and inorganic companions on earth but recognized with awe that they shared the planet as equals with animals, fish, birds, trees, rivers, bushes, stones, and such phenomena as weather and natural disasters" (Author's Note). Poems included in the collection go as far back as "Searching in the Britannia Tavern," from *New and Selected Poems* (1969). In the sections from *Collected Poems* that are included in this volume, Oberg saw the mythic stylelessness that "seems beyond the reach of art" (165), and John Gardner hailed these poems as "among the best Wagoner has ever written—some are among the best anyone has written" (10).

Reviewers of *Who Shall Be the Sun?* generally agreed with Oberg's and Gardner's observations. Anya Taylor, among others, detected parallels to poems from Ted Hughes's *Crow* (1970). Noting that "most white literature on Indian themes is suspect," Hayden Carruth, in *Harper's*, found Wagoner's poems "true," "compelling," and "very close to Indian sensibility." Peter Stitt, writing for the *Georgia Review*, recognized Wagoner's lack of due notice because of his career in the Pacific Northwest, "away from the dominant culture centers of the East" (704). Stitt sees the poems as "approaching the ontological strictly through the phenomenological; for him, the metaphysical can exist only within the physical" (699). But as Helen Carr noted in the *Times Literary Supplement*, for an American poet (or perhaps for any European, though she does not say so) to attempt to engage Indian culture is "hazardous." The culture is both alien and complex, as even the most casual student is likely to learn, and as Carr suggests, American guilt inclines—"compels"—us "to sentimentalize, to aestheticize, to sweeten." By "focusing upon the Indians as mystic ecologists," she concludes, Wagoner "evades the issue of what America has done, not just to the natural world, but to its inhabitants." The anonymous reviewer for the *Virginia Quarterly Review* adds that the almost inevitable "affectations" of these poems "will make some readers uncomfortable."

Overlooking the customary but still annoying inclination of European, and particularly English, critics to pretend that white Americans have somehow been more vicious exploiters of nature and more rapacious colonialists than their white European forebears and cousins, Carr makes a fundamental error in her critique. She attempts to impose her own ethical and political views of what *should* be said on what *is* said. Given the timing of Wagoner's book, just six years after the dramatic occupation of Wounded Knee by militants of the American Indian Movement (February 27 to May 8, 1973), it comes as no surprise that readers might expect poems pertaining to American Indians to be ipso facto political. Many white American poets and novelists, not to mention film makers, had in fact enacted the *mea culpa* well before the advent either of Dee Brown's *Bury My Heart at Wounded Knee* (1971) or the protest at the Oglala Sioux reservation. Had Wagoner followed that lead, in fact, he would doubtless have been excoriated by some critics for being "yet another" white American apologist for irreversible atrocities. Beyond that, of course, Carr clearly misses the implied message of the poems: that the intimate and meaningful relationship between humans and the natural world described in these poems has been destroyed by Western (not even the English are altogether guiltless) ignorance and greed.

One pertinent consequence of the lost relationship between people and their environment is that the poems of *Who Shall Be the Sun?* are among the most difficult to access for most readers of Wagoner's poetry. How we read them and what we make of them will depend very much upon what we bring to these poems. Wagoner dedicates the volume to noted anthropologist and student of Pacific Northwest Indian cultures, Franz Boas (1858–1942), whose guiding principle, as expressed in *The Mind of Primitive Man*, was: "There is no fundamental difference in the ways of thinking of primitive and civilized man" (17). Certainly there is nothing simplistic about the Indian lore as rendered by Wagoner. But his sentences in this collection are generally shorter and less complex in structure than elsewhere in his poems, and that may cause some readers to assume a conceptual simplicity which, in fact, is not the case. The opening stanza of "Only-One" (53–54) provides a rather extreme example of the syntax in *Who Shall Be the Sun?*:

> That boy wanted to be more than a boy.
> He gathered shells. They stayed hollow.
> He rattled birdbones. No birds would grow on them.
> His drumboard made a lost-in-the-wind sound,
> And no one would dance to it. He danced alone. (53)

These simple sentences recounting ordinary actions are not tantamount to conceptual simplicity, because as is common in oral narrative, information is elided along with transitions. The narrator presumes his audience is familiar with the story, and in his customary setting (at the council fire rather than at the anthropologist's office) it would be. The sometimes elusive character of Wagoner's poems in the Native American voice results from his conscious imitation of the voice he hears in his sources.

What happens in "Only-One" illustrates one other facet of Wagoner's Indian poems that might make them difficult for some non-Indian readers. An aura of unsolved mystery surrounds many of the Native American legends. Even a firm grounding in Greek and Roman mythology is not likely to prepare a reader for the peculiar world of a tale that portrays a boy named Only-One who sharpens the broken beak of a starving heron and who has his own eye promptly stabbed out as a result. Seeing the world now with only one eye, Only-One seems to see a girl standing at the water's edge on one leg: "One eye was beautiful. The other was darkness. / She lifted one arm, but the other stayed in shadow." When he presents her to his parents and to "the People," however, they see no one at all and think him crazy. At this point, she turns "half away" and vanishes. Only-One pursues her and finds her at last by the light of "cracked-in-half moon," standing "[a]gain in the shallows, preening blue feathers." He calls, and she flies toward him.

By comparison, even the most bizarre episodes of Ovid's *Metamorphoses* may seem mundane. Ovid's humans never cease to be human, even though they exist in a world of gods and demigods and even though they may be related to deities. After all, given the nature of Greco-Roman anthropomorphism, we are generally more aware of the humanlikeness of the deities than we are of their godlikeness. Moreover, people may be transformed into nightingales or flowers by this or that deity, but both the rationale and the moral in most cases are quite clear. Homer's Odysseus deals with deities and monsters, but for all his superhuman heroic powers, he never ceases to be human. Native American tales and legends, however, concentrate on the world before the coming of man, and the lines that distinguish the prehumans from the animistic nature deities are blurred, as the following passage from an Eskimo poem indicates:

> *In the very earliest time,*
> *when both people and animals lived on earth,*
> *a person could become an animal if he wanted to*
> *and an animal could become a human being.*
> *Sometimes they were people*

> *and sometimes animals*
> *and there was no difference.*
> ("Shaking the Pumpkin" 45)

As Ella E. Clark observes in *Indian Legends from the Northern Rockies* (1966), "Because of this close relationship between the Indian and nature, it is not surprising that most of his tales were about animals and birds. Rather, they are about 'animal people' or 'animal persons,' as English-speaking Indians refer to them today. These mythological beings lived on earth when it was young, 'when people had not come out yet'" (37). Accordingly, in any given legend such a character may seem human at one point and animal at another. Before the coming of humans, the animals lived in communities and carried on like humans; consequently, the distinctions often are lost in the oral transmissions.

If readers realize these circumstances, they may be at least somewhat less mystified by some of the striking events narrated in Wagoner's poems, but they may remain confounded by the point of this or that legend. As Boas observes, the line that distinguishes myth from folk tale is itself blurred (*Race, Language and Culture* 454), and Wagoner collects his most effective poems in the sections entitled "Plateau Indian Myths and Legends" and "Northwest Coast Indian Myths and Legends," thus adding to Boas's terms "myth" and "tale" the term "legend." The poems in these sections are reminiscent, in their mingling of the human and the supernatural, of Irish folklore with its magical, talking fish and shadowy horses that inspired the young William Butler Yeats. Even a cursory glance at the collections of Kwakiutl and other texts made by Boas and his followers will show both how extensive and how rich are the available materials. Native American poets, like Duane Niatum in *Ascending Red Cedar Moon* (1973), have, often at firsthand, availed themselves of this resource, and some Indians may resent a white American like Wagoner appropriating what they might conceive to be their birthright. I believe, however, that Wagoner's affectionate and powerful use of Native American lore is in fact a tribute to Indian culture. At the same time, these poems turn the attention of white American readers toward the Native American heritage in a profound way.

But the perspectives and apparent values of that culture do remain alien to some extent even in Wagoner's best poems, and that may be one of their primary virtues. The best poems do not strike us as translations or adaptations, even though they are, but as "tellings." That is, Wagoner does not compromise the magic or mystery of the legend in an effort to "make sense" to his non-Indian readers. "Salmon Boy" (66–67), for example, like several poems in the collection, concerns hunger, a theme that serves to remind us of the precarious state of the tribal people whose daily chore was often simply to assure their survival. "That boy was hungry" (66), the poem begins, but his mother gave him only the head of a dog salmon to eat. The boy carries the fish head to the mouth of the river, collapses, and turns into a salmon. He then joins the Salmon People and experiences their life in the ocean, where he "heard the long, high howling of Wolf Whale, / . . . Saw Loon Mother flying through branches of seaweed." The lyrical passage recounting Salmon Boy's life in the ocean is striking, and for three stanzas it would appear that the poem will simply celebrate the surreal dream of metamorphosis and the change of worlds. But then Salmon Boy leads the fish upriver to spawn:

> *He swam fastest of all. He leaped into the air*
> *And smacked his blue-green silvery side, crying,* Eyo!
> *I jump! again and again. Oh, he was Salmon Boy!*
> *He could breathe everything! He could see everything!*
> *He could eat everything! And then his father speared him.*
>
> *He lay on the riverbank with his eyes open,*
> *Saying nothing while his father emptied his belly.*
> *He said nothing when his mother opened him wide*
> *To dry in the sun. He was full of the sun.*
> *All day he dried on sticks, staring upriver.* (67)

The events of the poem are similar in some ways to Kwakiutl and Bella Bella narratives recorded by Boas, but I can not pinpoint a single tale as the source. John Bierhorst describes a Haida tale that is very close to the details of Wagoner's poem: the boy scorns the fish given him by his mother, drowns and is carried to the home of the salmon people; when he returns in the spring with the salmon, he is caught by his mother, but she recognizes her son by a copper necklace, and after six days the boy emerges from the fish skin and becomes a shaman (48–49). The spearing of Salmon Boy by his father in Wagoner's poem is typical, though, in being both startling and without explanation. Originally, the story may have related to a fertility myth, and certainly it teaches the necessity of respecting nature. Wagoner's version stresses the ironies of the myth and perhaps elaborates them.

Wagoner insists that his poems are not translations but that those concerning the myths and legends "might be called retellings" (Author's Note). Moreover, as he points out, the narratives exist in many versions, depending upon both their tribal origins and the teller, and no apology is due from him any more than from a Native American teller for embellishment. Wagoner's poem, "How Coyote Learned the Five Songs of Water" (39), is very close to the Okanogon tale concerning the origin of the Columbia River, as collected by James Teit and reproduced in the *Memoirs of the American Folk-Lore Society*. Teit's rendition begins:

> Coyote was travelling, and heard water dropping. He said, 'I will go and beat it.' He sat down near it, and cried, 'Hox-hox-hox-hox!' in imitation of water dripping. He tried four times, but the noise never ceased. He became very angry, arose, and kicked the place where the water dropped. The noise ceased. He thought he had beaten it, and laughed, saying, 'I beat you. No more shall water drip thus and make noise.' Shortly after he had gone, the water began to drip as before. He became angry, and said, 'Did I not say water shall not run and make a noise?' The water was coming after him, and increased in volume as it flowed. (65)

The foregoing constitutes only about one fourth of the tale as passed on by Teit. Coyote subsequently becomes thirsty, and he finds a creek and drinks, but as he returns for more water, he keeps getting thirstier and the creek keeps getting larger. He keeps getting closer to the river, and after a while he wades in. Teit's version concludes: "Finally he had drunk so much that he lost consciousness. Thus the water got even with Coyote for kicking it; and thus from a few drops of water originated the Columbia River" (67).

Wagoner's poem runs 25 lines, and while it is fairly close to this version, he may in fact have drawn on other narratives. Teit's rendition is close enough, however, for us to get a clear sense of what Wagoner's artful use of his sources has achieved. The portion I have quoted above Wagoner appropriates for the first three stanzas of "How Coyote Learned the Five Songs of Water":

When he heard that song, Coyote was sleeping.
It was Water dripping on stone. He listened
As he lay on the dry creekbed. It kept dripping
Till it filled his head, and he went to find it.
He said, "That song is over! Be quiet!"

But Water dripped on stone, so Coyote licked it.
He said, "I will sing that song myself if I want it."
But Water went on dripping, so Coyote drank it,
Saying, "Sing a new song in my belly!" But that Water
Kept dripping and dripping. Coyote kicked it.

He moved down slope in the dust, stiff-legged, sleepy.
Now he was thirsty. He had never felt so thirsty.
When he lay down, that song was in his head
Still dripping and dripping on the stone of his tongue.
Then he heard Water running after him. (39)

Except for the obvious economy of Wagoner's poetic version, his alterations of the source or sources seem slight. Coyote is sleeping instead of walking, but that sort of detail alters with the teller. The transmutation of noise into song, however, is the work of a poet, as is the metaphor of water dripping "on the stone of his tongue." Water has sung the songs of noise (a nuisance), of ordinary slaking of thirst, and of life-saving meeting of need as we approach the final two stanzas:

It trickled toward him, and he licked it all,
Saying, "Water, you are singing a good song!"
Now it flowed up his chest. He tried to drink it,
Choking and saying, "Three songs are too many!"
But it came pouring its fourth song, brown and angry.

Coyote drank his belly full, filled his whole heart,
His throat, his eyes. Oh, he was drinking
Deeper than he was tall. He was hearing Water
Singing inside out. In his ears that Water was singing
Its last song for the drowning of Coyote. (39)

Wagoner makes no reference to the forming of the Columbia River in his version but instead turns the point to a familiar folk motif: not enough, then too much. In Coyote's drowning Wagoner is committing no excess against his Indian sources, for such creatures as Coyote may die and return many times in Indian mythology.

Wagoner's poem, "How Raven Stole Light" (94–95), is very close to a Bella Bella tale recorded by Franz Boas, in which a great chief and his only daughter keep the sun in a box, allowing the People only the moon (*Bella Bella Tales* 3–4). In Wagoner's poem, the chief and his daughter keep the sun, the moon, and the stars. In the Bella Bella tale, Raven must transform himself three times, first into a cedar leaf, then into a salmon berry, and finally into a trout fry, before he can dupe the chief's daughter into swallowing him. In Wagoner's poem, Raven succeeds after his first transformation into a hemlock needle. In both versions, the girl becomes pregnant and Raven is born to her, and in both versions he receives the light by crying for it as if he were a baby. But the Indian narratives have little of the vivid detail that makes the poem and story itself appealing to a reader: "He flew through a sky as dark as his own feathers / And found a lodge surrounded by daylight." "That chief doted on Raven: his black eyes gleamed, / His beak and tongue were quick, he would play with furs / And bundles of dried light." Raven opened the box of stars, "and there, like herring eggs, / The Stars glistened in clusters, and Raven laughed, / Tossing them through the smoke-hole where they tumbled / Across the sky forever." In the Bella Bella story, Raven transforms some of the people who refuse to feed him into frogs, an element of the tale which is irrelevant to the story that Wagoner wishes to tell.

The status of *Who Shall Be the Sun?* among Wagoner's poems is difficult to ascertain. He has returned to that voice only rarely since the book appeared, but it has influenced a number of his poems. The animal poems in *First Light* (1983), for example, including a poem entitled "Under the Raven's Nest," show little impact of Wagoner's interest in Native American lore. But the "Land Behind the Wind" sequence in that book appears to be strongly influenced by it, as the title suggests. Its influence is also evident in specific poems from *In Broken Country* (1979) and *Landfall* (1981). In the last lines of "Burial Song" (125), the concluding poem in *Who Shall Be the Sun?*, Wagoner's speaker may be indirectly addressing just that issue when he says:

My body has stopped.
Now yours will go forward,
But mine will stay in this Now, exactly here.
. . . you will not see it . . .
Yet it will lie in wait for you to remember
Like a dream stiffened with danger. (125)

In her review essay for *Magill's Literary Annual 1979* Mary Jo Shea comments on "the board impact and timelessness which is appropriate to the mythological" in these poems (852). She also observes that Wagoner's customary humor is supplanted with "quiet irony" (854). While she cautions that Wagoner's admirers might be disconcerted by such departures from his usual voice, she commends the poems for constituting "a kind of religious statement" and for conveying lessons in humility in which we discover our role as part of nature rather than lord of it (856). The voice we hear in *Who Shall Be the Sun?* is indeed a different one for David Wagoner, but this portrayal of the proper role of humans in the world has been consistent throughout his work.

"The Spinning Ladies" and
The Hanging Garden

Between 1968 and 1981 David Wagoner saw no fewer than fifteen books to press, ranging from his edition of Roethke's notebooks in 1972 to the chapbook of poems, *Travelling Light*, the *Collected Poems*, and the Western novel *Whole Hog*, all published in 1976. Always a prolific writer in two genres, Wagoner in his forties and fifties was in his prime—he had established his voice and found his place—but his marriage was disintegrating. One might speculate that as he experienced stress in personal life, he compensated by absorbing himself in his work, and in his autobiographical essay Wagoner concedes that during his last years with Patt he had been "writing even more than usual, partly as an effort to shield [himself]" (*Contemporary Authors* 410). Wagoner's short, stark novel, *The Hanging Garden*, his most recently published novel at present, appeared in 1980. (His agent is seeking a publisher for what will be his eleventh novel, titled "Early and Often," which is set in the political and theatrical milieu of Chicago in 1893.)

Standing apart from his other fiction by virtue of their generic singularity and to some extent their lyricism, are *The Hanging Garden* and its antitype, "The Spinning Ladies," the unusual novella which appeared in volume 21 of Lippincott's *New World Writing* in 1962. Wagoner's distinguished company in the Lippincott collection included an essay on the painting of Mark Rothko by French novelist and critic, Michel Butor, and poems by James Dickey and Wendell Berry. William Schaefer describes the novella as "slight": "It maintains a light happy mood of summertime joy and nostalgia" (83). But Schaefer also notes that this whimsical celebration of "the spiritual rebirth of an old man" is the "brightest" (84) of Wagoner's fictional efforts. This pronouncement, which Schaefer made in 1966, before Wagoner had written his comic Westerns, remains valid, for the novella is unmarked by the occasional ominous and violent episodes of the comic novels.

Although Schaefer describes the sixty-seven-year-old Angelo Fenster-maker as "a kind of Blakean angel" (83), he neglects the full significance of Wagoner's epigraph, which is taken from Blake's *Visions of the Daughters of Albion* (1793). Oothon, who represents thwarted love and the ideal of physical freedom, is the feminine emanation of Theotormon, who repre-sents desire. She is told by the nymph of Leutha's vale that "the soul of sweet delight / Can never pass away" (Blake 189; Damon 308). She is raped by Bromion (reason, law) and is rejected by the jealous Theotor-mon, to whom she laments:

> Arise, my Theotormon, I am pure,
> Because the night is gone that clos'd me in its deadly black.
> They told me that the night & day were all that I could see;
> They told me that I had five senses to inclose me up. (191)

Blake rejects the conventional moral view that the body, the five senses, constitutes a prison for the soul. In fact, his epigraph to the Visions is: "The Eye sees more than the Heart knows." Wagoner's epigraph, the penulti-mate line in the passage above, suggests that Angelo, like Oothon, pos-sesses a visionary sense beyond the ordinary limits of night and day and is modeled on something more explicit than the vague "Blakean angel" that Schaefer suggests.

1. "THE SPINNING LADIES"

The title of Wagoner's novella obviously points toward the three sister Fates, and the protagonist, a bachelor who lives with his three spinster sis-ters, might be seen as a man directed by some special destiny. Wagoner goes to some lengths in the first sections of the story to show that the sis-ters direct Angelo's life in some ways. He has been ill and they are caring for him, and they see to it that he is properly dressed for any occasion. Yet their impact on his life after the first two sections appears to be minimal. The opening sentence sets both the theme and the tone of the novella: "The day Angelo Fenstermaker fell in love with himself had dawned out of the usually pulp-colored east like a sunset, amber and magnificent, and he descended the three flights of squeaking stairs almost buoyantly and went into the yard to have a look at things" (58). As the epigraph from Blake may imply, night and day become one—dawn and sunset appear alike—to the person with true vision. Put another way, one might say that limitations of time vanish for the visionary. Angelo explains to his sisters that he feels like Adam, specifically on the day he awakened to discover the creation of Eve (who might be seen as Adam's emanation). The "spinning sisters," however, appear indifferent to Angelo's peculiar new sense of things. "We have business to attend to," observes Stephanie; and the third sister, Theresa—the one who might occupy the place of irresistible Atropos, cutter of the thread of life—says simply, "Do what you care to, within reason" (60). What Angelo does is walk down the block to a ladies' cooperative apartment and acquire an invitation to a Presbyterian Church social, a picnic arranged by a number of elderly ladies to whom he feels drawn "in a kind, sexual, fatherly way" (62).

Angelo promises to take motion pictures of their outing, and although he has no real experience in such things, he is resourceful enough to arrange for the loan of a camera from a photographer's shop. He leaves the shop commenting that "it's certainly a lovely morning for seeing things" (65), an echo of the last phrase of the first sentence in the novella. In fact, Angelo's vision is remarkably acute throughout the work, and from the first he is extraordinarily sensitive to images; for example, the attire of his sisters (60) and a night crawler on the sidewalk (62). Moreover, he is keenly aware of reflected images: the mirrorlike underside of an airplane overhead, himself in front of the hallway mirror, his face in a circular flash reflector at the photographer's shop. As he notes early in the story, "this was a day for enjoying both light and shadow" (59). That is to say, we are told again and again in the first pages of the novella that Angelo Fenstermaker, whose surname in German means "window-maker," is on the threshold of some clarifying insight into himself, the result of which will be a presumably healthy form of self-love. Moreover, we are given abundant hints that his enlightenment will involve his relations with women.

If Angelo's given name suggests someone "angelic," we soon learn that such a reading is Wagoner's joke. Angelo pokes one of the ladies, the officious organizer, Miss Rice, with his movie camera as he moves toward the car, and he takes an instant dislike to a pushy fat man, Mr. Zimmerman, who elbows his way between a couple ladies in the back seat. Angelo needles Mr. Zimmerman (the characters refer to one another quite formally throughout the novella) by aiming his camera at him, then aims it at the driver, Mr. Zeiler, upon which the driver loses control and bumps the car ahead of him. When Angelo suggests that a hayride would have been "more romantic" (69), Mr. Zeiler, an irascible former barber, objects that he suffers from hay fever. Throughout the picnic, Angelo's intention appears to be to tease these unplayful men with an impish sort of innocence while he flirts with the attractive women. Like Theotormon in Blake's prophetic work, the men are jealous kill-joys strictly bound by convention. The German that lurks behind the names Zimmerman and Zeiler are "room" (or apartment) and "row" (line or lane), both of which suggest limitation and conformity. Angelo, at times, seems not unlike one of Blake's devils as he intentionally irritates his companions.

Examining the world and his experiences through the camera lens, Angelo sees what the others overlook or willfully ignore, and he reveals the picnickers to each other and to us. He detects, for example, the attractiveness of the older women, which escapes the petulant Mr. Zeiler, but when a few of the women begin to pose for his film "with a terrible, artificial joy" (73), Angelo pans away to a catbird on a maple branch. Zeiler claims that having been a barber gives him "a funny view of things. . . . It makes you suspicious," (76) but Angelo's experiences have given him a much broader perspective. He tests Zeiler by making a casual observation about woodspurge, a flower that "has a cup of three" (75), as he learned it from the poet, Dante Gabriel Rossetti, but the erstwhile barber is annoyed with extraneous information of any sort. Angelo observes: "One doesn't speculate and probe as much as I have in sixty-seven years without learning a great deal. And I've made it my occupation to trust everybody, whether they're emphatic or not" (76). But Angelo is not content merely to have had his say. He calls Zeiler's attention to a weed, and as he does so he allows the end of his cane to jab Zeiler in the stomach. Zeiler then drops the banjo belonging to the angry Zimmerman, who picks it up and holds it "like a giant lollipop" (76). Wagoner's simile implies an editorial criticism of Mr. Zimmerman as "childish." Angelo's placid apology adds to the comedy of the scene.

Throughout dinner Angelo continues with his eccentric observations and proposed activities, most of which appear to offend someone or other at the table. The Presbyterians all seem bent on having a conventional picnic, just like the ones they have had before, but Angelo suggests youthful games, a sack race or a creek-jumping contest, arguing in Faustian fashion that "[t]he human soul isn't complete unless it's striving" (78). When someone at the table complains of gastric pains, Angelo is quick to remark that most people confuse their stomach with their small intestine, scarcely conventional dinner conversation, and later he inquires, not maliciously but with boyish curiosity, how many calories the rotund Zimmerman has consumed. On a walk after lunch he finds occasion to quote from Marlowe's "The Passionate Shepherd to His Love," but the forward redhead, Miss Helen Ressler, misses the point, as she does Angelo's injunction that she exercise her imagination. *"Et in Arcadia ego,"* Angelo/Adam says (83), and he reflects upon the biblical story of Ruth, which the flirtatious Miss Ressler also fails to catch. Even as she undoes the top buttons of her dress, Angelo's attention is distracted from her: "He didn't have her centered in the picture because a bowl-shaped cloud of gold gadflies in the left background seemed exciting too" (84). It is not that Angelo is unaware or unappreciative of Miss Ressler's attraction to him, but rather that he sees beyond it. He is, in effect, in another world. When she complains that they "may not get another chance" to be alone together, Angelo confidently says they will, kisses her lightly on the neck, and observes, "This is a permanent day" (87). That is, Angelo, like Blake's Oothon, possesses an awareness of eternity.

When the curious orchestra of stringed instruments begins to play (it includes a mandolin, a mandola, and a zither in addition to the usual guitars, banjo, and ukulele), Angelo first requests "Jesu, Joy of Man's Desiring," a song composed by J. S. Bach, then an old English madrigal entitled "Mother, I Will Have a Husband." The latter request draws Miss Ressler even closer to Angelo. But the eight men who make up the orchestra are capable only of such popular tunes as "Nola" and "Beautiful Ohio" or hymns. Miss Ressler proceeds to tease Mr. Zimmerman, who plays banjo, bringing about a reprimand from Miss Rice to the effect that she must love her neighbor and "be respectable at the same time" (89), or else leave the cooperative. After that, Angelo appropriately requests "There's a Hole in My Bucket," but the ladies do not appreciate his wit.

The tense moment passes, however, as all join in singing "Nearer, My God, to Thee." Angelo uses up the remainder of his first reel of film "in the direction of the sun," then sits down "waiting for something else to happen" and "perfectly willing to undertake any role assigned to him" (90). That role comes to him in the voice of God: "The furthest phantom in an angel yet to be dared" (90). The voice, heard only by Angelo, comes without warning or preparation. When he asks what that means, the voice of God responds, "And win the name all day" (90). If the "name" referred to is his own, Angelo is being confirmed in his sense that it is his duty to act as a messenger of sorts to the unloving, convention-bound picnickers, who react predictably by assuming that Angelo is out of his mind. God's final message is, "And how shall the heads of the portals be raised up?" (91). I assume that this interrogative form of Psalms 24:7, "Lift up your heads, o ye gates," constitutes God's directive to Angelo. *The Interpreter's Bible* indicates that "above all, the gates of the human heart barred against God" (4:134) are those that must be raised. Hearing Angelo's announcement that he has had a "mystic experience," the picnickers assume he is sick, but Angelo advises them to go on with their music and to "forget about it" (92) although he does not forget. Rather, he sees that "the ladies had returned to separately genteel postures" (92), and shortly Mr. Zeiler quips that they all got too near to God. They then turn from hymns to "a semi-slow version of *Chinatown*" (92).

Miss Rice suggests that with the coming of evening, "vespers time," everybody "should think about being nice" (93), but the other picnickers favor leaving prayers till Sunday. This gives Angelo an opportunity to rephrase his message about the "permanent day": "You can't save something for a day that may never exist. . . . Really, what we ought to do is go on and on and on" (93). But again his message is shunted aside. As the picnic winds down, Mr. Zeiler passes out spiked lemonade, which he assures the ladies is non-alcoholic, and Angelo disputes with a former businessman over the question of human honesty. Miss Ressler observes, "It's been a frightening day, but I hate to have it end," to which Angelo confidently responds, "It won't" (100). He is not yet finished, however. He deftly picks up Mr. Zimmerman's banjo, takes it into the shadows outside the picnic pavilion, and then calls out to the picnickers to arrange a treasure hunt. Perhaps at one level he is implying that one must become a child again in order to enter the kingdom of heaven; at another, that play is necessary for the release of tension and escape from the mundane. However one perceives Angelo's intentions, only Miss Ressler is willing to participate.

The treasure hunt for Zimmerman's banjo *appears* to be Angelo's last attempt to "raise up the heads of the portals," and if that is the case, he fails in his mission, at least in part. As he searches for and finds Miss Ressler, who has discovered the banjo and broken it against a tree, the others drive away leaving them together at the darkened pavilion. Angelo explains, "I wanted everyone to rise above himself. Herself. But apparently it didn't work" (107). Angelo has succeeded, however, with Miss Ressler, who refers to herself as a "spinster" (109) as she sits beside him and appears to assume the role of a "spinning lady." Together they share what

amounts to a "permanent day." Like Oothon, they sit on the bank of a
stream, but while Oothon sings a lament over Theotormon's jealousy, Angelo and Helen celebrate their new found love.

2. THE HANGING GARDEN

Wagoner's most recent novel, *The Hanging Garden* (1980), occupies the
pole opposite that of "The Spinning Ladies." The dust jacket describes the
novel as "a nightmare of terror, perversion—and worse" and promises that
the reader, before putting it down, "will have arrived at a truer understanding of the bestial." Wagoner himself describes it as "a grisly gothic
horror story full of dead animals" (*Contemporary Authors* 410). He had
flirted with the thriller in his early urban Midwest novels, coming closest
with his first, *The Man in the Middle* (1954), but he had not yielded utterly
to the temptation. A comic strain appears in each of those novels, even in
the largely serious *Rock* (1958), justifying Schaefer's description of them
as comedies of the absurd (72). After the early midwest novels Wagoner
followed up on the characters and motifs established in *The Escape Artist*
(1965) in the four comic Westerns. The last of these, however, *Whole Hog*
(1976), interweaves the light with the dark, the funny with the frightening,
more thoroughly than any of his previously published novels. In *Whole
Hog* Wagoner showed that he could draw bizarre, pathological evil in his
portrait of the multinamed "buckskin man." In *The Hanging Garden* the
villain is the elderly, psychopathic head of the local historical society, Mrs.
Cutter.

The protagonist of the novel is forty-nine-year-old Simon Burrows, the
soon-to-be-divorced former mayor of a large city, apparently somewhere
in the Midwest. A dog fancier, he has recently begun breeding bull terriers
at his place in the country, where he has retired from the pressures of politics and his wife, who is now running for mayor herself. With him is Diane
Lee, a twenty-five-year-old handler he meets at a dog show. It is tempting
to speculate on autobiographical echoes in this novel, since Wagoner's
marriage of nearly twenty years was then in the process of rapid disinte-
gration. He may already have been falling in love with a former student of
his, Robin Seyfried, whom he married in the summer of 1982; or the tentative, almost shy relationship between Simon and Diane may be altogether a product of Wagoner's vivid imagination. But perhaps the closest
of Wagoner's works to a tour de force of imagination verging on fantasy is

"The Spinning Ladies," and for all its gothic horror, *The Hanging Garden* is firmly founded on the quotidian.

With "The Spinning Ladies," *Rock*, and *The Road to Many a Wonder* (1974), *The Hanging Garden* is a relatively rare example of a successful romantic relationship in Wagoner's fiction. Most of his protagonists are loners, the older males either reaching out to women without success or already having given up, and the younger ones only just beginning to recognize the attractions of women and concentrating on their search for a father figure. The developing relationship between Simon and Diane, however, works as a subplot, important primarily because Diane's presence adds to the danger of the situation. With her safety to consider, even though she is a remarkably capable woman and reminiscent in some ways of the resourceful Millie Slaughter of *The Road to Many a Wonder*, Simon must act cautiously at certain crucial moments in the novel. As the story progresses, Simon actually solves two mysteries, that of the missing dogs and that of Diane herself.

Simon awakens one morning to find that his two bull terriers have died during the night under mysterious circumstances and that his caretaker, an evasive old redneck named Dorff, is using his kennels to house strays from the pound, and planning to sell them for medical research. The pound is run by Dorff's sadistic son, Scratch and, as Simon and Diane discover, it is connected with the county historical society. When they go to the museum to borrow a shovel to bury a dead dog they found in the neglected kennels, they meet the apparently retarded Alma and her mother, Mrs. Cutter, an aristocratic anachronism who recognizes Simon as a distant but suspicious relative.

When Simon interrogates the drunken Dorff, we learn that his father was executed by hanging, though the crime he committed is never specified. Simon also discovers that Scratch likes to turn his violence on animals, so he informs the mayor, who fires Scratch and closes the pound. The sense of mystery increases until, near the midpoint of the novel, following an erotic picnic episode, Simon and Diane come upon the "hanging garden" of the title. In effect, Wagoner creates here a grim pun, for this is not the luxuriant hanging gardens built by Nebuchadnezzar, but a literal garden of hanging animals, a "hanging garden without a Babylon" (94). The sinister Scratch apparently has arranged a grotesque parody of the great chain of being with a display of animals ranging from two dogs and a "stiff weatherbeaten tiger cat," to fieldmice and a turtle "the size of a watch" (93), to a beetle and a spider. Only later do we learn that the hanging garden is the creation of Mrs. Cutter.

Wagoner's fondness for puns has often been noted—and sometimes deplored—in his poems, and he has used them before this point in the novel. In his first meeting with Diane, Simon notes that she is a "professional handler" (4). She responds that she has all she can "handle" in town. Simon, doubtless intending the double entendre, appeals "[B]e *my* handler." Referring to the problems of his work as mayor of a large city, Simon speaks of "urban refusal" (31) instead of "urban renewal" and the "effluent society" (48) instead of the "affluent society." When Mrs. Cutter tells Mayor Caldwell she thinks he is "hysterical," he replies that as president of the "County Hysterical Society" (76), she ought to know. In effect, then, such corny, obvious puns help to set up the central, one might say symbolic, pun of the novel.

From the discovery of the hanging garden, the pace of the novel becomes even more rapid. It is perhaps the fastest moving of Wagoner's novels, though *Baby, Come on Inside* (1968) also moves very quickly. When Simon informs the mayor of their discovery, he finds that the ramshackle farmhouse near the hanging garden was the site of a former lover's lane and after that of an apparent suicide by hanging. As the circumstances become more threatening, Diane becomes adamant, refusing to leave the stray dogs that have been left in their care. Her strength, we learn just before the discovery of the hanging garden, is borne of hard experience. Early in the novel, when Simon asks her how she makes her living, she says she works for a caterer: "There was no pleasure in her smile now. 'I cater to people. I—we try to help people have a good time'" (18). At the picnic Simon sees that she has an abdominal scar from "one too many abortions, trying to please people" (89). This way, she points out bitterly, both she and her mother could still pretend to be virgins. Clearly, then, another ironic pun in the novel is Wagoner's selection of her name, an echo of Diana, the goddess of chastity. Like the mythical goddess, however, Diane is the protectress of animals.

Finding Scratch in the kennels at night, Simon goes to his house for his pistol, but Scratch releases the dogs and escapes. Diane pursues him to retrieve a pregnant beagle, then Simon follows him to the hanging garden. Throughout the novel, and even in the midst of his angry pursuit in the dark, Simon reflects upon his recent departure from politics, and Wagoner suggests the inevitable corruption in politics as he does in his other novels:

"He felt like the mayor of his own guts, and he'd never been that before" (127). Like Diane, Simon has compromised himself in catering to others. It is to be again his own man that Simon has so drastically changed his life, but he nearly loses it on the threshold of gaining self-possession. Always cautious, he approaches the gruesome garden animal-like, on all fours. There he sees a bizarre scene: Mrs. Cutter apparently dancing with Mayor Caldwell.

> He'd come by himself like an idiot instead of bringing help, maybe wanting to destroy some bad publicity before anyone could take pictures of it, and he'd wound up posing as one of the exhibits. Not even hung in effigy like any public figure, but in the flesh. (129)

Simon hardly comprehends what he has seen when Mrs. Cutter's daughter shows up with a tranquilizer gun and shoots him.

Inside the hut he finds Dorff, who is near death, and the two deranged women attempt to feed Simon a ghastly witch's feast before he passes out. Simon's delirious response to the grotesque proceedings is perhaps the best moment in the novel, as he sees everything from the perspective of a mayor. He awakens in a dark cage in Scratch's pound after a strange dream in which he sees himself as a hanging scarecrow. As he comes to he is confronted by what appears to be Scratch but turns out to be Mrs. Cutter, who disposed of Scratch some time ago and assumed his identity. After a second tranquilizer shot, Simon rides a wheelchair through the museum, in his delirium interpreting the experience in the rhetoric of a public official: "It was therefore with great reluctance yet with a feeling of pleasurable exhaustion that he reached what he gathered was his point of departure: the foot of the broad, shiny main stairway" (155).

When he again regains consciousness, Simon is strapped to a bed in the upstairs of the museum with Mrs. Cutter seated nearby in a rocking chair. She addresses Simon in a voice that alternates between Scratch's nasal Appalachian dialect and the refined, cultured speech of a southern lady. When he realizes, however, that she is bitter over Mayor Caldwell's refusal to accept her proposal of a convenience marriage, Simon abruptly proposes, offering her what she really wants, which is what his wife wants—power. Threatened by men like Dorff, who fathered the illegitimate Alma, and by her own imperious father, Mrs. Cutter longs to possess something of their power and authority. Since he is himself a master of political rhetoric, the former mayor proves convincing, at least to the demented Mrs. Cutter, and he works his way free of his bonds in time to assist the sheriff with her arrest. Simon and Diane decide to open an animal shelter and devote themselves to catering to each other.

Despite its gothic elements and some moments of polished writing, *The Hanging Garden* is the least intriguing or engaging of Wagoner's novels. Diane Lee may well be his most convincing female character, but in fact she has relatively little competition in his fiction. Millie Slaughter of *The Road to Many a Wonder* alone shares center stage with Wagoner's male protagonists, but she is arguably too good to be true, a heroine believable only in a romantic comedy. Simon Burrows is a considerably more mature and competent protagonist than we encounter in most of Wagoner's novels, and *The Hanging Garden* might have served as a pilot for a series of detective thrillers, though Wagoner has not indicated any such intention. Perhaps Simon's easy self-confidence is his undoing. He is an uninteresting character, experiencing none of the confusion, despite the fact that he is refabricating his life, that plagues Charlie Bell, Willy Grier, Max Fallon, or Popsy Meadows. And his age alone puts him in a different world from that of Danny Masters or the adolescent protagonists of the comic Westerns. Moreover, while he does confront the unknown horrors of a dangerous psychopath, he does not face the issues of corrupting materialism or urban blight or adolescent desperation. Nor is he searching for a father figure, trying to discover or prove his manhood, or seeking love—he simply happens upon it, and accepts it as it comes. Simon Burrows is depicted, perhaps, as Wagoner regards himself and certainly as many others regard him: handsome, physically fit, intelligent, witty, capable of attracting "a girl about half his age" (20). He has a good sense of humor, and he handles the occasional harassment of his soon-to-be ex-wife compassionately but coolly. If he is haunted by anything it would appear to be some annoyance with himself over having wasted an important part of his life on politics.

What we miss in *The Hanging Garden* is that conflict in values between the often ill-at-ease protagonist and the confident, though frequently bumbling antagonist. If, as I have surmised, Wagoner has drawn Simon to more closely resemble himself than he has his other protagonists, that might explain Simon's lack of impact as a fictional character. David Wagoner has been in most ways a successful and fortunate man. If he has not won the fame and admiration that he may desire and indeed deserve, he has not had to endure the hardships of a Franz Kafka, a Theodore Roethke, a James Wright or a Joseph Conrad, to name four writers whose work he particularly admires. Some of Wagoner's success, combined with his very private nature, has aroused envy and resentment, and that has doubtless abbreviated his list of admirers. He is, to put it simply, a hard man with whom to empathize. This is not to promote that old canard that great literature comes only from writers who have suffered greatly, but it may account for the failure of Simon Burrows as a character, if my premise is correct. The result, at any rate, is that *The Hanging Garden* may appeal as a thriller, but it lacks thematic focus and weight, and it has little of that tension within and between characters which we expect of good, serious fiction.

NEW LIGHTS:

From *In Broken Country* to *Walt Whitman Bathing*

IN AN INTERVIEW WITH THE *University of Washington Daily* in 1977 David Wagoner, then working on the poems that would comprise *Who Shall Be the Sun?* (1978), said, "[T]he voice that's coming out of these poems is not my own at all" (32). Some poets would be disturbed over such a development, concerned that they had lost their true voice, that they had become imitative or that they could no longer compose in their accustomed style. Such a fear might in fact be predictable in the case of a writer like Wagoner, preparing to publish his ninth collection of poems, five of which had appeared within a ten-year period. But as he pointed out in the interview, he has "more than one style" (32). He explained his use of varied voices simply as "a characteristic of people who write drama and fiction. They have to be able to talk like more than one person. This has spilled over into my poetry" (32). For Wagoner, the poems of *Who Shall Be the Sun?* certainly were not imitative and did not constitute a loss or repudiation of former voices and styles, as demonstrated the next year when *In Broken Country* appeared.

1. IN BROKEN COUNTRY

In many ways the most interesting review of *In Broken Country* is that of fellow Northwest poet, Richard Hugo, himself a former student of Theodore Roethke. Hugo describes Wagoner as "a poet of Elizabethan wisdom and wit" ("David Wagoner" 1). By this he means not only that Wagoner is something of a Renaissance man, but also that he writes "as if for him, as for the Elizabethans, the language is a recent development" (1). Hugo notes that "[t]he rest of us pursue that elusive quality we call 'voice' in our poems, assuming somewhere we find one that is ours" (1), but Wagoner "writes more kinds of poems than most of us can, and he finds his poems in a wider variety of sources than do the rest of us" (3).

It may be argued, on the other hand, that Wagoner's ability to assume various voices in his poems indicates uncertainty or something short of full commitment to a firm set of values, point of view, or vision. Some of the poems of *In Broken Country*, as of other collections by other poets, do fall short. But virtually all of Wagoner's poems are well made. Wagoner is and has been for a number of years too sound a craftsman to turn out a technically incompetent poem. But this is not tantamount to saying that all the poems in his later collections are fine works that will stand the test of time and vicissitudes of taste. Of the 63 poems in the collection, R. W. Flint draws the line at page 65, suggesting that the poems which "justify" the book may be selected from roughly the last third (61).

The first section of *In Broken Country*, comprising 21 poems, presents us with a familiar array of voices. The first person speaker predominates, and in many cases he is indistinguishable from Wagoner himself; in fact, the first ten poems appear to be quite openly autobiographical. The voice we hear is generally personable and personal, often playful, self-deprecatory, and reflective. In the opening poem, "After the Speech to the Librarians" (3–4), the speaker finds himself lost at the end of a road after having spoken to some librarians: "Something about reading and writing / And not enough about listening and singing." He is struck by the scene before him: a dozen horses browsing on the hillsides, a marsh hawk on a post, and "hundreds of sparrow-sized water pipits." Although the gate before him is locked, "Everything is trespassing as easily / As the hazy sunlight." In the second section of the poem the speaker reviews the components of his reverie in reverse order: the pipits perch beside the hawk, "extremely happy / To be where they are and what they are"; the unsaddled horses "have opened their own gates for the winter"; the librarians are "going back to their books" in schools "where children / Will be reading and writing and keeping quiet / Maybe and listening to how not to be so childish."

Some poets might have been satisfied to have ended the poem at the last line I have just quoted. It ties up neatly and it scores; he has made his point. But Wagoner, in the third section, sets the static scene in motion. His impulse to dramatize mitigates against the simply pictorial. The hawk suddenly glides across the field, swoops down but takes no prey, then soars away crying out sharply. The water pipits answer, "thin as fencewire." The speaker then grasps a message that overshadows the one he had been consciously nursing earlier in the poem, and the impact is startling, if only because of its obviousness: "Isn't it wonderful not to be dead yet?" One reaction to that line may be simply to question why Wagoner did not write: "Isn't it wonderful to be alive?" The rhetorical question, as he poses it, undercuts any Wordsworthian moment of joy in what is, after all, a glimpse of the organic unity of the universe. The speaker does move on to connect the birds to the horse, himself, the librarians, and the children through the medium of the air taken in by the hawk and released as song. Subtly suggested, too, is a sort of kinship between the two figures of the hawk and the speaker, the poet himself. But what stays with us in this poem is the rhetorical question, menacing for all its wonder, and perhaps only partly compromised in the concluding fantasy (a possibility as opposed to a certainty) that "we all might sing for the children."

In such poems as "After the Speech to the Librarians" Wagoner successfully builds on an apparently trivial moment, his best weapon being quiet understatement. In some of his less successful efforts one might say that he tries too hard. He grasps after language, seeks out supercharged puns, and forces the poem. The results are not so much irksome as they are simply unsatisfying, perhaps in the way that a conversation with a genuinely clever person can become cloying, too much of a good thing. "The Junior High Band Concert" (9–10), for example, opens with an almost sophomoric pun, "When our semi-conductor / Raised his baton," and it concludes, "But meanwhile here we were: / A lesson in everything minor, / Decomposing our first composer." In "My Father's Wall" (13), where he reflects on pouring cement with his father to build a basement garage, the first stanza ends: "When the truck backed in / With two yards of ready-mix jumbling in its drum / And the chute swung over, we thought we'd be all set." Confronted with such a line at a cocktail party, we are probably inclined to say, "Yeah, okay. I get it." A fine line separates effective or powerful wordplay from the easy pun, but measuring that line requires a feel for the context. The boyish puns of "The Junior High Band Concert," for example, are appropriate for the adolescent experience reflected in the poem. When he likens the "you" of "Standing in the Middle of a Desert" (97) to a cactus and puns, "You don't have enough essential qualities / To vegetate here," he may be straining the reader's patience.

More problematic are the many poems which Wagoner contrives from random sources and leaves with clear marks of their contrivance. The overmanipulation of form in "The Death of the Moon" (23) is one example, as Wagoner follows the lunar eclipse in shrinking line and stanza from five, 10– to 12–syllable lines in the opening stanza, to four shorter lines in the next, to three lines shorter still, to two lines, to one line, "Her darkness." The form in such a poem becomes obtrusive, both overcalculated and too obvious to be effective. Other poems may be regarded appropriately as *jeux d'esprit*. These poems are generally well made, and perhaps such poems are inevitable in most poets' repertoires, but the first two sections of *In Broken Country* contain too many of them. "Into the Nameless Places" (18–19), for example, takes its cue from a notice on the wall of a nursing home. The questions are intended to help a patient who is "undergoing Reality Orientation," and they are irresistible to a poet like Wagoner, who has a penchant for the found poem and who delights in serious play: "*Your name is?* / Not on the tip of my tongue, but slipping away," / "*The weather is?* / On the other side of the window," / "*Tomorrow is?* / As it may be or as it was / Yesterday, and ever shall be in the beginning." The poem ends more soberly: "and no one / Asks out of politeness why I stare at nothing / As if it were really here." Serious and painful experiences are touched on in this poem, but the reader never loses his or her awareness that the poem is a sort of exercise—David Wagoner out walking his wit.

A similar promenade of wit occurs in "The Singers" (22), which begins with an epigraph from a manual, "Correct Methods of Vocal Study," advising against smiling while singing. The advice, offered in stilted and dated English, is engaging, but the poem does not go beyond play. A poem like "Thistledown" (24), although well wrought, also has the marks of the poetic exercise. In this minor-key meditation, a tuft of thistledown floats into the speaker's car, then slips back out the window. There is in Wagoner, then, that fascination for the trivial things of life that leads him to write, occasionally, a trivial poem. "Book Sale—Five Cents Each!" (40), on a Salvation Army book store, is one such poem, as is "To the Fly in My Drink" (52) and, despite their curiosity, the set of five stunt poems (43–48). These poems are not bad, really, but their playfulness is not always worth the carriage, and if Wagoner's reputation were to rest on them, he would mean no more to our age than Matthew Prior means to the eighteenth century. At their worst, they tend to justify at least some of the critical laceration dealt by Robert Peters in his review of *Landfall* (1981), in which he says of a similar poem: "On a certain level, it is fun to read; on another, it is self-indulgent and coy, and might better have been restricted to the eyes of his wife or of his friends" (270). Wagoner's "wry humor," as Peters observes, can turn "precious" (269).

The series of love poems that rounds out the first section of *In Broken Country* offers better evidence of Wagoner's skill, if only because in them we no longer sense either *jeu d'esprit* or exercise. The series—not really a sequence—begins with "Elegy While Pruning Roses" (26–27), a very personal poem which opens with an epigraph from Roethke's "Cuttings (later)" (*Collected Poems* 35). The speaker, clearly Wagoner himself, regrets not having time to transplant the pruned rose cuttings, and he vows to remember the "dying branches tumbling downhill together" when he cuts bouquets. Only in the last section, twenty-eight lines into the poem, does the speaker address the poem directly to Roethke, and in the process enter the elegiac mode:

> *Ted, you told me once there were days and days*
> *When you had to garden, to get your hands*
> *Down into literal dirt and bury them*
> *Like roots to remind yourself what you might do*
> *Or be next time, with luck. I've searched for that mindless*
> *Ripeness and found it.* (27)

At this point, in the center of the most powerful section, Wagoner shifts the focus for just a line and a half: "Later, some of these flowers / Will go to the bedside of the woman I love." This short passage triggers the six love poems that follow, but the speaker immediately turns back to the elegy: "The rest are for you, who weren't cut off in your prime / But near the end of a long good growing season." It is a feeling tribute to the mentor and friend who, as Wagoner continues, "knew where roots belonged" and "what mysterious roses / Come from and were meant for: thanks, / Apology, praise, celebration, wonder, / And love, in memory of the flourishing dead."

"The Gift" and "For a Woman Who Said Her Soul Was Lost" (28,29) are especially personal poems, the first concerning a birthday present for his wife, Patt, to whom the book is dedicated, on her "most frightening birthday" (presumably her fiftieth). While the second person is often intentionally ambiguous in Wagoner's poems, devised to suggest people in general as well as the reader, it is not in these. The title in "The Gift" refers both to his present for his wife, this poem, which she is seen as unfolding in the opening line, and to "All the gifts" she was born with, including her "phantasmagorical heart." The second poem begins, "You wept past midnight like a ghost in an old novel." Both poems also concern his wife's bout with breast cancer in 1974; she died in 1984. In "The Gift" he hopes she can forget those days "When all you asked as a gift / Was not wanting to die." In "For a Woman" he confesses that as she wept in pain, he took her soul early in the morning "into the woods, into the mountains" where they used to listen to birds together.

The next two poems, "Looking Up" (30) and "Watching the Harbor Seals" (31), locate troubled lovers at a familiar site, Dungeness Bay, a hallowed place in Wagoner's poems, sacred to love. But in the wintry "Looking Up," the couple are "vacant of love" and are likened to their "bone-white shelter" of driftwood and to the "empty shell" and "bleached feather" nearby (30). Only when a large flock of geese takes flight and passes over them do we sense the possibility of healing. In "Watching the Harbor Seals," the couple observe eleven seals "feeding together" at the "bright end of summer" (31). The 24–line poem, alternating long and short lines (up to fourteen syllables and as little as five), rhymes -*er* throughout. In this scene sea and sky seem one in a "blue-green shimmer" and the gulls and cormorants and seals in their "glistening" feathers and fur seem to have found their "place under the sun." But although the poem ends with the lovers "[h]olding each other," the seals recognize the couple as "The ones who suffer / There on the dry stones in the empty air / From a different hunger."

The last two love poems in the series are also paired: "For a Woman Who Dreamed All the Horses Were Dying" (32) and "Love Song After a Nightmare" (33–34). In the first poem, against his beloved's frightening dream of dead grass, dying horses, and emptiness, the speaker offers his own dream of them together in an unfenced field where small wild horses shyly approach to "muzzle our trembling hands." In "Love Song After a Nightmare," the speaker gently awakens his beloved after a nightmare that has "hobbled" her heart. Love, he insists, "has come back alive" and will need only "what we bring together / On this, our first day / On earth, to make its garden." This allusion to Eden is reminiscent of the Dungeness Bay settings of both "A Guide to Dungeness Spit" and "An Offering for Dungeness Bay" (*Collected Poems* 20–21, 201–2), where Wagoner also creates a scenario of a couple beginning or setting out from paradise. The love poems of *In Broken Country* are haunted, however, by the fear of impending death and perhaps, as well, by what Wagoner describes as "Patt's lifelong hypochondria" (*Contemporary Authors* 409).

The first section of *In Broken Country*, then, concludes strongly with this series of poems in which love is salvaged from fear and death, or perhaps from fear of death. Throughout these poems there is an intimacy and

even an intensity that induces credibility. The poems are short and un-
complicated, yet powerful in their sincerity (to use a term long absent
from serious literary criticism). The second section opens with "Elegy for
a Minor Romantic Poet" (37–39), a poem which Richard Hugo calls "fascinating" and "important" ("David Wagoner" 3). Hugo perceives a similarity with Wallace Stevens's Crispin of "The Comedian as the Letter C,"
"striking poses, growing a mustache, leading his life the way he feels is demanded by the role of poet" (3). But Hugo also observes that the poem is
"frightening and sad": "Most of all, in the life and work of the failed poet
we find the real depository of the fears of all of us who write" (3). Having
failed to transform his love into "Earth Mother, / Madonna, or Bitch Goddess," the poet has left her "[a]s stiff in print as in her coffin." The "critical
eyes" have ignored his "painful message" and "decided *real* poetry is
something different," so the poet is on the verge of realizing his worst
fears, "[b]eing unknown and unread." The speaker does not gloat over the
demise of this minor poet, however, but reads his work "with care and
fear." Hugo suggests that Wagoner's sympathy comes of his "honest recognition of parts of himself in the minor poet" (3). Perhaps most of all Wagoner can sympathize with the poet who thought he had "beaten" his way
through "into a suddenly sweet light-dazzled clearing / Where no one had
ever been" so that he would "never again be merely those doubtful selves"
he had caught before, only to have time prove it an "illusion."

A series of five poems concerning birds breaks through the miscellany
near the middle of the second section when the speaker focuses on barn
swallows at the end of "Meditation on the Union Bay Garbage Fill"
(58–59), but these poems are low-voltage affairs with the notable exception of "Sitting by a Swamp" (64). Unlike Dungeness Bay, the wilderness
setting—swamp, forest, mountain, desert—is not usually a meeting place
for lovers, but rather a solitary place for meditation and confrontation of
the self. From a dead silence and stillness at his entry into the swamp (first
stanza), the fauna gradually come to life (sunfish, frog, and marsh wren in
the second stanza), and then (third stanza) a fox sparrow recognizes the
speaker's presence,

> *At a wary time, where I wait*
> *To be what they want me to be:*
> *Less human. A dragonfly*
> *Burns green at my elbow.* (64)

The combination in the last three lines of this poem of conceptual assertion (the speaker's desire to be "less human") with a vivid, exact image (the
dragonfly burning green)—without transition—is the sort of leap that typifies Wagoner at his best.

Two more series of poems make up the second section. "Cutting Down
a Tree" (65–66) initiates a set of four poems assailing the timber industry.
In "Judging Logs" (67), the "slow log-scaler" with his "understanding /
Pitiless eye," is presented as "the resurrection / But lifeless." In "An Address to Weyerhaeuser, The Tree-Growing Company" (68–69), reminiscent of poems from *Sleeping in the Woods* (1974), the speaker is "too mad
to be lyrical about it." Speaking for the wrens driven out of the clear-cut
woods, he concludes by addressing "Mr. Weyerhaeuser": "each song /
Lasts seven seconds and forever. Think what you might manage / To move
if you could sing or even listen." In "At the Edge of a Clear-Cut Forest"
(70), the speaker surveys the rubble left by a logging operation, but at the
end of the poem he finds a puddle in a wheel rut where "tadpoles swim,
transforming themselves, persisting." Wagoner's political stance, in short,
remains both consistent and clear: As in his novels set amidst the Midwest
urban blight, humans are destroying their own world, but the cause is not
yet lost. Of course there is nothing novel about this sentiment; Rousseau
felt this way, so did Wordsworth, and so did Thoreau. Man's corruption
and destruction of nature has been condemned and lamented for cen-
turies now. Wagoner, some might say, simply adds his voice to those others
crying in—and about—the wilderness. A fine ode to the forest products
industry or to the exploitation of nature has yet to be written.

Wagoner's series of five poems dealing with hunting and trapping, starting with "Buck Fever" (71–72), are of a piece with his poems on the timber industry. In these poems, however, Wagoner is consistent in his use of
the second person, the voice of the instructor now dedicated to thwarting
the aims of the hunter and trapper. In "Buck Fever," the speaker asserts
that the hunter's wits are his "lightest equipment" and that the hunter's
craft is "uninitiated." As with his comments on the log scaler, Wagoner,
speaking through his persona in such poems, is not at all reluctant to insult
the occupation and implicitly those who work at such jobs, even though
they are common to the economy of the Pacific Northwest. This may explain why he has never been widely embraced as a regional poet at home,
though he is often considered so in other parts of the country.

Following the hunter's preparation for the shot, the speaker stops at the moment of pulling the trigger and proposes a pair of conditions: "If you hear an explosion," he says, you will "see your trophy leaping / And slumping to its knees / And coughing blood and falling, then lying still." If, on the other hand, something inside chooses "To remain silent / And your game escapes before your eyes / . . . / You can stalk away for good, crackling and whistling, / Enjoying buck fever." The wordplay in these lines is carefully calculated. No longer stalking game, the hunter is seen as stalking off in the colloquial sense of leaving the scene, and the phrase "for good" does not mean simply "once and for all," but "for the better." In "Setting a Snare" (75) the speaker depicts a trapper as an executioner erecting a "gallows" along a familiar path for a "small game animal": "Like you, he's fond of walking old paths and playing / Safe under cover." Again, Wagoner selects his words carefully, imparting to the animal such humanlike traits as a fondness for "old paths" and for play. At the end of the poem he taunts the trapper for his cowardice, for letting the noose handle the "unpleasant details" of "[t]he act of strangling." By the end of the poem the trapper has become not an executioner, but a murderer.

As in his anti-hunting and trapping poems, Wagoner uses the instructor's voice for the complex and powerful twelve-poem sequence that concludes *In Broken Country* (89–108). But in these poems the instructor does not accuse, and in fact the voice is more sympathetic to the subject's plight than in the "Travelling Light" sequence. The first poem, "Finding the Right Direction" (89–90), shows the subject, you, headed south, away from "bitter north." We have no clear sense of what the southward journey signifies, but we are given several clues as to the psychological or spiritual condition of the subject, who is encouraged to follow the path left by glacial drift "toward the end of your own ice age." This suggests emotional coldness, perhaps the freezing of passion, the death of love. The subject's eyes are "unmindful" of various natural signs, suggesting flawed vision, and the "surest compass" turns out to be a deserted cabin, under the southern eaves of which we find "A swallow's nest clinging to next to nothing / Like you, beginning now." The subject of the sequence, then, is associated with images of confusion and desolation as well as uncertainty as to direction.

In the next poem, "Walking in Broken Country" (91–92), the desolate scene is described as a "garden of dead gods when Apache tears / Burst out of lava." In this land of cinders and rubble, all is "sheerest guesswork." Here geometry itself seems confounded:

In this broken country
The shortest distance between two points doesn't exist.
Here, straight lines are an abstraction, an ideal
Not even to be hoped for
(As a crow flies, sometimes) except on the briefest of terms. (91)

Given the implications of the troubled love poems in the first section and Wagoner's comments in his autobiographical essay, one is tempted to read the sequence as reflective of his disintegrating marriage and his increasing sense of personal alienation. If this is the case, however, it is so only in the broadest sense: that is, the tone or emotional pitch of the poems may reflect some of the stress of Wagoner's private life. The poems, if they are autobiographical at all, may be so only indirectly, even unintentionally. The tribute to ideal love, spiritual union, and harmony in "Travelling Light" has lost its dazzle. The "you" in these poems is confronted now with "[a] whole clutch of directions to choose among," but realizes that "back-tracking from dead-ends is an end itself." Nothing adds up, for the "matter of all your sensible facts" is "[j]umbled to the horizon."

If the psychological and spiritual state of the subject is not that of David Wagoner himself undergoing the stress of a collapsing marriage, it is that of an individual enduring something very much akin to that. The subject must work his way through a threatening maze, come to grips with himself, and prepare to restart his life. In "Climbing Alone" (93–94), the third poem of the sequence, the subject attempts to maintain his "center of gravity" as he struggles upward against his "own judgment." In climbing a narrow formation known as a "chimney," the instructor's advice is to recall "the history of stress." But, the instructor points out, "when you stop to think or breathe, as you must," in order not to lose your mind, "[y]our best intentions seem more ludicrous than usual," and you come to the end of your rope, in effect, to find "nothing at the end of it / But the end of it." The next poem, "Crossing a River" (95–96), is something of a companion piece to "Climbing Alone," another dilemma to be faced. The surging river cuts off the subject from "the impossible place" he had "meant to go." The instructor advises against climbing the cliff to find the river's source; rather, he should follow it downstream where the water eventually "goes underground without you."

No sooner does the subject solve the problem of crossing the river than he is confronted by the opposite problem, "Standing in the Middle of a

Desert" (97). Here the subject attempts to take a stand, but he lacks the "essential qualities" to survive in a desert, so he must keep on the move, "[m]ore footloose than ever." But "At the Point of No Return" (98), the sixth poem in the sequence, warns that the "slips of the foot" can no longer be "taken back." The subject is now "Irresponsibly committed, / Refreshed by the absence of the power to choose." This condition appears to reflect a common stage of a person's thinking in the process of a marital breakup: frustration over the inability to control one's life yields to an oddly pleasant sense of futility. In the latter half of this poem Wagoner constructs a fascinating extended metaphor that suggests the slight comfort available to the alienated subject, who enjoys believing that the tracks he leaves in the "blowing sand" will create "thousands of shelters, / Small rooting places / For seeds" that without him "would have kept on tumbling / Unfulfilled downwind." His progress through life, then, "no matter how misdirected," can be justified, so he would like to believe, by this "equally erratic, / Interrupted, and inexplicable line of survivors." Perhaps Wagoner has in mind here his own writings. At any rate, the instructor exposes this rationalization for the wishful thinking it is, pointing out that such living memorials are doomed, in the broken country, to strain root and branch simply in order to "postpone their burial."

Near the end of "At the Point of No Return" the instructor refers to the subject's "Star-sighted, red-rimmed eyes." In the next poem, "Living Off the Land" (99–100), the subject's eyes "gnaw the land ahead for food" and in the desert his "natural disadvantages" become apparent. Hunger drives the subject to the knowledge of vultures and coyotes. "[p]raying for seeds / . . . / To sprout and take root" is a "waiting game" that the subject cannot play, for time is not on his side. By then the subject would have "turned into all you can eat, this air and this sand, / Faltering, flowing even without water / Uneventfully downwind." The last line of the poem echoes the line, "Unfulfilled downwind," of the previous poem, "At the Point of No Return."

"Reading the Landscape" (101) and "Seeing Things" (103) are the next two poems in the sequence and begin to trace the possibility of survival once the subject recognizes that he is "strangely at home / In the visible world, a place called Here and There," but he is warned that any thought that he is not lost is an illusion. Then sand enters the subject's mouth and eyes, "sharing your misunderstandings / Of what you say and see, reminding you / Your mind's voice and mind's eye / Are equally vulnerable in their pastimes and desolations." Now he is prepared to arise, "Ignoring all directions / But your own," and to "exercise your freedom of chance by aiming / Somewhere, keeping a constant Here beside you / As faithfully as your death." The notion of free choice is teased here, as is the idea of the faithful companion. The poem is a disillusioning experience, therefore, in several ways.

Now the subject is prepared to see things. But of course "seeing things" in the desert means coming to terms with mirages and illusions, and as the poems in the sequence have increasingly asserted, this self is "long since out of focus." The subject should be aware of mirages and be able to resist them because his "fondness for light, / For the earth's unlimited metamorphoses" should inform him of the earth's "disguises." In fact, the "burden of proof" shifts to "other beholders," presumably to the grazing antelope mentioned earlier in the poem, who may now see him, ironically, "As a menacing, blurred afrit, / A towering apparition wobbling toward them / Helplessly, their last hope, their disillusionment." The wandering, lost, helpless subject of the poem becomes a menace, as seen by others.

The tenth poem in the sequence, "Lying Awake in a Desert" (104), alters the conditions of the previous two poems, by placing the subject in the desert at night. Now he must rely on sound rather than sight, and whereas he appeared dangerous to the "beholders" in the previous poem, "Seeing Things," he is now "defenseless" by the light of the moon. The instructor offers little comfort, warning him that scorpions and sidewinders may wish to share his body's "residual heat," so he must waken in the morning "gently." But this poem does strike a hopeful note in the concluding image: "Meanwhile, get through this night of reckoning / By the irrational riches of starlight."

The subject drains the last drop of his canteen and then receives instructions on various ways of locating water in the desert in the next poem, "Looking for Water" (105–6). Although the subject's "blundering, rootless sense of territory" cannot match the "self-possession" of the cactus, the instructor leads him at the end to the life-sustaining water, which he shares communally with flies and bees:

> *Wait by that emptiness. If it trickles and fills,*
> *Your luck is only beginning.*
> *The flies and bees will join you in that bitter communion,*
> *Will take it with you, as drunk as true believers*
> *Sharing another kingdom.* (106)

As may be inferred from the conclusions to the previous two poems, by the end of the sequence the subject is at last "Getting There" (107–8): "You take a final step and, look, suddenly / You're there." But having arrived at "the one place all your drudgery was aimed for," the subject is uncertain as to what it was he wanted to be. As the instructor describes his condition, "You feel like tinder / Under a burning glass,/ A luminous point of change." This is the condition, as I see it, of the speaker in Roethke's "The Far Field" (*Collected Poems* 193–95), finding himself "at the field's end" (193), Roethke's first-person speaker discovers "[a]ll finite things reveal infinitude" (196). Wagoner's instructor-speaker is also at the edge, on the verge of a new beginning, apparently about to undergo a change in identity: "Like wind etching rock, you've made a lasting impression / On the self you were." The ordeal "would make an unpromising / Meandering lifeline," and the lessons learned will sink in only gradually. The instructor is firm at the end of the poem in complimenting the subject for having "earned" the new vision, "this worn-down, hard, incredible sight / Called Here and Now," but he is also cautionary. The subject in this poem has not arrived, as has the loving couple in "Travelling Light." "Getting There" is not a celebration of visionary enlightenment or of mystical union. Wagoner does not shift to the communal "we" in this poem as he did in "Travelling Light" or in "A Guide to Dungeness Spit." The relationship between instructor and subject remains intact, and "getting there" is not "being there," but a crucial stage of a process which means starting over and "beginning another / Journey without regret / Forever, being your own unpeaceable kingdom, / The end of endings" (108).

2. LANDFALL

The title of Wagoner's next book, *Landfall* (1981), suggests that he has indeed undertaken that journey and found a new place, a land beyond the broken country, where love is possible. The collection ends with a sequence of six poems entitled "A Sea Change," in which the voice is that of the lovers familiar to us in "A Guide to Dungeness Spit" and "Travelling Light." As Sara McAulay observes, relative to the sequence at the end of *In Broken Country*, the language and tone of these poems are "darker, more lyrical," the landscape "dreamlike, more explicitly metaphoric," and the "perils" less physical and more difficult to "remedy" (94). The speaker in the first poem of the sequence, "Going to Sea" (101), might again be autobiographical at one level, at least in the loose sense described above (the book is dedicated to Patt "downstream and upstream, with love"). He and his beloved are "born marooned," "castaways all our lives." The journey they are undertaking for themselves and for all of us requires that they bring only "what's necessary": "Relics of our bodies / And souls, what's left of our minds, remnants of our hearts." With these plus food and water, he says, "we can subsist . . . / After a dying fashion." Reversing the pirates' usual practice of privateering on the high seas, then burying their treasure and making a map with an *X* to mark the spot, they mark an X "At the crux of departure," burying "all we no longer treasure." That antitreasure is a dark collection of items pertaining to death, for example, "a dead-man's chest," "[s]ongs hollow as laughter," and last, "an empty bottle . . . holding the message / Of our light parting breath."

The journey seems quite explicitly to be a voyage beyond life, at least as the lovers have been accustomed to experiencing it. Their material wealth, "[p]ieces-of-eight and gold doubloons," is left behind as useless on this transcendental voyage. Reading the first poem of the sequence, it is difficult to avoid thoughts of such conventional symbolic associations as "the sea of eternity." The title of the sequence recalls to mind Ariel's song from *The Tempest*, which reflects on the ultimate change of death: "Nothing of him that doth fade / But doth suffer a seachange / Into something rich and strange" (I, ii, 403–5). The death, of course, is metaphoric, as is the journey at sea. Like the characters in Shakespeare's play or like Odysseus, "we" (accompanying the personas in the poems) will experience a transformation that will amount to a type of rebirth. In "Landfall" (109–10), the last poem of the "Sea Change" sequence, the speaker refers retrospectively to their setting out as "embarking on new lives." Now, he says, "all turns nameless again"; that is, all is as it was in the beginning, as in Eden. Therefore, we "must love to learn" (not "learn to love") "Once more how to point at the trees and birds and animals / We see around us, even our own hearts, / Naming, renaming them."

That is Wagoner's sustained and sustaining theme: We must not simply learn to love what we customarily call "nature," but we must "love to learn" it. More accurately, this amounts to relearning. As the poems of *Who Shall Be the Sun?* imply, we were once like the Indians with respect to our world. We were once an integral part of it; like the Indians we lived in harmony with nature and knew the names of the flora and fauna. We did not exploit nature then, but drew upon it for our needs and with reverence. The Indian invests nature with names (Coyote, Stump, Salmon-Boy) and invests himself with names drawn from nature (Crazy Horse, Black Elk, Red Cloud). As we "see" what is around us, Wagoner insists, we will see and comprehend "our own hearts." Some will object to this as an idyllic vision or Golden Age metaphysics, but it is the aim of virtually all nature poets who work at a level beyond the picturesque, that is, land-scape poetry, to project that hypothesis and to insist upon its reality.

Conceptually, Wagoner is in line with Wordsworth, though his perspective on nature is harder. Some might argue that he is typically American in conceiving of nature as a rough but necessary ally. In his playfully ill-tempered review of *Landfall*, Robert Peters calls Wagoner a "blackbird of American verse," a "fairly commonplace bird" rather than a "more flamboyant species" (267). Peters would have Wagoner be more like Charles Bukowski or Allen Ginsberg; he would like Wagoner to "risk disturbance, grotesqueries, and failures" (271). One suspects that Peters needs experience editing a literary magazine if he feels underdosed with grotesquery and failure, but be that as it may, his survey of Wagoner's sensibility does reopen the issue of the poet's vision or philosophy. I agree that if we read Wagoner's poems hoping to detect a fresh or startling angle on humankind's relations with nature, we will be disappointed. I would suggest, however, that while poems may be as close to philosophy as many readers ever get, the poet is not the ideal philosopher. It is not (at least not necessarily) the role of the poet to be an innovative thinker, or even, as the works of Bukowski and Ginsberg amply illustrate, to be profound.

It is important, however, that the poet's perspective be clear, and on that subject Wagoner has reiterated in interviews what is already evident in his poems. Speaking with the editors of *Crazy Horse* magazine in 1972, Wagoner said he measures himself "in terms of harmony or disharmony with the natural world": "In the woods, along mountain streams, by the seashore, I've tried hard to find my place *among* (not above, like most of our floundering, foundering fathers) all animate and inanimate matter" (41). As Wagoner surmises, this does make him a nature poet, and his insistence that he is not naive as to the benevolence of the wilderness does not change that label. As to the near universality of his views among nature poets, Justin Askins writes in his comments on two sequences in *Landfall* and *First Light*: "This movement from psychic disarray to psychic maturity, where the confusions of self-centeredness are cleared away through a glimpse into the hidden ordering of nature, where man is part and not paragon, is Wagoner's innermost vision. It is also at the core of all authentic nature poetry" (339). If we read Wagoner for a controversial or grotesque kind of nature poetry or for radical political stances, we read him for the wrong reasons.

But having called Wagoner "a nature poet," or even "mostly a nature poet," is not to have said very much. He is at least equally a poet of human nature. In fact, although they are generally well made, his least effective poems in *Landfall* are those nearly "pure" nature lyrics like "Nuthatch" (24), the clematis poems (25–26), "Bittern" (56), and "Craneflies" (60), which are devoid of human beings. *Landfall* includes too many poems like those for my taste, and too many like "Looking into a Pond" (62), in which the onlooker is little more than that. In such poems one is tempted to agree with Paul Breslin's observation that there is "too much nature and not enough poetry," that Wagoner does, occasionally at least, assume "that whatever he sees is interesting because he saw it" (31). Unfortunately, the book begins with five such self-indulgent poems, starting with "Under the Sign of Moth" (3–4), which locates the speaker in the comfortable domesticity of his garden where he snoozes until, in "Moth Song" (9), "I open, I become / Completely known, I blossom." By then it is too late, and the reader is inclined to agree with Peters that "Wagoner reflects a middle-class sensibility as that sensibility approaches middle age" (267).

But *Landfall* is redeemed, not only by the "Sea Change" sequence, but also by a number of poems in which the speaker interacts meaningfully and profoundly with nature; for example, "Return to the Swamp" (55), "Wading in a Marsh" (57–58), "Staying Found" (72–73), "Turning Back and Starting Over" (89–90), "Sleeping on Stones" (95–96), and "Downstream" (97–98). Moreover, as is usually the case with Wagoner's collections, this book includes a considerable number of poems that could not be designated nature poems at all. Among the best of these are the autobiographical poems that reflect upon Wagoner's father, particularly "My Fire" (10–11) and "My Father's Garden" (14).

In "My Fire," Wagoner compares his tending of the coal-burning furnace to his father's work as a smelter at the steel mills. Both processes involve a sort of magic, the boy's converting fire to steam for the radiator, his father's "melting and turning / Blood-colored ore to pigs / And men to something stranger." In the closing stanza Wagoner offers a symphony of sound and imagery in the description of his "spirit" swelling and singing inside the radiator pipes, where it would

Turn back to water and fall
To the fire again, turn white,
Rise hissing in every room
Against the windows to grow
Fronds and bone-white flowers,
All ice in a frozen garden. (11)

This is Wagoner at his best. The theme of metamorphosis in nature or elsewhere is prevalent in his work, and it operates in this poem on multiple levels. In the first stanza he sees himself tending the furnace where "black fossils of ferns / And, swamp-shaking dinosaurs" burn until he hauls out clinkers that have been transformed into "the vertebrae of monsters." In the last stanza his spirit is converted into steam, then into water, and back into steam after striking the fire again. But beyond that cycle he offers a more profound metamorphosis into a sort of art in the "frozen garden" that forms on the windows, with words like "fronds" and "bone-white" obviously reflecting the imagery of the opening stanza, "black fossils of fern." The sound patterns in these lines are also striking: the long *i* of fire/white/rise culminates in the word "ice"; groups of sounds resonate with each other (hissing/against, grow/bone/frozen); sibilants hiss throughout much of the poem, and alliteration helps knit together the last lines (fronds/flowers/frozen).

In "Staying Found" (72–73) Wagoner is also autobiographical, but he conceals the personal self at the center of the poem by using the third person. The poem begins with the epigraph from Bradford Angier's *How to Stay Alive in the Woods*: "We become lost not because of anything we do, but because of what we leave undone. . . . We stay found by knowing approximately where we are every moment." For Wagoner, whose double vision of the woods embraces both its actuality and its metaphoric identity, such a passage is irresistible. The persona in the poem is alone in a rain forest, "caught by its impossible / Greenness." He is "bewildered / By a wilderness he'd only half imagined / Among the mills and ruined lakes of his childhood." The wordplay here typifies Wagoner's work. It is neither his best nor his worst pun, but it is the sort of serious playfulness that a reader must either take in stride or avoid by reading some other poet. The memory of mills and ruined lakes clearly recalls Wagoner's boyhood in Whiting, Indiana, located in the industrial area between Gary and Chicago. In this new wilderness the persona walks "softly" and "quietly" on a "resurrected / Earth whose fire was wildflowers" rather than "the open hearth where white-hot steel / Boiled against furnace walls" ("My Father's Garden" 14). The central symbol of the poem is a nurse log, as in "Waiting in a Rain Forest" from the "Travelling Light" sequence, representative of new life "young cedars" emerge from death. This symbol was not available to Wagoner when he described the often sterile landscape of *Dry Sun, Dry Wind* during the early 1950's, before he moved to Seattle. The "children" of the "virgin forest" are paradoxically "perfectly neglected / And cared-for," and among them he finds himself. He is "healed."

A moment later, however, the persona turns, and immediately he is lost. His healing involves forgetting the "defeated trees, the flowers starving / In poisonous wind and rain, the dead ground" of his youth. But in "another moment" he learns a "different way of dying / Called Here and Now, called There and Where and Nowhere." In short, the realities of change and death cannot simply be consigned to oblivion, but the empty and futile death of nature described in the early poems and the urban Midwest fiction is not the only way, certainly not the universal way, of death. The persona discovers, therefore, that when he stumbles onto the road again "his mind / Had changed." Now he will no longer be lost in the woods or in cities, but will "stay found."

Although a poem like "Staying Found" might be described as autobiographical in only a general way, the events clearly proceed from personal experience, and it is likely that some such transforming event served as a necessary foundation. The same may be said for Wagoner's powerful love poems, many of which he wrote, according to his autobiographical essay, as his marriage was disintegrating and his personal life was running counter to that implied by both the poems and the dedications that open his books. *Landfall* is dedicated to his wife, yet they separated in the summer of 1981, the year the collection was published, and Wagoner remarried a year later. The lovers in Wagoner's poems might be said to represent, then, not love as it actually is, but as it could be or should be.

"By a Lost Riverside" (94) and its companion poem, "Sleeping on Stones," (95–96), may proceed from a recollected summer evening, or they may be wholly a product of Wagoner's imagination, despite their apparently firm anchor in actual experience. As in "Riverbed," the title poem of his 1972 collection, the lovers lie down by a stream where nesting salmon spawn and die. At the end of "By a Lost Riverside" the speaker calls upon his beloved to recognize the metamorphoses:

> *Love, remember: dry,*
> *Those stones were gray, but in rain*
> *Lay speckled like the eggs*
> *Of wild, bountiful, barely*
> *Imaginable birds*
> *In an enduring nest.* (94)

Not only does rain transform the actual appearance of the stones, making them more colorful, but also it alters their metaphoric possibilities. Curiously, the eggs the speaker is reminded of are not salmon eggs, but bird eggs, and the result is that the poem rises at the end.

Technically, the last lines of "By a Lost Riverside" offer further testimony to Wagoner's craftsmanship. His use of enjambment often leads to line breaks which represent the necessary occasional surprises of well-made free verse (rain/Lay, barely/Imaginable), at the same time that they strengthen the left margin, in effect protecting it from becoming a flat series of function words—articles, prepositions, and conjunctions. Again, we have evidence of a subtle accentual line; the first four are 3-stress lines, the last two are 2-stress. And again we witness Wagoner's remarkable ear. Assonance (gray/rain/lay/eggs) and alliteration (bountiful/barely/ imaginable/birds) are the most prominent sound patterns in the closing lines, but beneath them, in the sense that they are less obtrusive, are the continuing m and n sounds, from "bountiful" and "imaginable" to the entire last line: "In an enduring nest." The poem ends with the very softness that the idea of nesting suggests.

"Sleeping on Stones" (95–96) also locates the lovers in a riverbed, but the premise of human lovers somehow imitating the spawning of a salmon would be ludicrous if it were not for the fact that life and death are involved. The lovers watch the salmon "restlessly," in two senses of the term, because they know she will later "drift downstream and ashore and lie / Still in a way that was still beyond us." A close reading of this poem will indicate how untranslatable a poet Wagoner is, for his phrasing is, I would say, absolutely idiomatic. I know of no other poet whose words and phrases are so dependent on colloquial English and, more specifically, on the American idiom. In the opening stanza we are told that the stones "wouldn't give in / Easily" and that our bodies are "nonconforming members." In the second stanza we are told that the rounded stones seem "easy / To go along with, comfortable, as comforting / To the touch as polished carvings." But the river has "lodged them close." From this colloquialism, Wagoner builds, or rather rebuilds, a somewhat extended metaphor, something of a conceit. The river has left the stones "Like the foundation of a ruin that nothing / But us at the moment would try to build on." The salmon in the next stanza is "hard at her labor," both in the sense of doing hard work and in the sense of giving birth. The fourth stanza begins: "At last, we'd made our bed, and we lay in it." The origin of this metaphor is in folk wisdom: You've made your bed, now lay in it. (The more grammatical "lie" rarely appears in this context.) The lovers' eyes are "wide open," not simply in the physiological sense but in the sense that they are prepared for understanding, and they are "losing / Touch" not only physically, but also metaphorically, as one "loses touch" with reality. At the end of this pivotal stanza, the lovers no longer move stones, but join them by assuming their heaviness.

The next stanza begins with the speaker's observation that the stones "had found their places," aided by the river. Now the lovers must find their proper place, not helped by the current but by its sound. In the sixth stanza the water flows "over the gray stones in our skulls," smoothes them, turns them over, and beds them down "into one streambed." Most readers would probably accept Wagoner's metaphor unhesitantly, without considering its source in another piece of folk wisdom: You have rocks in your head. At this crucial point in the poem, the mind of the lovers has become one with the streambed, which has previously seemed hard and alien. The salmon now enters and begins nesting, metaphorically in the transformed mind of the lovers.

Following "Sleeping on Stones," the last poem in this section of *Landfall*, "Downstream" (97–98), culminates the vision of the lovers, who "give in to the persuasions of the river" and float downstream. Unlike the two previous poems, "Downstream" offers the dramatic immediacy of the present tense, and the lovers appear to be floating in a boat of some sort, but the lesson is unchanged: "Nothing is the same / Ever." The lovers have been brought to realize the necessity of change and death. They see that the windbreak of alders, "gravely leaning paleboned," is "another river, its bed channelled by seasons." Wagoner's vision of the interrelatedness of change and death, however, is never ugly or foreboding, but bright and hopeful. The poem ends: "We cross a pool, / Translucent, the stones below us / Glimmering, remaining."

3. FIRST LIGHT

Wagoner's love affair with light is nowhere more evident than in the poems of his next collection, *First Light* (1983), the first of his books to be dedicated to his new wife, Robin Seyfried—whom Wagoner had known for about five years, first as his student in poetry workshops, before their marriage in the summer of 1982. The collection is also dedicated to the memory of his father and mother, both of whom figure in some of the autobiographical poems in the first section. Divided into seven sections, *First Light* is the most varied of his twelve previous books (counting the "Travelling Light" sequence as part of *Collected Poems*), but most of the voices are familiar to those who have read much of Wagoner's work.

In his review of the book for *Magill's Literary Annual 1984* Daniel Mark Fogel praises Wagoner as "a major American poet" and "a virtuoso," and he outlines Wagoner's "extraordinary" range in both technique and content (299). A brief survey of the 87 poems distributed over seven sections amply illustrates the latter point. In section 1, eight poems range over subjects from a day spent with Wagoner's grandfather, who was working as a truant officer, to elegiac poems for his parents. Section 2 is a seventeen-poem menagerie of everything from octopus to elephant, from winter wren to peacock. Section 3 comprises sixteen poems, which Fogel categorizes as written in a "sardonic, bitter, satirical voice" (302). These are narratives for the most part, odd anecdotes like "The Naval Trainees Learn How to Jump Overboard" (49–50) and "In the Booking Room" (52), and retold myths and fairy tales, usually with a twist, such as "Medusa's Lover" ("she couldn't do a thing with her snaky hair" [41]) and "Jack and the Beanstalk" (46–47), in which Jack's mother turns a tidy profit selling beans at the market.

The fourteen poems of section 4 Fogel describes as poems of "precise observation" related to William Carlos Williams's "legacy of 'no ideas but in things'" (302). In this section, however, the poems resist such easy classification. The first concerns what fortune tellers call a "cold reading" (a generalized fortune used when the teller has no information on the subject), the next concerns a magician who creates the illusion of a floating woman, the third is a proposal for an unusual sculpture of a stairway haunted by various plaster figures, and the fourth, "Poem About Breath" (63–64), is a peculiar memory of Elizabeth Bishop. At this point a poem entitled "Stump Speech" (64–65) traces the life of a tree, based on the model of the nursery rhyme, "The House that Jack Built": "This is the bark, which is always dead." The poem moves on to phloem, cambium, xylem, and heartwood until the speaker locates himself by the stump, "a dream of a tree forever dead." The next half dozen poems, like "The Water Lily" (66) and "The Caterpillar" (67), fit Fogel's description well enough, but the section ends with three dreamlike poems, including "Writing an Elegy in My Sleep" (71) and "Walking on the Ceiling" (74). J.D. McClatchy describes half the poems in *First Light* as "never less than clever but rarely more." Certainly using that fraction is over-censorious, even for the poems in the fourth section, but there is an occasional product of mere ingenuity in the book.

Section 5, a sequence entitled "The Land Behind the Wind," has been generally recognized as offering the strongest poems in *First Light*. The lovers, this time described in the third person rather than the familiar first person "we," move through a dream-filled and dreamlike winter landscape in search of "a place to stand behind the wind" (86). The title of the sequence refers to the Native American term for the afterlife or the spirit world. Section 6 is made up of thirteen poems that Fogel calls "allegories or moralized landscapes bearing on Wagoner's central themes of staying alive and of doing so through poetry" (302). Of the thirteen poems all but three mention light in some way or other, usually in the sense of enlightenment or clarification of vision and understanding, as in "A Young Girl with a Pitcher Full of Water" (91), in which, as the girl pours, "She grows / More and more light. She lightens. She sees it flowing / Away from her to fill her earth to the brim." In the nineteen lines of "Aerial Act" (90), some form of the word "light" appears thirteen times. Fogel describes the ten love poems of section 7, written for Wagoner's new wife, as reflecting "a love between a man and a woman upheld by an organic view of human wholeness with other humans and with nature" (302).

Some critics have complained of redundancy in Wagoner's subjects and themes or have decried what they see as stylistic flatness. Although Mc-Clatchy praises the poems of the "Land Behind the Wind" sequence, he feels that Wagoner is "pacing off familiar ground" in *First Light*. Sanford Pinsker, in his study of three Northwest poets—Richard Hugo, William Stafford, and Wagoner—mentions that Wagoner was once concerned about "repeating himself, even about self-parody," but as Pinsker also notes, "nobody criticizes composers or painters for working out variations on a theme" (*Northwest Poets* 107). Moreover, as we have seen, Wagoner has almost as many themes as he has voices. Paul Breslin and Robert Peters may be numbered among several critics who have found Wagoner insufficient as an innovator in technique. In a positive review of *First Light*, W. Pratt writes, a "pleasing monotone, laconic and wistful, is Wagoner's sure American style." I suggest, however, that this rather faint praise is inaccurate. Especially in his stylistic experiments, Wagoner frequently tries out something new, even as he continues with that which has served him so well over the years.

The subtle elegy to his father, "My Father in the Basement" (*First Light* 11), which appears superficially to concern an ordinary repair job, represents Wagoner as a sort of free-verse formalist, if that phrase is not too great a paradox. The lines vary in length from ten to thirteen syllables, and they are arranged in four tight five-line stanzas. Although a dozen lines show no end punctuation, the principle of line is clearly grammatical rather than subjective, as reference to the left margin (all capitalized, as usual in Wagoner's poems) will attest. The second stanza illustrates my point:

> /   /   /   /   /
> *None of the fuses had blown as dark as storms*
> /   /   /   /
> *At their tiny portholes. Nothing was on fire*
> /   /   /   /
> *But the fire in the furnace, and nothing was frozen*
> /   /   /   /
> *But the humming freezer and the concrete floor*
> /   /   /   /
> *And the hands he'd poured it with, now cold and hard.* (11)

Note that the enjambment here occurs at natural grammatical junctions that will cause the reader no disruption. After the first line the left margin is a collection of one preposition and three conjunctions. The result is a sort of formality, a lack of surprises, no flashy line breaks, no clever or startling transitions for the reader. With relatively slight exception or uncertainty, I think, most readers proficient in scansion would accept the primary stresses as I have marked them. In short, with occasional exceptions, Wagoner composes here a four-stress accentual line. Throughout his career, in fact, the accentual line has been Wagoner's standard. It offers a pulse without being predictable. The poem ends with his father lying down on the floor because "nothing was worth doing / Unless he did it himself" and "[b]ecause if he couldn't fix it, nobody could."

A linguist might observe that Wagoner rarely breaks up the nuclear sentences in his lines, a stylistic trait that typifies the work of such breath-line poets as Charles Olson. Against that fixed stanzaic structure with its often predictable line breaks, however, Wagoner offers various nonstanzaic poems typified by a line that seems to ramble loosely, expanding and contracting throughout, though always according to a pattern (see chapter 3). Denise Levertov has observed that the "deployment of the poem on the page" may be regarded as a "score, that is, as the visual instructions for auditory effects" (32). The way a line breaks, Levertov adds, affects not only the rhythm but also the musical pitch of the line. Some of the most effective poems in *First Light* are composed in lines that work like the following from "The Source" (83–84), part of the "Land Behind the Wind" sequence. The lovers climb a mountain

> *Through lupine, through snow, the light a snowfall,*
> *A blue-white daylight the color of snow-melt*
> *Shimmering by their feet,*
> *Still only half persuaded not to be ice*
> *But to give in to the full beginning*
> *Of flowing. At the rim*
> *Of a pond near the foot of steep snow-drifted talus,*
> *Half-frozen, they knelt where the foot-wide creek*
> *Was now being born*
> *Again and again under their eyes. They drank*
> *From the source. . . . (84)*

The communal drinking, sealed with a "strange kiss," leads to the lovers' awareness that they are on the threshold of the spiritual country they have been seeking, the land behind the wind. The two poems which follow, concluding the sequence, are "Seeing the Wind" (85) and "Walking into the Wind," in which wind encircles the lovers as they turn in circles, lost and confused, until they see, in the last line, "[t]here lay the wind at their feet like a pathway" (86).

Both of Wagoner's predominant techniques of line composition suggest that he has remained a formalist of sorts. It should be no surprise to those aware of his skilled craftsmanship that he would turn out a fine villanelle, "Canticle for Xmas Eve" (56), somewhere along the way, and it should be no surprise either that his villanelle would take liberties with the conventional form. Wagoner's villanelle is without rhyme, although it has the typical alternating refrain lines. But even the refrain lines are transformed as they are repeated throughout the poem so that by the end, when the first and third lines come together, this sinister Christmas carol appears to resolve into madness. It is not uncommon for Wagoner to compose his shorter poems (up to thirty or so lines) in a single sentence, as he does in this canticle, thus making quotation an awkward affair. The poem begins

> *o holy night as it, was in the beginning*
> *Under silent stars for the butchering of sheep*
> *And shepherds, is now and ever shall be, night, . . .* (56)

The fourth line, beginning the next tercet, draws from the familiar hymn, "O Little Town of Bethlehem": "How still we see thee lying under the angels / In twisted wreckage." The concluding quatrain of the villanelle proceeds from the phrase, "what is and shall be for this night,"

> *Of bludgeons and hopes, of skulls and fears laid open*
> *To the mercies of our fathers burning in heaven,*
> *o little town of bedlam in the beginning*
> *Of the end as it was, as it is to all, good night.* (56)

The holy town of Bethlehem, never mentioned by name in the poem, but implied by allusion to the hymn, becomes the insane asylum of Elizabethan England, now synonymous with madness.

If Wagoner's fascination with form might enable us to anticipate his interest in the villanelle, his equal curiosity about the limits of form might lead us to predict what he offers in "The Bad Uncle" (5–6) and several other poems in this collection: no punctuation except for the period at the end of the last line. His one-sentence poems and those that feature the expanding and contracting lines indicate Wagoner's attraction to the idea of flux. The imagery of flowing streams, advancing and receding tides, and shifting winds is common to his poems, and a cast of symbolic travelers, wanderers, or lovers populates that shifting landscape. Although Wagoner personally may strike us as a firmly rooted individual, most at home in his suburban Seattle backyard, his fictional characters and his poetic personas are typically footloose in the world. The unpunctuated poem offers particular advantages to a poet like Wagoner who enjoys comedy and who understands the workings of line. The following passage from "The Bad Uncle" illustrates some of the fun:

That Fourth of July it was impossible
To hear themselves think except out loud
With potash and sulfur paste between two bricks
Across the road by the cowshed swinging a spikemaul
Down to explode that horrible sandwich
Boom till cows and chickens wouldn't come home
To roost at milk-time the neighbors wandered in
To see what in thunder the big commotion oh
Emmett stop it he gobbled up half the pie
Before nephews and nieces got started for heaven
Sakes . . . (5)

The impression created is close to that of the stream-of-consciousness novel. Events tumble over comments about Uncle Emmett and about what is happening. Time appears to spill, to run over in this happily fluid world, and the unpunctuated lines contribute importantly to the overall impression. Wagoner creates in this poem a delightfully chaotic holiday reminiscent of moments in Eudora Welty's *Delta Wedding*.

It is obvious that Wagoner returns to a number of familiar topical and thematic patterns in his poems: his parents, particularly his father; his own boyhood, especially his adolescent years, with an ever present ability to laugh at himself; his personal protest against exploitation of the environment, usually by loggers or hunters; himself at rest and meditative in his own backyard or garden; an individual lost in rugged country; a couple wandering or traveling in the wilderness or at sea; a single insect or animal in the wilds or in a zoo; reconstructed history, myth, or fairy tale; the magician or related artist/entertainer whose specialty is sleight of hand or delicate balance or deception; the Native American animist song or legend. This list accounts for ten recurring topics and themes in Wagoner's poems. A fair representation of his poetic achievement should consider all of these, and it should account for his particular skill with the sequence, and it should also reflect on his shifting perspective or point of view (he/she, you, I/we).

Yet it is equally true, to the consternation of some critics and fellow poets, that David Wagoner can find a poem almost anywhere, in anything, in anyone. Virtually every new collection of his poems includes work in several of the familiar veins mentioned above, but experienced readers nearly always discover something quite different. For example, in the sixth section of *First Light* we find four short poems, varying in length from eleven to sixteen lines, all of which are portraits of females: "A Young Girl with a Pitcher Full of Water," "A Woman Standing in the Surf," "A Young Woman Found in the Woods," "A Woman Feeding Gulls" (91–93). The poems do not form a sequence like "Travelling Light" or "Sea Change," and in fact all four were published in different periodicals, but they have in common not only their brevity and focus, but also their vision of the nurturing female. Although she carries the water "unsteadily," the young girl with a pitcher leans "as if to pour herself," and she seems actually to be capable of growing light; we leave her "smiling above flowers" (91). The woman standing in the surf is depicted "[t]high-deep in the sea" as she rises to meet the incoming waves "crying out of fear / Of her desire." The portrait is clearly sexual, the poem ending with the woman spreading her arms out and welcoming the waves "[a]gainst her, against her" (92).

The next poem, "A Young Woman Found in the Woods" (92), is the most startling of the four. The first line strikes us as simultaneously pastoral and funereal: "Lying among flowers in a green shadow." She could be asleep or she could be dead. The next line resolves any doubt: "She has left the cage that held her breath and her heart." The wordplay suggests the traditional view of the body as the prison of the soul, while literally it refers to the ribcage. What is left is a "hovel" where not blood, but rain is flowing "[b]reathlessly, heartlessly." Read in the context of "A Woman Standing in the Surf," this line may recall, rhythmically, the last line of that poem even as it recalls the early image in that poem of the woman feeling the "Breathless baffling / Of winds by the moon" (91). The dead woman's eyes are now "more hollow / Than when they wondered where on earth they were," and they are now "[t]urned inward" to "no horizon." The last image of this haunting poem depicts the woman "smiling at strangers / More openly than ever at any lover." Again, in the context, we may recall the concluding image of the smiling girl in "A Young Girl with a Pitcher Full of Water." "A Young Woman Found in the Woods" ends with the flat statement that she now "has no secrets." Wagoner offers no real clue in the poem as to the cause of the young woman's death: accident, starvation, murder (perhaps a sexual crime)? We may surmise, given the hint about "smiling at strangers" or the "lover," but that would be mere speculation. There is an odd chill about this poem that combines with its aura of mystery to sustain its unique power. The last line underscores the deep irony of the poem, for although she now "has no secrets," in one sense of the word, we are left totally mystified.

"A Woman Feeding Gulls" (93) seems intended as a sort of antithetical mate to "A Young Woman Found in the Woods." Here the woman is alive, offering food, and surrounded by noise and motion. The long *i* sounds of the opening lines may suggest the shrill cries of the gulls:

> They cry out at the sight of her and come flying
> Over the tidal flats from miles away,
> Sideslipping and wheeling
> In sloping gray-and-white interwoven spirals
> Whose center is her. . . . (93)

This poem is a single, continuous 14–line sentence powered by gerunds and participles, whereas "A Young Woman Found in the Woods" is set up in three four-line stanzas, each concluding with a period. The erratic variations in line length may suggest the flight of the feeding gulls. The line length in "A Young Woman Found in the Woods" also varies, but it follows a pattern: three lengthy lines, then a single short line providing a chillingly terse ending for each stanza. "A Woman Feeding Gulls" ends on a reference to the ongoing cycle of time—day and night—and feeding, "the endlessly hungry opening and closing / Of wings and arms and shore and the turning sky."

4. THROUGH THE FOREST

Wagoner's next collection of poems, *Through the Forest: New and Selected Poems, 1977–1987*, drew slight attention from critics and reviewers, perhaps because the book featured only thirty-one new poems. Reviewers like Bill Ott, for *Booklist*, and Daniel L. Guillory, for *Library Journal*, joined previous commentators in commending Wagoner as one of the finest nature poets. Ott reminded readers of Wagoner's "talent for writing about human beings" (1713) and Guillory reflected on "the pleasures of [the poet's] craftsmanship" (130). The anonymous reviewer for *Publishers Weekly*, however, observed that "this new volume reorganizes his poetry thematically into a summa of his life and work" (68), suggesting that the new placement of the poems is itself significant. Still, for most readers of any poet launching into what amounts to his thirteenth collection over thirty-four years, the question is, "What is new?"

Predictably, Wagoner draws most heavily on his most recent collection, *First Light* (1983), from which he takes 55 of the 87 poems. From *In Bro-*

ken Country (1979) he selects 37 of 63 and from *Landfall* (1981), 39 of 76. He includes the three sequences from those collections, though he deletes one poem, "Climbing Alone," from the sequence of *In Broken Country*. Rather than simply run the selected poems in order of publication, as he did in *New and Selected Poems* (1969) and in *Collected Poems* (1976), Wagoner carefully arranges them along with the new poems in five sections divided by four sequences, one of which, "Acts of War" is new. One innovation, then, is the context in which the earlier poems now appear, a point which reviewers have largely overlooked.

Consider, for example, the environment of the lead poem, "After the Speech to the Librarians," in *Through the Forest* relative to *In Broken Country*, where it was also the opening poem. In the latter collection the poem precedes such autobiographical titles as "Boy Jesus" and "Jeremiad" (concerning Wagoner's boyhood roles in church programs), "The Junior Highschool Band Concert" (where "I played cornet, seventh chair"), and "My Father's Wall." In *Through the Forest* the poem begins a section of thirty-two nature poems. The five poems that follow "After the Speech to the Librarians" provide evidence of how eclectic Wagoner has been in setting up this collection: "Sharp-Shin," a new poem about a sharp-shinned hawk, "Return to the Swamp" (*Landfall* 55); "The Author of *American Ornithology* Sketches a Bird, Now Extinct" (*First Light* 22); "A Remarkable Exhibition" (*First Light* 23); and "Thoreau and the Snapping Turtle," a new poem which, like the two previous ones, takes its origin from Wagoner's extensive reading in natural history. The nature of the poem does not change, of course, simply by virtue of its relationship to other poems in its vicinity, but as William Stafford has observed about language contexts, poems "resonate" with each other (35), and if a reader encounters "After the Speech to the Librarians" in its new context, I think he or she is likely to regard it somewhat differently than a reader who meets it as the lead poem of *In Broken Country*.

The same can be said for many poems in *Through the Forest*. Here, for example, "Winter Wren" and "Kingfisher" from *First Light* (33, 34) are set just before and after "Marsh Hawk" from *Landfall* (65). Two dozen poems, eight of them new, make up a powerful autobiographical section which should help Wagoner escape such potentially, though not necessarily, limiting labels as "nature poet" (as in "just another . . .") or "Northwest regionalist" (as in "mere . . ."). The concluding five poems again testify to Wagoner's calculated alignment: "My Father's Ghost" (*Landfall* 15); "Elegy for My Mother" (*First Light* 12); "Songs My Mother Taught Me" (*In Broken Country* 20); "In the Dream House," a new poem, a 26–line sentence on his father, who looks at his mother now "Out of pride with open eyes, / Which he no longer has" (89); and "Their Bodies" (*First Light* 13).

The third section, following the "Land Behind the Wind" sequence, consists of seventeen nature poems, three of which are new, and then the new five-poem sequence, "Acts of War." The section begins with "Stump Speech," from *First Light* (64), and includes other poems, such as "An Address to Weyerhaeuser, the Tree-Growing Company" (*In Broken Country* 68) and "Staying Alive in a Clear-cut Forest" (*Landfall* 79), which reflect Wagoner's environmental politics. But as in the other sections, it is his arrangement of the poems that is particularly striking. He brings together "Looking into a Pond" and "Algae" from *Landfall* (62, 59) and expands the moment with "The Water Lily" from *First Light* (66). Later, he alternates between running water and rain by selecting poems from all three collections: "Waterfall" (*In Broken Country* 81), "Trying to Sing in the Rain" (*Landfall* 82), "Three Ways of a River" (*First Light* 69), and "Making a Fire in the Rain" (*In Broken Country* 82).

Section 4 returns to the autobiographical motif at first, but these poems do not concern Wagoner's boyhood or his family. The twenty-nine poems in this division actually comprise something of a miscellany. Poems like "After Reading Too Many Poems, I Watch a Robin Taking a Bath" (*In Broken Country* 61) and "Neighbors"—a new poem that begins, "My neighbor tells me I'm the worst, the rudest / Person he's ever met" (141)—reflect on Wagoner's day-to-day experiences. In fact, it is Wagoner's preoccupation with such seemingly trivial events as a bathing robin that so riles his neighbors; he prefers nature to human nature. The section is predominantly given over to what might be called studies in human nature: elegies and eulogies for Richard Hugo (both new poems) and Theodore Roethke; a new poem called "The Astronomer's Apprentice," which takes its origin from a passage in the *Monthly Notices* of the Royal Astronomical Society for 1870; four poems drawn from mythology or fairy tales, including a new title, the 104–line "Prince Charming"; and several poems pertaining to unusual human feats, among them "The Naval Trainees Learn How to Jump Overboard," from *First Light* (49) and "Stiltwalker" and "The Excursion of the Speech and Hearing Class," both new additions.

The fifth and concluding section of twenty-nine poems consists for the most part of lyrics devoted to gardening or love. Only three poems in this section are new: "Ode to Twelve Yards of Unscreened Fill Dirt," "For a Third Anniversary," and "In a Garden at the End of Winter." Fourteen of the remaining poems are drawn from *First Light* and only two are from *In Broken Country*. The fifth section comes across as domestic, and the love celebrated is not so much passionately romantic as it is quiet and deep. "We sleep," Wagoner writes in a poem from *First Light* ("In Love"), "[a]nd wake in the wildly abandoned countrysides / Of our bodies, embodying / Whole days and nights while Time keeps time, keeps time / With our pre-occupied hearts" (190). The lovers are in tune with nature; their romance takes place out of doors, under the stars, in a lakeside cabin visited at night by a weasel.

As in several poems from *First Light*, Wagoner here tests the patterns of idiomatic phrases, and his readers' wits, with unpunctuated poems, reminiscent in some ways of e e cummings. One of the most effective of these is "Coming Home Late with the Bad Young Man" (75). The opening lines show the rich playfulness of the technique, as Wagoner weaves in an allusion to Kipling's "If," a poem painfully familiar to those who occasionally browse among greeting cards.

> *So many tangled feet from home among toads*
> *No bigger than junebugs hopping at mosquitoes*
> *Dizzily we could keep our head while all*
> *About us the wobbly sprinklers were losing theirs*
> *To the night over lawns like upside-down chandeliers*
> *Along the sidewalk to make it glassy-eyed*
> *To the steps. . . .* (75)

If we place mental commas in the first line after "home" and at the end of the second line, we will receive one set of meanings: the speaker wanders home dizzily, his feet tangled, stumbling at night among toads and junebugs. But if we read the lines as they stand, unpunctuated, we are invited to entertain some possible "misreadings," which is precisely what Wagoner expects of us. For example, we may read of a "home among toads" which are no bigger than junebugs that hop at mosquitoes; or we may place the mental comma after "junebugs" and find the speaker "hopping at mosquitoes." But we know, after all, that it's the toads, not the speaker or the junebugs, that are hopping at those mosquitoes. Now the word "dizzily," which begins the third line, can also apply ambiguously either to the toads or to "we" or possibly even to the junebugs or the mosquitoes.

Wagoner offers us here, and in other poems presented in this mode, a syntactic puzzle. At the third line we acquire the nuclear sentence, which is the allusion to Kipling, except that the plural subject does not acquire a plural objective noun; the "we" appears to concern not the speaker and his literal brother, but the speaker and the "bad young man" or "sneaky brother" who lives inside his head, as we learn in line 17 of the poem. The "we" also applies to the reader, who in effect is now accompanying the "bad young man" home after a night on the town. The play on words that substitutes the "wobbly sprinklers" for Kipling's "others" seems at first to conclude at the end of the fourth line, but Wagoner extends the confusion with the prepositional phrase, "to the night," making it seem that the sprinklers, rather than he himself, have lost their heads to the night, while the sprinklers have actually lost their heads "over lawns." He then adds the simile, "like upside-down chandeliers," apparently applying to the sprinklers, but when we finally make it "to the steps," it is "glassy-eyed," as if we were the chandeliers by metaphoric extension.

At this point in the poem we may well find ourselves yearning for a period, or at least a nice semicolon, but it is not to be. For the remaining twenty lines of the poem, the participial phrases mount up, complicated by strings of prepositional phrases and all branching from the kernel statement, which could be rephrased as follows: Although we were dizzy, we could keep ourselves under control till we got home. Many of the participial phrases are cast as negatives: "not stopping soaked" (line 7), "not saying prayers" (line 18), "not thinking" (line 19), "not washing" (line 22). When the speaker tries his key, it is "under the gasp of the screendoor stopper / As soft as the click of the nightlatch being good / At keeping strictly quiet the bad young man . . ." (75). In effect, then, the metaphor makes sense as it applies both to the screen door and to the speaker, but is the gasp "as soft," or is it the "stopper," or is it "the click of the nightlatch," or is it his "first try" to fit the key? We hardly have the chance to think of that ambiguity before we are confronted with another, less subtle one. Clearly, that is, the nightlatch is not "being good," but the "bad young man" is; that is, he is "good" at "keeping strictly quiet." But the paradox has been established, at least in a playful way.

At line 12 the "bad young man" is described as "[a]mounting to nothing risking hell tiptoeing" down the hall. The four *-ing* word endings crammed into one line are part of the fun. The speaker, "breathless with beer," makes it past his father's bedroom, but he is caught by his mother, whose arms stretch out "for the sneaky brother / Who lived inside our head not saying prayers / Not thinking purely of girls who believed in virgins / Tom-catting out to lead us gladly astray" (75). The mischievous inner self could be read as a literal older brother. Wagoner does have a brother nine years older than he, but I think the poem implies nothing as literally autobiographical as that. Rather, Wagoner is speaking for "us," and especially for those of us who have not thought "purely of girls." This statement is obviously ambiguous, suggesting on the one hand "only" and on the other hand "morally," but the real trick of the sentence is the clause, "who believed in virgins." At first it seems to apply to the girls, the nearest noun, but we readily perceive that connection to be unlikely. Next, it might occur to us that it applies to the speaker ("we") and that it parallels the previous clause, pertaining to the sneaky brother "who lived inside our head." But it could also relate to "our mother's forgiving and unforgetful ears." Only the next line will help us resolve our dilemma, probably in favor of the second possibility: the sneaky brother who lives inside our heads quite probably does believe in virgins who are out tomcatting around, trying to lead him (us) astray. The use of "tomcatting" to apply to females, however, introduces another layer of ambiguity.

Wagoner next supplies an allusion to the popular song, "Show Me the Way to Go Home." The tomcatting virgins will "show us the way to go home." Then he builds dependent clauses again—"who didn't brush our teeth" (line 22), "who couldn't find / Our pajamas" (lines 23–24), "who lay there staring" (line 24)—and the poem ends with "us" staring, "Like a mind's eye groggily dimly at the ceiling / As we turned to fall disgraced into the morning." The poem is nothing short of a deconstructionist's dream.

Four of the new poems are written in this unpunctuated style that Wagoner handles masterfully and that seems particularly well suited to his wit and his love of verbal play, but he does not limit his use of this style to playful poems. "Our Father" (63–64) offers a portrait of a hard man in fifty-four short lines, beginning

> *He held so much*
> *Anger in him quiet*
> *Heavy nobody*
> *Had ever hit him*
> *Once he never had to*
> *Hit anybody either*

> But would just look
> Hard in the face. . . . (63)

This portrait does appear to be biographical. The father who played foot-ball at Washington and Jefferson, a lineman who graduated *magna cum laude* in classics, was to turn down an offer to teach and coach at V.M.I. and instead worked all his life in "the rumble / Screech clank slam / Of the rusty steelmill." Wagoner depicts him in this and in several other poems in earlier collections as a burned-out man, perhaps disappointed with the de-cisions he had made about his life. At the end of the poem, Wagoner por-trays his older brother, "The star outfielder the star / Center the scholar I wanted / To be" (64), as frightened, trying to awaken him in order to share his fear. Wagoner's poems in the last two collections have become more di-rectly and explicitly self-revelatory.

Wagoner rarely abandons modes at which he was succeeded, and at least since 1976, with the publication in chapbook form of *Travelling Light*, the sequence has been his bread and butter. In *Through the Forest* he offers a new sequence, "Acts of War," but it is not as ambitious as his earlier efforts. The sequence in *Landfall* (101–10) consists of only six po-ems, but the shortest runs 24 lines, while "Acts of War" consists of just five poems, ranging from as little as 7 to 55 lines. Quantity, of course, is not the measure of value when it comes to a sequence of poems. Much more im-portant are such matters as coherence, focus, and conceptual or thematic development, and in these respects the new sequence is sound.

For the first poem, "In Enemy Territory" (126–27), Wagoner uses the ternary form that he devised about twenty-five years earlier for "A Guide to Dungeness Spit" and that he has employed in all of his sequences, be-ginning with "Travelling Light." He also establishes in this poem the fa-miliar voice of the detached speaker:

> *There comes a time in going to war when the earth underfoot*
> *Is yours no longer, when the country ahead*
> *Is enemy territory.* (126)

Even the predicament of the persona (you) in the poem is familiar—dis-orientation in a hostile world that had formerly appeared comfortable and had been taken for granted. The speaker in this poem is less an instructor, perhaps, than a sort of omniscient journalist who can describe the condi-tions and penetrate the mind of the persona without becoming personally involved. The speaker's observations that you "must assume sharp hostile eyes / Are aimed your way" is not so much an order as it is a statement of fact. Under these circumstances, as with the characters Wagoner has shown us lost in forests or deserts, the individual has no thoughts of heroism, "[n]o gestures or brave postures for the sake of monuments," but only a "straightforward face" in search of "some doubtful sanctuary." The sanctuary is a tree, under which the persona receives a "bombardment / Of light that mottles and riddles your body / To innocent pieces." Bombarded by light, the persona experiences a sort of revelation by way of his memory of "the land you left behind," where he could wander freely day and night without fear of enemies. Wagoner then depicts the combat that would make the enemy "yours / In death signaling speechlessly / His utter surrender." This "nightmare / Of the execution of love," we are told, "could end this war" if we were not to "fight to the finish" but to yield, to take refuge and learn

> *What your already fallen and transformed companions,*
> *The flowers of generations, have been learning*
> *To do without you.* (127)

That is, in effect, "a more perfect union / In your heart's conflict." It is, then, both here and in some of the other sequences, the divided self that is at war, a war between the self and the universe, and the only victory is, in the words of the old spiritual, "to study war no more." That would mean

> *Going to ground again and quickening with the dead*
> *To prove the gold green neutral fire of the sun*
> *Is enough to live by.* (127)

The next poem in the sequence, "Securing a House" (128–29) is set up in five 9–line stanzas. The speaker retains the relationship with the persona in the poem; that is, he states matters of fact and can be said to teach or instruct only indirectly. It is almost as if two aspects of the self were in conversation, the one having been through it all before, and the other (like us, the readers) inexperienced and ignorant but not stupid or unwilling to learn. The first line, though, could be taken two ways, either as a command or as a statement: "You can't ignore that house." The speaker then explains that it "may become a nest / For the enemy behind you," so now you "turn to the doorway." The house, with its conventional associations of ease and security, as suggested by the title, has been taken for granted, like so much else that is vital to us in the world. Now, we are told, "you prime yourself / For anything": no one at all; a person to be rescued; "a burst of fire / Out of nowhere, breaking / The heart of your position"; or a booby trap that would leave you "a *tableau mort* / In memoriam of your war." The sinister wordplay at the end of this poem is Wagoner at his best. The breaking heart is associated with lost love a fraction of a second in the reader's mind before the phrase is completed, "the heart of your position," and at the same time we recognize the literal heartbreak caused by the bullet. The phrase *"tableau mort"* recalls *"tableau vivant,"* a term commonly used in drama, so we are reminded that what we have just experienced in this poem is a sort of scenario. "In memoriam," of course, reminds us of the grave, but the memory is not to be of our valor or patriotism, but of "your war." The rhyming of "war" with the French *"mort"* nicely underscores Wagoner's message.

The third poem in the sequence, "To the Last Man" (129–30), begins with two plays on idiomatic phrases, "the fortunes of war" and "the pitch and toss of battle," now rendered as "the misfortunes / Of war" and "the pitch and tossing-away of battle." The reader, the "you" of the poem, now becomes the "last man," and "your sense of direction turns / Against you," while the puns continue. We are told that the "chain of command" no longer connects us to our superiors, "[b]ut ends at its weakest link," implicitly us, alone, surrounded by "wreckage and mud, the decay of comrades / At peace now in their newly disarmed divisions." At the midpoint of the poem, Wagoner pivots, breaking the first block of sixteen lines and beginning the second section with "yet." Though the persona may despair and think now of death, he may be "the single unpredictable crucial / Element at a point of counterattack." This attack is not the glorious arrival of the cavalry to the rescue, but his own voice "come back from a body count of the dead" to give a "reckoning," "[n]ot carcasses of the truth but the whole truth," of which he is "the insane / Defender," telling his magic, holy, otherworldly story, which is "As dreadful as the world that dreamed it among / Ancestral voices prophesying you." The allusion to Coleridge's "Kubla Khan" might prompt us to associate the persona with the poet, but the wordplay also suggests the internal conflict between the two, for most readers will notice the substitution of "you" for "war" as the object of prophecy. The speaker concludes, "Even with no one listening, you must tell it." The poet, prophet/seer/bard, must speak, even if the audience thinks him or her mad, and even if the poet can find no audience at all.

After "To the Last Man," come the seven long, unpunctuated lines of "Victory" (130), a brief, breathless celebration in which Wagoner playfully juggles metaphors: "the exhausted hoofbeats of the drums in the earth," "the bugles of engines," "the parapet of your mouth." The poem's brevity suggests not only the momentary nature of victory, but also its deception. The concluding phrase of the poem is ironic: "it was all yours now." We do not see the irony, however, until we read "At Peace" (130–31), the final poem in the sequence. The first of the two sections (thirteen lines) is a conventional celebration of the end of war. "After the splitting earth- / Work-battering nightmare," the persona, you, breaks into the open and discovers that "each hill, each pathway, / Each grove and wellspring . . . Is yours for the asking." But as the second section (nineteen lines) makes clear, the persona has learned from this war that peace means not only the exchange of barbed wire barricades for cattle fences, artillery fire for thunder, and the sound of bugles for the cries of geese, but also a change in himself. He returns not as a hero or "star-born conqueror," but as a "living message, / Speechless and empty-handed." He is not intent upon possessing the territory or making personal or political gains from the internal conflict for which the war has been an elaborate metaphor. Because his inner strife has been quelled and the alienated self reunited with the human community, the persona can become a "living message" which, in effect, is what we all are.

An anonymous reviewer of *Through the Forest* writing for *Publisher's Weekly* noted that, like William Carlos Williams, Wagoner "celebrates the commonplace in poems so straightforward and self-effacing that the reader is only barely aware of them as artifacts." The concluding noun of that opening sentence has, I believe, something of a chilling effect, even if it was intended as a compliment. This reviewer, perhaps not inadvertently, consigns Wagoner's poems to the museum, and, although he hails the book as "a summa of his life and work," concludes that "[h]is achievement is a modest but solid one. He aims not to excite or arouse, but to comfort and please." One senses something of the distance that separates the dramatic metaphysical poems of Donne from the gentle Cavalier lyrics of Herrick. "In a stormy and stress-filled age," the reviewer adds, Wagoner offers "an alternative version of the world as a garden of natural wonders."

Although they did not express it directly, what the handful of reviewers may have been saying is that they could see nothing fresh or new in the poems of *Through the Forest*. Of course, what is new about the book, aside from the contexts already described, is thirty-one poems, but the themes of the new poems and sequences are not markedly different from Wagoner's earlier work. Again and again Wagoner has shown us an individual alone in the world, or occasionally with his beloved, enduring hardships, and winning through to a quietly triumphant acceptance of the universe and an understanding of his place in it. In the "Travelling Light" sequence, the lovers discover "where we began," the "amazing / World of our first selves where believing is once more seeing / The cold speech of the earth in the colder air / And knowing it by heart" (*Collected Poems* 261). In the sequence from *In Broken Country*, formerly untitled, but now entitled "The Journey," the last poem concludes that what has been won is the "worn-down, hard, incredible sight / Called Here and Now," and that means always to be starting over, for "The life in your hands is neither here nor there / But getting there" (*Through the Forest* 54). In "A Sea Change," from *Landfall*, the couple learns that they must love each other in order to learn "Once more how to point at the trees and birds and animals / We see around us, even our own hearts, / Naming, renaming them" (186). And in the "Land Behind the Wind" sequence, from *First Light*, the lovers find that the wind itself is their pathway to the land they have dreamed of.

5. WALT WHITMAN BATHING

Of course it is risky to speculate as to how reviewers will react to Wagoner's next collection of poems, due for release in 1996 and presently sitting before me in manuscript form. Entitled "Walt Whitman Bathing," this collection of forty-four new poems, including a nine-poem sequence, might be described as paradigmatic. The poems of the first section are apparently autobiographical, ranging from the opening poem, "The Pink Boy," which concerns an early childhood memory of a funeral for a boy who had "[s]ome milk from a bad cow," to "My Father Laughing in the Chicago Theater," in which we encounter the familiar figure of the poet's father: "The tears would dribble / From under his bifocals, as real as sweat. / He would gape and gag, go limp, and spring back to life." Familiar, too, is the speaker's ambivalent response: "I would laugh too, but partly at him, afraid / Of becoming him." The first section concludes with "At the Mouth of a Creek," a love poem reminiscent of both "Riverbed," the title poem of his 1972 collection, and "The First Place," from *Sleeping in the Woods* (1974).

The ten poems of the second section, including the powerful title poem of the volume, involve personae other than the speaker in his first-person voice. "The Rosebush," for example, is a memory of Wagoner's mentor, Theodore Roethke, and "Love Still Has Something of the Sea" involves Aldous Huxley and Thomas Mann. In "Deportment for Young Gentlemen," Wagoner resorts to what one might call "found" text, as he often has in the past, for example, in "A Police Manual," from *Riverbed* (1972), and "In Distress," from *Landfall* (1981). The new poems also represent Wagoner's considerable formal range. "A Young Woman Trying on a Victorian Hat," for example, is carefully arranged in tercets, while the next two poems, "Old Men Going to Bed" and "Let Us Put You in Your Dream Car," are unpunctuated celebrations of the inclination of language to deconstruct before our eyes. Then, in "The Padded Cell" Wagoner alternates long and short lines, one of his favorite rhythmic techniques.

The portrait of Whitman bathing focuses on an imagined incident after "the good gray poet's" stroke in January of 1873. Those familiar with the eleventh section of "Song of Myself," in which Whitman identifies himself with a lonely twenty-eight-year-old woman watching young men bathing at the seashore, a mildly erotic moment, will find Wagoner's portrait of the old poet bathing at a pond in the woods quite moving. After bathing himself gently with "his good right hand," Whitman dances "A few light steps, his right leg leading the way / Unsteadily but considerately for the left / As if with an awkward partner." The elderly poet, whose correspondence for years following his stroke is filled with complaints of loneliness, then stares at the water "for an hour as if expecting / Something to emerge, some new reflection / In place of the old." Presumably, Whitman's dilemma is not simply his disability, but that of all artists and poets (if not of people generally) in old age: to come up with something new, something different. Wagoner does not imply that Whitman succeeds in his meditation. He examines "[t]he postures of wildflowers" and "[t]he workings of small leaves," but these only leave him "mumbling inaudibly." Wagoner's concluding image is of the old poet, "patiently / As he might have dressed the wounded or the dead," leading himself "toward home like a dear companion." Implicitly, the poet and indeed all humans are ultimately alone.

The dozen poems that comprise the third section of "Walt Whitman Bathing" are located out-of-doors, and the first poem, "Bear," will inevitably remind veteran readers of "Meeting a Bear" from the "Travelling

Light" sequence, dating back twenty years. The animal life in this section ranges widely from a gray fox in a zoo to a pair of barn owls hunting, snakes, a burro named Clancy, and barnacles. Wagoner then turns from fauna to flora, concluding the section with four poems on wild roses, vine maples, a willow, and shield fern. These poems move the reader from "Bear's" confrontation with the perils of nature in the wild to the quiet pleasures of domesticated nature in the fern that the speaker removes from the forest to transplant into his garden.

The new collection ends with a nine-poem sequence entitled "Land-scapes," and here, too, the voice is familiar, occasionally even echoing passages from former sequences, for instance, in "Mapmaking": "How hard it is to fabricate broken country." As is most often the case with Wagoner's sequences, the second person (you) is dominant, and the three-line "stanza" (two longer lines and a short one) appears in four of the poems. When we read "In the Woods," we feel we have been there, with David Wagoner, before:

> *No matter where you were when you began, no matter*
> *Where you thought you were when you turned*
> *This way and that*
> *To lurch downslope, uphill, forcing yourself to choose*
> *Breathlessly when you lost the trail or in luck*
> *At ease, breathing*
> *Again when you found it, this was the certain be-all*
> *And end-all of the woods: a clearing chosen*
> *At random by your feet. . . .*

Now the speaker, who helps guide us toward coming to terms with our surroundings, invites us to make ourselves "at home" in the woods "by do-ing without / The pointless heroics of moving, by remaining / Quiet." We are led in this poem to a "fulfillment" in "a meeting place / Of silence and resonance" where we can hear what we were "meant to hear—birdsong, wingbeats, / The voices of animals." We will emerge

> *like that ancestor*
> *Who first set foot on earth at the foot of his tree and dared*
> *To remember he had learned in high branches*
> *To carry the light*
> *Through the skin of each leaf, the eye of every needle*

Down through a maze of intricate web-fine roots
To feed on darkness.

Increasingly, one is tempted to say that Wagoner should not be so inclined to reject the title of "visionary" that Hyatt Waggoner offered in his revision of *American Poets: From the Puritans to the Present* about a dozen years ago (624).

If the foregoing commentary on Wagoner's soon-to-be-published collection of poems sounds like a book review, perhaps that is appropriate. Reviewers might be tempted to bewail that this book offers "nothing new," but the challenge to provide something different with each volume seems to me one that Wagoner has long since outgrown. What he has been offering in his last several collections is a consistent vision in a now familiar voice—or, more accurately, an ensemble of voices—and its qualities should by now be quite clear.

To reiterate Wagoner's principles, humans live in a condition of becoming rather than being; therefore, they must remain in motion, discovering their world and reestablishing their relationship with it throughout their lives. Their best tools are humility, alertness and perceptivity, resilience, and love. In describing Wagoner as a visionary poet, Hyatt Waggoner reminds us that the visionary poem appears to begin in direct perception rather than reflection, and it "does not assume a dichotomy between the perceiver and the perceived. . . . It implies rather that responsible imaginative vision may be noetic, may disclose or uncover previously hidden aspects of being" (*American Visionary Poets* 12). Visionary poetry, Waggoner argues, "sees us as participants in the world, part and parcel of it, neither objective observers of it nor homeless in it" (7). In Wagoner's sequences and in many other important poems, such as "A Guide to Dungeness Spit," "Sleeping in the Woods," and "Staying Found" it is this lesson that the personae must learn, the ultimate survival lesson, and that should be enough for any poet to offer.

SOME OBSERVATIONS AND SPECULATIONS

In addition to his novels and collections of poems, David Wagoner has seen nine of his short stories in print since the publication of "Holiday" in the *Kenyon Review* in 1949. Most of these appeared between 1978 and 1980, and they suggest one of the directions Wagoner might take, although he presently has a novel set in Chicago in 1893 that is not yet published. "The Bird Watcher," which appeared in the *Georgia Review* in 1980, is reminiscent of Wagoner's environmental protest poems aimed at loggers and hunters. The protagonist, a bird watcher who is trying to lose his "city-self" and "trying to be less human" (41), encounters a hang-glider enthusiast on a logging road in the Cascades, and he offers first aid when the man crashes into a swamp. The focus of the story is on the vision of the bird watcher, and his vision is Wagoner's. He is a loner, aware that most people can not or do not share his interests or values, which involve simply "*being* somewhere natural . . . where he could look and learn and renew a powerful and healing sense of belonging momentarily to a dependable order." He has not come to meditate, but to "drive out of a man-made and man-damaged world and find a place where other older processes were still at work." He describes it as "an intimate joining with the Here and Now" (44).

The protagonist seems passive, or perhaps impassive, and one senses that the aid he administers to the fallen flyer will not be effective. Even if the flyer survives his severe back injuries, he is not likely to learn the lessons implicit in the bird watcher's humble admiration of the miraculous here and now. The quiet, understated celebration of that miracle, sometimes magnified by an equally modulated love between a man and a woman, is what David Wagoner's poetry and fiction are all about.

In this there is something admirably self-effacing, yet at the same time almost annoyingly defensive. Recalling his first meeting with David Wagoner, Sanford Pinsker records a disappointment that was probably inevitable, given the circumstances. Pinsker had come to the University of Washington in Seattle in the fall of 1963 to study with the notorious, manic-depressive, charismatic Theodore Roethke. Instead, as he tells it, he saw before him in the classroom an awkward, shy, overly handsome man in his mid-thirties: "He wore clothes too well, coifed his hair a touch too much" ("The Poem is Quicker Than the Eye" 110). Wagoner was not a vatic poet debilitated by irrational fears and alcohol. He had been at the university for about nine years by then and had three collections of poems and three novels to his credit, but he was not a presence on the campus. Years from now we will not uncover an apocrypha of "Wagoner stories" passed down by successive generations of graduate students and inflated with time. A box in Jay Parini's article on Theodore Roethke, "Madness and Meter," is captioned, "Fantastic Stories: Punchlines from Life" (22): Roethke prancing on a window ledge and clambering out a flag pole; a University of Washington professor following Roethke around campus picking up ten dollar bills as fast as the poet could throw them out. There will be Wagoner anecdotes, but probably no such extravagant legends.

Despite the echoes of Roethke in some of his earlier poems, Wagoner was not and is not "Roethkean." Many other poets are or have been Roethkean, though. Yeats was and Bly is, or has been. But many poets have not been stung to madness by the muse. Wallace Stevens wasn't nor was William Stafford. Richard Hugo was somewhat like Roethke, but Dave Smith and Robert Hass are not. Wagoner is not the bearish, lovable, infuriating, sad, boisterous, angry bundle of raw nerve endings that was Theodore Roethke and quite a long list of other renowned poets. For those who firmly embrace the myth that all true poets are mad, David Wagoner will never be a poet. This romantic fallacy, grotesque as it may seem to some, remains as much intact today as it was some two hundred years ago. It is another aspect of the age-old quarrel over humankind's double nature.

In an interview with *Yes* magazine published more than twenty years ago, Wagoner goes at least part way in accepting the myth: "I think a person making a poem must be a species of madman-dreamer" (26–27). But he cannot fully embrace the implications of that myth, for he adds that the poet must be "then a craftsman, then finally selfcritic" (27). If a line of descent may be drawn from Blake, roughly, through Coleridge, Whitman, Yeats, Roethke, and Dylan Thomas, that line will demarcate not simply a kind of madness, but a high sense of craft as well. In an interview with the editors of *Crazy Horse* magazine in 1972, Wagoner quite forcefully defended himself against the editors' classification of his temperament as "classical" rather than "romantic" (42–43). Specifically, Wagoner allied himself with the following traits, which he identified with a romantic sensibility: the belief that human emotions can be trusted when reason fails; attempting to achieve the sublime, daring to be mysterious in the process; admiration of flux rather than the status quo; the belief in the natural goodness of man uncorrupted by civilization; commitment to individualism, even at the risk of self-exposure; preference of the organic to the artificial, specifically with respect to poetic form (42). Wagoner's description of the romantic sensibility is of less moment to us here than his poetic self-concept.

His personal views are, of course, implicit and often explicit in his work. In a world that has lost (if it ever had) the Native American's intuitive, unitive, animistic vision, Wagoner would, ideally at least, reassert that vision. Like Frank Waters and most writers of Native American fiction and poetry, Wagoner proposes a synthesis of the material and the spiritual, the rational and the intuitive, the conscious and the unconscious, the masculine and the feminine. Poems like "A Guide to Dungeness Spit" and the "Travelling Light" sequence are typical in their movement from the physical toward the spiritual. In novels like *The Road to Many a Wonder*, the rational, materialistic male is made whole by the intuitive, spiritual female. Against the ravages of Weyerhaeuser or personal stress, he can offer only the hope for survival and love.

The love which informs so many of Wagoner's poems is intensely personal rather than social, private rather than public. Wagoner himself is more likely to take a step back than he is to take a step forward in his relations with others. He has been aptly characterized as a loner, and in a recent poem, "Neighbors," from *Through the Forest*, he confronts one of the costs of his love of privacy. Challenged by an irate neighbor, Wagoner explains in this poem what he probably could not explain to that person in actuality (assuming of course, that the occasion of the poem is from his own experience):

> *I'm afraid to tell him*
> *I'm trying hard to listen to other voices*
> *In my private head, not necessarily*
> *Including his, to say I'm too wrapped up*

In my own thoughts for fear he'll challenge me
To name one. I can't tell him I see things
Like trees instead of his face, that I hear birds
Instead of his wife because I imagine
Myself belonging among those strange neighbors. (141)

The humor, of course, is as much a part of Wagoner as his fascination with nature. Since I first met him in 1981 when he came to the University of Idaho to speak to the graduating class at the law school, Wagoner has struck me as a man who is utterly preoccupied. He is affable, even personable, but his mind and heart are elsewhere. Some people, like his neighbors and probably including some of his students, colleagues, and fellow writers, cannot tolerate that sort of distance. They will interpret it as aloofness, even arrogance, and they will be offended by it. How can an individual who keeps so apart succeed as a teacher? It has been argued over the past several years that creative writing programs have spawned two types (varying, of course, in degree of polarization): the writer who teaches and the teacher who writes. Wagoner seems clearly to be the former, but rather than rely on hearsay, I inquired of three of his former students, all now successful poets by one definition or another, and one of whom, Mary Ann Waters, died recently after the publication of her first book.

Sandra McPherson, who directs the creative writing program at the University of California at Davis, characterized Wagoner as "a really earnest teacher" who "conveyed a passionate interest in his joy of writing poetry." Tess Gallagher, who lives in Port Townsend, Washington and has taught at Syracuse University, took Wagoner's writing workshops after having studied with Mark Strand in 1970 (a "pivotal experience" for her as a poet) and with Stanley Kunitz. She writes: "While I felt strongly that he enjoyed his time in the classroom then, I also understood that he had very few ego needs as regarded the experience. He wanted to keep his relationships with students pretty closely circumscribed to the classroom." The result, Gallagher notes, was that the class sessions were "very intense," with no wasted moments. She mentions his thorough preparedness, and she recalls his "line by line fidelity as we worked on our poems in the workshop. He was very thorough in asking for an exactness in language and diction as well. And just as he emphasized punctuality and conservation in matters of time, he also required this of us in examining our poems. The 'timing' of the poem had to be right."

In her account, Gallagher, who has now been teaching workshops for more than twenty years herself, describes the friendships she has sustained with her former students, exchanges of letters and visits that have extended outside the classroom. These she has found "nourishing." But the needs of writers, as of all individuals, vary: "Mr. Wagoner's production is really the amazement you must focus on if you are to understand him in the classroom. One simply could not accomplish what he does and maintain relationships with students beyond the classroom." But she also recounts a visit to one of his classes in which Wagoner was "visibly flustered . . . affected and moved" by the demonstration of his students' "need to commemorate this last meeting" by bringing refreshments. She adds that he "seemed warmer and more able to be affectionate with his ever-present humor" than he had been when she was his student in the early seventies.

Mary Ann Waters, a more recent student in Wagoner's workshops, says that she ended up "liking the distance" that he created, a distance that she describes as "a magic space around him that a person just cannot invade." Beneath that, she notes, she could sense "that he liked me, but, more important, that he was interested in my work and would be a fair judge of it." Perhaps only those experienced in such workshops can fully appreciate the worth of that sort of distance. Tess Gallagher offers an outline of a class session in which Wagoner placed the students in the role of poetry editor, judging submissions by the opening lines of several poems. The experience taught her that her poems "were to be read by real flesh and blood people whose time was limited, whose attention needed to be courted and engaged immediately." Part of the distance that separates Wagoner from his students, then, might be called "editorial distance," the sort of distance that has made him for some thirty years one of the most respected poetry editors in the country.

Mary Ann Waters' observations are of particular interest because she provides several quotations from David Wagoner out of her journals of that period:

Anybody can be coherent; it's what the makers of dictionaries do.

You can always get the meaning right later if you have the rhythm right—I worry about the rhythm—if you have meaning but no rhythm you have a botch.

He has an ear like a sewing machine. [on a beginning poet]

You have to give names to the trees. The living things that got
here before you.

Wait a minute, I shouldn't be so certain. Let me put that as a
question.

A new volume of David Wagoner's collected poems is scheduled for
publication in 1997 or 1998. It appears at a time in the evolving history of
American poetry when writers like Joseph Epstein and Dana Gioia, himself a poet, are asking "Who Killed Poetry?" (*Commentary* August 1988)
and "Can Poetry Matter?" (*The Atlantic* May 1991). In 1996 the National
Council of Teachers of English published Jed Rasula's *The American Poetry Wax Museum*, in which he writes, "Poetry is a receptacle of the most
archaic associations of the linguistic function, which makes it seem inept if
not simply irrelevant today" (40). In *After the Death of Poetry* (1993) Vernon Shetley argues that the best course for poetry is away from subjectivity—especially given the trends in critical theory toward denial of an
autonomous self—and toward "making poetry more difficult" (3). He
adds, "[T]he most fruitful paths for American poetry seem to lie between
the erasure of subjectivity toward which Language poetry often seems to
aspire and the unexamined belief in the power of subjectivity to shape
meaningful poetic forms[,] often seen among the MFA mainstream[,] or
the New Formalist faith in the power of traditional poetic forms to give
valid shapes to subjectivity" (19–20). Finally, Paul Hoover, editor of the recent *Postmodern American Poetry* anthology for Norton (1994), noting
"the loss of individuality in a consumer society" (xxvi), promotes language
poetry and performance poetry, particularly with respect to the "multicul-
turalism" of the latter.

Presumably, as we near the turn of the century, significant trends are
underway which might "save" poetry in America, or at least alter it radi-
cally. If that does happen, Wagoner's work may be lost in the shuffle, as he
is neither New Formalist nor Language poet, neither Ethnic (i.e., Asian-
or African-American, Chicano, or Native American) nor Performance
poet. Of course, such spokesmen as Epstein, Gioia, Rasula, Shetley, and
Hoover might argue that if something startling does not happen soon, poetry itself will not survive in America, if it has not indeed already perished,
so the point will be moot. Proponents of what has been called "the well-
made poem" have been described, usually pejoratively, as Academic. Re-

gardless of their individual voices or inflections, poets as different as Donald Hall, Sharon Olds, Mary Oliver, William Meredith, Rita Dove, Stephen Dobyns, Dave Smith, Marilyn Hacker, Charles Wright, Amy Clampitt, Maxine Kumin, Robert Hass, W. S. Merwin, Edward Hirsch, Stanley Plumly, Pattiann Rogers, Carolyn Kizer, Norman Dubie, Li-Young Lee, and William Matthews, to list twenty—in short, many of the best known and most frequently read and widely anthologized poets writing today—could be thought of as members of this "academia" club, irrespective, by the way, of age, gender, race or ethnicity. Given the rise of postmodernism and the extension of cyberspace, it is conceivable that the next century will have no taste for the well-made poem, that writers who indulge in such notions as individual identity and subjectivity will be regarded as outmoded and self-indulgent, and that late capitalism will indeed prove to have no cultural logic at all. But to concede possibility is not the same thing as to concede probability. The premise of this book, after all, is that the poems and fiction of David Wagoner probably *will* survive, at least "[i]n the valley of [their] making."

In a recent letter (13 June 1996) Wagoner mentions that in addition to the manuscript of a novel presently with his agent, he has written "a whole book of 'poems' adopted from Thoreau's *Journal* which a local theatrical actor-director-dramaturge-exec (Kurt Beattie of the Seattle Rep) and [he] are going to make into a one-man play this summer with production (not at the Rep) very likely locally." He had just turned seventy the previous week, but he describes himself as going strong, still teaching full-time and editing *Poetry Northwest*. He describes his wife, Robin, who suffers from lupus, as "a wonderful mother" to their adoptive daughters, Adrienne (age four) and Alexandra (age six). He adds, "We're going to Disneyland (my God!) in August. Pray for me." William Butler Yeats was in his mid-fifties when his first child was born, but then, he did not have to cope with Disneyland.

Bibliography

PRIMARY SOURCES

Poetry

Dry Sun, Dry Wind. Bloomington: Indiana UP, 1953.
A Place to Stand. Bloomington: Indiana UP, 1958.
The Nesting Ground. Bloomington: Indiana UP, 1963.
Staying Alive. Bloomington: Indiana UP, 1966.
New and Selected Poems. Bloomington: Indiana UP, 1969.
Working Against Time. London: Rapp and Whiting, 1970. British Edition
    from *New and Selected Poems*.
Riverbed. Bloomington: Indiana UP, 1972.
Sleeping in the Woods. Bloomington: Indiana UP, 1974.
Collected Poems 1956–1976. Bloomington: Indiana UP, 1976.
Travelling Light. Chapbook. Port Townsend, WA: Graywolf, 1976.
Who Shall Be the Sun? Bloomington: Indiana UP, 1978.
In Broken Country. Boston: Atlantic-Little, Brown, 1979.
Landfall. Boston: Atlantic-Little, Brown, 1981.
First Light. Boston: Atlantic-Little, Brown, 1983.
Through the Forest: New and Selected Poems, 1977–1987. New York:
    Atlantic Monthly, 1987.
Walt Whitman Bathing: Poems. Champaign, IL: U of Illinois P, 1996.

Novels

The Man in the Middle. New York: Harcourt, 1954.
Money Money Money. New York: Harcourt, 1955.
Rock. New York: Viking, 1958.
The Escape Artist. New York: Farrar, 1965.
Baby, Come on Inside. New York: Farrar, 1968.
Where is My Wandering Boy Tonight? New York: Farrar, 1970.

The Road to Many a Wonder. New York: Farrar, 1974.
Tracker. Boston: Atlantic-Little, Brown, 1975.
Whole Hog. Boston: Atlantic-Little, Brown, 1976.
The Hanging Garden. Boston: Atlantic-Little, Brown, 1980.

Novella

"The Spinning Ladies." *New World Writing* Vol. 21. Philadelphia: Lippin-
    cott, 1962: 58–110.

International Editions of Novels

La Lampiste. Casablanca: Société Cheritienne d'Éditions et de Diffusion,
    Presses de la Cité, Paris, 1955. French Translation of *The Man in the
    Middle*.
The Man in the Middle. London: Victor Gollancz, 1955.
Juventad Desnuda. Barcelona: Editorial Fermo, 1963. Spanish translation of
    Rock.
The Escape Artist. London: Victor Gollancz, 1965.
Kdepak Se Dnes Vecer Toula Mui Kiuk? Prague: Odeon, 1974. Czech transla-
    tion of *Where is My Wandering Boy Tonight?*
Les Chasseurs d'empreintes. Paris: Hachette, 1979. French translation of
    Tracker.

Edition

Straw for the Fire: From the Notebooks of Theodore Roethke. New York:
    Doubleday, 1972.

One-Act Play

The Song of Songs Which is Sheba's. Slackwater Review. Special David Wag-
    oner Issue (1981): 52–87. Performed with two other one-act plays as *An
    Eye For An Eye For An Eye* at the University of Washington in 1979.

Short Stories

"The Red Hat." *Folio* 14 (February 1949): 49–56.
"Holiday." *Kenyon Review* 11 (Summer 1949): 441–50
"The Escape Artist." *Harper's Magazine* 230 (May 1965): 102–20. Adaptation
    from the novel by the same title.
"An Afternoon on the Ground." *Prairie Schooner* 52 (Fall 1978): 213–22.
"Wild Goose Chase." *Georgia Review* 32 (Fall 1978): 531–39.

"Mr. Wallender's Romance." *Hudson Review* 32 (Spring 1979): 45–63.

"Cornet Solo." *Boston Sunday Globe*. 20 May 1979, Sec. 10: 41–42. Rpt. in *Slackwater Review*, Special David Wagoner Issue (1981): 34–42.

"The Water Strider." *Boston Sunday Globe*. 14 October 1979, Sec. 28–29: 37–38. Rpt. in *Slackwater Review*, Special David Wagoner Issue (1981): 43–51.

"Fly Boy." *Ohio Review* no. 25 (1980): 86–95.

"The Bird Watcher." *Georgia Review* 34 (Spring 1980): 41–50.

"Snake Hunt." *Western Humanities Review* 34 (Winter 1980): 22–36.

Essays

"The Liberation." *Coraddi*. Arts Festival Issue of Women's College of the University of North Carolina, 1949. n.p.

Untitled contribution to Ezra Pound symposium. *Nueva Corrente* 5–6 (Genoa, Italy). (1956): 234.

"Finding the Good Green Earth . . . Fresh Air . . . and Adventure in America." *Mademoiselle* 72 (April 1971): 246, 272.

"The Journey of Carl Morris." *Malahat Review* 32 (October 1974):5–8.

"The Literature of Legerdemain." *Times Literary Supplement*. 24 December 1976: 1598–99.

"Roughing It in the Sandwich Islands." *Times Literary Supplement*. 8 April 1977: 422.

"David Wagoner." *Contemporary Authors Autobiography Series* Vol. 3. Detroit: Gale Research, 1986: 397–412.

Recordings

"'A Valedictory to Standard Oil of Indiana' and Other Poems." Aural Poems. Western Michigan University, January 1966.

"Poets of Today." Folkway Records-Scholastic Magazine, Spring 1968.

"100 Modern American Poets Reading Their Poems." Spoken Arts Treasury, Vol. 16, 1969.

"Carolyn Kizer & David Wagoner." Audiotape Archives. Academy of American Poets, 1994.

Interviews

"An Interview with David Wagoner." *Crazy Horse* 12 (Autumn 1972): 38–46.

"Conversation with David Wagoner." *Yes* (1973): 21–28.

Feuerstein, Rob. "A Guide to the Central Figure for the Poetic Art of the Northwest." *University of Washington Daily*. 29 Mar. 1977: 32.

McFarland, Ron. "An Epistolary Interview with David Wagoner." *Slackwater Review*. Special David Wagoner Issue (1981): 11–18.

Henderson, Mike. "Writer's Talent Outweighs Fame." *Everett Herald* [Everett, WA]. 12 Apr. 1981, Venture Sec.: 14–16.

Dacey, Phil. "David Wagoner." *American Poetry Observed: Poets on Their Work*. Ed. Joe David Bellamy. Urbana: U of Illinois P, 1984: 266–74.

O'Connell, Nicholas. "David Wagoner." *At the Field's End: Interviews with 20 Pacific Northwest Writers*. Seattle:Madrona Publishers, 1987: 39–57.

Film

The Escape Artist. Prod. Francis Ford Coppola. Dir. Caleb Deschanel. Zoetrope Studios. Released and distributed by Orion Pictures-Warner Brothers, 1982–83.

SECONDARY SOURCES

Abbey, Edward. Review of *Where is My Wandering Boy Tonight?* *New York Times Book Review*, 22 November 1970, 58.

Anonymous. Review of *Through the Forest*. *Publishers Weekly* 231 (26 June 1987): 68.

—. Review of *Who Shall Be the Sun?* *Virginia Quarterly Review* 56 (Winter 1980): 26.

Askins, Justin. "Mild Delight." *Parnassus* 12 (Fall 1984): 331–41.

Auden, W. H. *Collected Longer Poems*. New York: Random, 1969.

Bierhorst, John. *The Mythology of North America*. New York: William Morrow, 1985.

Bishop, Elizabeth. *The Complete Poems: 1927–1979*. New York: Noonday, 1993.

Boas, Franz. *Bella Bella Tales*. Memoirs of the American Folklore Society, Vol. 25. New York: B. E. Stechert, 1932.

—. *The Mind of Primitive Man*. Rev. ed. New York: Free Press, 1963.

—. *Race, Language, and Culture*. New York: Macmillan, 1940.

Boucher, Anthony. Review of *The Man in the Middle*. *New York Times Book Review*, 15 October 1954, 15.

Boyers, Robert. "The Poetry of David Wagoner." *Kenyon Review* 32 (1970): 176–81.

Breslin, Paul. Review of *Landfall*. *New York Times Book Review*, 22 March
    1981, 14+.

Brown, Norman O. *Life Against Death*. Middletown: Wesleyan UP, 1959.

Carr, Helen. Review of *Who Shall Be the Sun?* *Times Literary Supplement*,
    25 April 1980, 477.

Carruth, Hayden. Review of *Who Shall Be the Sun?* *Harper's Magazine* 258
    (May 1979): 89.

Ciardi, John. Review of *Dry Sun, Dry Wind*. *New York Times Book Review*,
    26 June 1953, 10.

Clark, Ella E. *Indian Legends of the Northern Rockies*. Norman: U of Okla-
    homa P, 1966.

Cording, Robert K. "David Wagoner." *American Poets Since World War II*.
    Vol. 5, part 2. Detroit: Bale Research, 1980: 348–55.

Curley, Thomas F. Review of *Rock*. *Commonweal* 68 (22 August 1958): 523.

Damon, S. Foster. *A Blake Dictionary*. Providence: Brown UP, 1965.

Dickey, James. Review of *The Nesting Ground*. *New York Times Book
    Review*, 22 December 1963, 4.

Dobyns, Stephen. Review of *New and Selected Poems*. *Poetry* 117 (March
    1971): 397–98.

Donne, John. *The Elegies and the Songs and Sonnets*. Ed. Helen Gardner.
    Oxford: Clarendon, 1965.

Engle, Paul, and Joseph Langland, eds. *Poet's Choice*. New York: Dial, 1962.

Flint, R. W. Review of *In Broken Country*. *Parnassus* 8 (1980): 59–62.

Fogel, Daniel Mark. Review of *First Light*. *Magill's Literary Annual 1984*.
    Englewood Cliffs, NJ: Salem, 1984: 299–303.

Frankel, Haskel. Review of *The Escape Artist*. *Saturday Review* 48 (28 Au-
    gust 1965): 66.

Gallagher, Tess. Personal communication with the author. 19 August 1986.

Gardner, John. Review of *Whole Hog* and *Collected Poems*. *New York Times
    Book Review*, 2 January 1977, 7+.

Guillory, Daniel L. Review of *Through the Forest*. *Library Journal* 112 (Au-
    gust 1987): 130.

Gunn, Thom. Review of *A Place to Stand*. *Yale Review* 48 (December 1958):
    302.

Hoover, Paul, ed. "Introduction." *Postmodern American Poetry*. New York:
    Norton, 1994.

Howard, Richard. *Alone with America*. Enlarged edition. New York:
    Atheneum, 1980.

Hughes, John W. Review of *Riverbed*. *Saturday Review* 55 (26 February 1972): 62.

Hugo, Richard. "David Wagoner: A Poet of Elizabethan Wisdom and Wit." *The Weekly's Reader*, November 1979: 1+. Rpt. in *Slackwater Review*. Special David Wagoner Issue (1981): 119–23.

—. "Some Stray Thoughts on Roethke and Teaching." *American Poetry Review* 3 (January/February 1974): 50. Rpt. in *The Triggering Town*. New York: Norton, 1979.

Irwin, John T. "The Crisis of Regular Forms." *Sewanee Review* 81 (Winter 1973): 158–69.

Jarrell, Randall. *Poetry and the Age*. New York: Knopf, 1953.

Kennedy, X. J. "Pelting Dark Windows." *Parnassus* 5 (Spring/Summer 1977): 133–40.

Keynes, Geoffrey, ed. *The Complete Writings of William Blake*. London: Oxford UP, 1966.

Levertov, Denise. "On the Function of Line." *Chicago Review* 30 (Winter 1979): 30–36.

Lieberman, Laurence. *Unassigned Frequencies*. Urbana: U of Illinois P, 1977.

McAulay, Sara. "'Getting There' and Going Beyond: David Wagoner's Journey Without Regret." *Literary Review* 28 (Fall 1984): 93–98.

McClatchy, J. D. Review of *First Light*. *New York Times Book Review*, 22 January 1984, 12.

McFarland, Ronald E. *David Wagoner*. Western Writer's Series no. 88 Boise: Boise State UP, 1989. 55-page pamphlet.

—. "David Wagoner's Comic Westerns." *Critique* 28 (Fall 1986):5–18.

—. "David Wagoner's Dynamic Form." *Contemporary Poetry* 5 (1983): 41–50.

—. "David Wagoner's Environmental Advocacy." *Rocky Mountain Review of Language and Literature* 44 (1990): 7–16.

—. "Learning to Laugh at Being a Flop: David Wagoner's Poems of Adolescence." *California English* 28 (January/February 1992): 6–7, 30–31.

—, ed. *Slackwater Review*. Special David Wagoner Issue (1981).

McPherson, Sandra. Personal communication with the author. 13 September 1986.

Malkoff, Karl. "Wagoner." *Crowell's Handbook of Contemporary American Poetry*. New York: Thomas Y. Crowell, 1973: 313–16.

Meredith, William. Review of *A Place to Stand*. *New York Times Book Review*, 8 February 1959, 10.

Oberg, Arthur. Review of *Collected Poems. Poetry* 130 (June 1977): 162–67.

Ott, Bill. Review of *Through the Forest. Book List* 83 (August 1987): 1713.

Parini, Jay. "Madness and Meter: Life with Theodore Roethke, The Great American Poet of His Generation." *Pacific Northwest* 20 (December 1986): 20–23, 69.

Peters, Robert. "Thirteen Ways of Looking at David Wagoner's New Poems." *Western Humanities Review* 35 (Autumn 1981): 267–72. Rpt. in *The Great American Poetry Bake-Off* 2nd Series. Metuchen, NJ: Scarecrow, 1982.

Phelps, Robert. Review of *Rock. New York Herald Tribune Book Review*, 17 August 1958, 3.

Pinsker, Sanford. "The Achievement of David Wagoner." *Connecticut Review* 8 (October 1974): 42–47.

—. "David Wagoner: The Poem is Quicker Than the Eye." *Slackwater Review*. Special David Wagoner Issue (1981): 109–18.

—. "On David Wagoner." *Contemporary Poetry in America*. Ed. Robert Boyers. New York: Schocken, 1974: 360–68.

—. *Three Pacific Northwest Poets: William Stafford, Richard Hugo, and David Wagoner*. Boston: G. K. Hall, 1987: 99–124.

Powers, Dennis. Review of *Baby, Come on Inside. Saturday Review* 51 (17 August 1968): 26.

Pratt, W. Review of *First Light. World Literature Today* 58 (Summer 1984): 424.

Rasula, Jed. *The American Poetry Wax Museum*. Urbana, IL: NCTE, 1996.

Rilke, Rainer Maria. *The Duino Elegies*. Trans. J. B. Leishman and Stephen Spender. New York: Norton, 1967.

Roethke, Theodore. *Collected Poems*. Garden City: Doubleday, 1975.

—. "Some Remarks on Rhythm." *Poetry* 117 (October 1960): 35–46. Rpt. in *On the Poet and His Craft*. Ed. Ralph J. Mills, Jr. Seattle: U of Washington P, 1965.

Rothenberg, Jerome, ed. *Shaking the Pumpkin*. Garden City: Doubleday, 1972.

Sale, Roger. Review of *The Road to Many a Wonder. Hudson Review* 27 (Winter 1964–75): 625–26.

Sandol, James. Review of *The Man in the Middle. New York Herald Tribune Book Review*, 15 August 1954, 8.

Schaefer, William J. "David Wagoner's Fiction: In the Mills of Satan." *Critique* 9 (1966): 71–89.

Scott, W. T. Review of *A Place to Stand*. *Saturday Review* 42 (3 January 1959): 13.

Shea, Mary Jo. Review of *Who Shall Be the Sun?* *Magill's Literary Annual 1979*. Englewood Cliffs, NJ: Salem, 1979.

Shetley, Vernon. *After the Death of Poetry*. Durham: Duke UP, 1993.

Stafford, William. *Writing the Australian Crawl*. Ann Arbor: U of Michigan P, 1978.

Stallings, Sylvia. Review of *Money Money Money*. *New York Herald Tribune Book Review*, 2 October 1955, 3.

Stitt, Peter. Review of *Who Shall Be the Sun?* *Georgia Review* 33 (Fall 1979): 699–704.

Studebaker, William. "Focusing on the Double: Irony in Wagoner's Poetry." *Slackwater Review*. Special David Wagoner Issue (1981): 100–108.

Taylor, Anya. Review of *Who Shall Be the Sun?* *Commonweal* 107 (14 March 1980): 155.

Teit, James A. *Folk-Tales of Salishan and Sahaptin Tribes*. Memoirs of the American Folk-Lore Society, Vol. 11. New York: G. E. Stechert, 1917.

Thomas, Dylan. *Collected Poems*. Revised edition. New York: New Directions, 1956.

—. *Quite Early One Morning*. In Kreshner, R. B., Jr. *Dylan Thomas: The Poet and His Critics*. Chicago: ALA, 1976: 119–20.

Thoreau, Henry David. *Walden and "Civil Disobedience."* Ed. Sherman Paul. New York: Houghton, 1960.

Van Duyn, Mona. Review of *The Escape Artist*. *Poetry* 109 (February 1967): 332.

Waggoner, Hyatt. *American Poets: From the Puritans to the Present*. Revised edition. Baton Rouge: Louisiana State UP, 1984.

—. *American Visionary Poetry*. Baton Rouge: Louisiana State UP, 1982.

Wallace, Ronald. *God Be with the Clown*. Columbia: U of Missouri P, 1984.

Waters, Mary Ann. Personal communication with the author. 27 September 1986.

Williams, William Carlos. *Selected Poems*. New York: New Directions, 1969.

Wright, James. Review of *A Place to Stand*. *Poetry* 93 (October 1958): 49.

INDEX